Silvia Stoller (Ed.)
Simone de Beauvoir's Philosophy of Age

Simone de Beauvoir's Philosophy of Age

Gender, Ethics, and Time

Edited by
Silvia Stoller

DE GRUYTER

ISBN 978-3-11-048172-3
e-ISBN 978-3-11-033914-7

Library of Congress Cataloging-in-Publication Data
A CIP catalog record for this book has been applied for at the Library of Congress.

Bibliographic information published by the Deutsche Nationalbibliothek
The Deutsche Nationalbibliothek lists this publication in the Deutsche Nationalbibliografie;
detailed bibliographic data are available in the Internet at http://dnb.dnb.de.

© 2014 Walter de Gruyter GmbH, Berlin/Boston
Druck und Bindung: CPI buch bücher.de GmbH, Birkach
♾ Gedruckt auf säurefreiem Papier
Printed in Germany

www.degruyter.com

To my mother
Herta Stoller

Acknowledgments

This book publication would not have been possible in this form if not for the support of many academic and public institutions and of close friends and colleagues. Since it was initiated in line with a research position I held at the University of Vienna, I first of all wish to thank the Austrian Science Fund (FWF) for generously funding my research. Concerning friends, I first wish to thank Ida Černe, my oldest best friend in Vienna, for her untiring commitment from the very beginning of this project to the very end of the book manuscript. Secondly, my thanks go to my friend and colleague Elisabeth Schäfer for her invaluable support at an early stage of the book project when sharing my experiences on editing this volume while jogging in the beautiful gardens at Schönbrunn in Vienna. Further, I would like to express my deepest gratitude to my friends Gertrude Postl, Veronica Vasterling, Reinhard Stremayr and my dear parents for additional help in various ways. Each of them had her and his own way of contributing to this book project. Finally my thanks go to my colleagues Helen Fielding, Dorothea Olkowski and Christina Schües who shared much of their time and professional experience in reading and commenting on the manuscript.

First versions of these essays were originally presented at an international conference on *Age/Aging* on the occasion of Simone de Beauvoir's 100th birthday at the University of Vienna in 2008. The papers were extensively revised when the plan for a publication developed, and they finally went through several review processes. I would like to thank the authors for their professional co-operation, their patience and their tremendous encouragement I received while working on the manuscript. I am indebted to the Austrian Science Fund (FWF) for generously financing the conference. Furthermore, my thanks go to the Austrian Federal Ministry of Science and Research, the Federal Ministry of Social Affairs and Consumer Protection, the "Gruppe Phänomenologie" as well as the City of Vienna (Cultural Department, Science and Research Promotion), and the University of Vienna for co-financing the conference.

Finally, I would like to take this opportunity to thank Christoph Schirmer from De Gruyter for his interest in this publication and his invaluable assistance during the publication process. Last but not least I wish to express my sincere delight that this book on Beauvoir has finally been included into the program of De Gruyter.

Table of Contents

Part Three: **Age and Time**

Silvia Stoller
Beauvoir's *The Coming of Age*

For much too long, Beauvoir's brilliant treatise *The Coming of Age* has stood in the shadow of her groundbreaking work *The Second Sex*. It is no secret that Beauvoir's study on aging has not received the recognition it deserves. Contemporary Beauvoir researchers mostly agree on this point. The contributions in this volume try to make up for this by focusing on *The Coming of Age*. Such a focus is essential within the scope of Beauvoir research. Only this way can the full meaning of Beauvoir's *Coming of Age* be made visible. Moreover, such a focus will not only help to illustrate the full meaning of Beauvoir's *Coming of Age*, but it will also shed light on Beauvoir's collected works and their place in twentieth-century philosophy.

According to their specialization, each author has addressed Beauvoir's reflections on age from different angles of feminist philosophy. This is important because feminist philosophy has not placed sufficient emphasis on this study on aging. In addition, most of the essays collected in this volume share a phenomenological background. This means that they aim at reflecting upon *The Coming of Age* from a phenomenological or existential perspective.[1] As such, this volume accords with the academic tradition of reading Beauvoir either as a phenomenologist and a philosopher whose work is influenced by phenomenology and existential phenomenology, or of interpreting her work by means of phenomenology. In so doing, the phenomenological reflections on Beauvoir's *The Coming of Age* presented here provide a helpful frame which attempts to do justice to one of Beauvoir's most important methodological approaches: phenomenological existentialism.

To the best of my knowledge, this volume is the first one to focus exclusively on *The Coming of Age*. It pursues three objectives: first and foremost, the volume contributes to the uniqueness of Beauvoir's philosophical work in its entirety. Second, it attempts to explore the phenomenological implications of Beauvoir's essay on old age and, as such, can be characterized as another inquiry in feminist phenomenology. Third, the volume supports Beauvoir's own claim of "breaking the silence" about age and aging, a claim that, even 40 years later, continues to be pertinent, and it seeks to promote future research in this field.

---

1 Most of the contributors to this volume are members of the international network of experts in phenomenology and feminist philosophy, "Feminist Phenomenology Group," which was originally founded on the occasion of the international workshop on "Feminist Phenomenology" at the Institute of Science and Art in Vienna in 2000.

Beauvoir's Groundbreaking Essays on Gender and Age

Besides her impressive literary and autobiographical works, Simone de Beauvoir wrote several philosophical works. Among them there are two outstanding philosophical studies that are highly relevant both socially and politically. The first one, *The Second Sex* (*Le deuxième sexe*, 1949), focuses on the existence of women in times of omnipresent gender inequality and the discrimination against women in patriarchal societies. The second one, *The Coming of Age* (*La vieillesse*, 1970), which appeared 21 years later, deals with the issue of age and aging in times of prevalent marginalization and devaluation of old people in Western industrialized societies. Both books attest to Beauvoir's prodigious lifelong social and political engagement with regard to people in democratic societies who are considered secondary and consequently have been widely marginalized, subordinated, ignored, and oppressed. They also illustrate the characteristic aspects of Beauvoir's philosophical thinking throughout her life, namely that she was ahead of her time. Finally, they share a couple of apparently strong similarities which are worth mentioning again.

When it first appeared, *The Second Sex* was censored by the Catholic Church and placed on a list of prohibited books, the *Index Librorum Prohibitorum*. Its publication was met with horror, incomprehension, and defamation by colleagues and the media. Nevertheless, Beauvoir became the leading figure for a whole generation of women: a model for the movement of modern women, a classic of feminist philosophy, and a public icon. Not only did she have her finger on the pulse and spirit of the time, but she also presented her era with something that time would further mature. Similarly, and this is also true of *The Coming of Age*, Beauvoir was ahead of her time. Unlike *The Second Sex*, this study was not met with a wave of indignation; but it also quickly became a bestseller. Its publication preceded by decades the establishment of modern gerontology as a new academic discipline, long before Age Studies were established in academia. The book came out at a time when the question of aging was not yet a topic of political debate and government policies and when the problem of aging had not yet entered public consciousness.[2]

The similarities between these two philosophical essays are striking. Each comprising several hundreds of pages, both essays are extraordinarily long

---

[2] Elaine Marks describes this characteristic of Beauvoir, in other words and in terms of psychology, as "her tendency to transgress boundaries" (Marks 1986, 190), meaning: transgressing the boundaries of accepted discourses.

and cover a large scope of scientific, historical, literary, and philosophical material. Methodologically, Beauvoir decided to treat the issues of gender and age in
very similar ways, and to divide each of her books into two main parts. Both
times, the first part presents the results of scientific, biological, anthropological,
and historical research, as well as leading views of the contemporary capitalist
society of her time. In the case of the study on aging, the first section is entitled
"Old Age Seen from Without" (French: "Le point de vue de l'extériorité"). Without meaning to diminish the results of the objective sciences, Beauvoir writes
that old people are treated as mere objects seen from an external standpoint:
the elderly appear as objects of knowledge. While the first part introduces a scientific understanding of the issue at stake and thus starts with an outsider's perspective, the second part regards the topic from the view of lived experience, that
is to say, the first-person perspective. This part is titled "The Being-in-the-World"
(French: "L'Être-dans-le-monde"). One could also say: "Old Age Seen from Within." As in her book on *The Second Sex*, such an approach deals with the issue of
how elderly people live their age on their own terms, with the individual regarded
not only as an object but also as a subject.

From the philosophical point of view, Beauvoir argues that in our societies,
women as well as old people are "the Other." Penelope Deutscher's statement
summarizes this striking parallel very well: "Where she argued in *The Second
Sex* that woman is the Other, in *Old Age* [*The Other Sex*] she would argue that
the aged are, in a similar sense, the marginalized Other" (1999, 6). Thus, it
does not come as a surprise that feminist philosophers agree in their readings
of Beauvoir, stating that her making the "marginalized otherness" a topic of discussion in *The Second Sex* and *The Coming of Age* is "remarkably similar" (Bergoffen 2004, 19).

However, another remarkable similarity should be taken into consideration.
In her main work, *The Second Sex*, Beauvoir argues that one "is not born, but
rather becomes, a woman" (1989, 267). With this central thesis she anticipated
one of the topics of modern gender research, namely, that "woman" or "femininity" is a social construction. This means that being a woman is first and foremost
a question of social values and standards, primarily mediated through education. Applying this insight into construction to the question of old age in her
essay *The Coming of Age*, Beauvoir assures us that: "old age can only be understood as a whole: it is not solely a biological, but also a cultural fact" (1996, 13).
Culture and cultural norms define what age is. Thus, Beauvoir emphasizes the
relevance of culture not only for a definition of "woman," but also for the experience of "old age." Without diminishing natural and physiological facts, Beauvoir places emphasis on the cultural dimension of the "second sex" and "old

age," arguing that the meaning of both is a result of cultural interpretations.[3] Even more, the negative meaning of old age is imposed on the elderly. Beauvoir herself relates the construction of gender to the construction of age and draws a parallel between *The Second Sex* and *The Coming of Age:*

> The most important fact to emphasize is that the status of the old man is never *won* but always *granted*. In *The Second Sex* I showed that, where women derive great standing from their magic powers, they owe it in fact to the men. This is equally true for the aged in relation to the adults (1996, 85).

Remarkably, both essays aim at social groups which, both in Western societies and elsewhere, are oppressed and marginalized. Beauvoir raises her voice against their oppression and marginalization as well as against the injustice that women and the aged suffer from to this day, across the globe. Both essays attest to the actuality and imperative of her claims. The outlined similarities between these books are striking, and it was Beauvoir herself who once said in one of her autobiographies that she could imagine her future essay on *The Coming of Age* as forming a symmetric "counterpart" to *The Second Sex* (1993, 130).[4]

The Forgotten Study on Age

Yet, compared with *The Second Sex*, Beauvoir's book *The Coming of Age* never received the academic attention that it deserves. In fact, from the 1970s, her study on age has remained widely unnoticed within the context of feminist Beauvoir research. On this point scholars agree. Given the striking parallels outlined above as well as the importance and innovation of these studies, one wonders how Beauvoir's *The Coming of Age* could be so ignored for such a long time by feminist philosophers.[5] Yet, although this neglect seems to come as a surprise for the academic world, there are several reasons for its omission.

---

3 See more on the similarities between *The Second Sex* and *The Coming of Age* in Bergoffen 1997, 186–90, and Bergoffen 2004, 17–18, and Deutscher 1999 and 2003.
4 While, in this section, I put emphasis on the similarities between Beauvoir's *The Second Sex* and *The Coming of Age*, in his study *Age Rage and Going Gently* Oliver Davis has stressed some remarkable differences (cf. Davis 2006, 35–40).
5 Another forgotten work in this respect is the seventy-minute documentary film *A Walk through the Land of Old Age*, directed by the Swedish filmmaker Marianne Ahrne in 1974. The film is devoted to the situation of older people in post-war France and based on Beauvoir's essay *The Coming of Age*. Beauvoir herself does not only appear throughout the film, she was also involved in the project from the very beginning, including script-writing. The British philosopher Oliver

First, for decades there has been a general neglect of age in feminist philosophy. In the past, feminist philosophy used to deal with issues other than age. And although contemporary feminist philosophers have become aware not only of the constitutive role of age as a category of identity, but also of the intersection of gender and age, age in some cases is still regarded as being secondary, and in my opinion it still tends to lack scientific acknowledgment in feminist philosophy. Perhaps the most famous example is the *Companion to Feminist Philosophy* (Jaggar and Young 1998) which does not contain a single article dedicated to the topic of aging. Surprisingly, aging is mentioned only once, namely in the article on "Disability." The same is true for more recent publications in feminist philosophy, as can been seen from *The Feminist Philosophy Reader* (Bailey and Cuomo 2008) which serves as standard reading for students and scholars in the United States and other English-speaking countries. There is a section on "Race and Racism" included, however a section on "Age," along with other categories of identity, is missing. What counts for feminist philosophy is also true for feminist theory in general. As Marilyn Pearsall says in the introduction to her edited book on feminist explorations of women and aging: "Part of the problem with aging from a feminist perspective is that as an issue it has been relatively neglected by contemporary feminism" (Pearsall 1997, 1).

Indeed, feminist scholars in the past have given little attention to *old* women. The primary focus of feminist philosophers has mostly been on young adults or middle-aged women or girls. Today's leading feminist age theorists confirm this specific neglect in feminist research. As Calasanti and Slevin have argued in their book *Age Matters*, "Feminists consider age but rarely old people and age relations" (Calasanti and Slevin 2006). Consequently, this also affected feminist research on Beauvoir. As Woodward points out, Beauvoir's *The Coming of Age* was largely ignored by feminists because for a long time they were primarily concerned with women's issues regarding exclusively the earlier years of female adulthood (Woodward 1993, 23). Ironically, the charge of ignoring *very* old age in feminist discourses was also directed against Beauvoir herself. As Pe-

---

Davis of Warwick University has analyzed this film in chapter five of his study *Age Race and Going Gently*, "Beauvoir as biographer and autobiographer of the ageing subject" (Davis 2006a, 145–70), and he has also conducted an interview with the Swedish filmmaker Ahrne which is included in his book (Davis 2006b). Recently, the transcript of the documentary film was printed in an edited volume on Beauvoir's political writings by Margaret A. Simons and Marybeth Timmermann (Simons and Timmermann 2012, 339–63; Beauvoir 2012); Davis wrote an introduction to this film and the transcript (Davis 2012). Without any doubt, *A Walk through the Land of Old Age* serves as an important additional document with respect to the research topic of Beauvoir and aging.

nelope Deutscher in her article in this volume argues, Beauvoir neglected "to discuss at any real length the experiences of *very aged* women" (29, emphasis added).

Another obstacle for an appropriate acknowledgment of Beauvoir's *The Coming of Age* by feminist scholars can be seen in the fact that it is not a "feminist" book in the narrower sense of the word. While *The Second Sex* in particular is about women, *The Coming of Age* is about aging in general and does not aim at a gender-specific treatment of the topic. Consequently, because of this gender-indifferent theoretical approach, feminist scholars have considered Beauvoir's book on old age to be less relevant, while simultaneously overlooking the chapter "From Maturity to Old Age" of the second book of *The Second Sex* (1989, 575–96) in their feminist reception.[6]

Another reason for the academic neglect of Beauvoir's reflections on old age is her own focus on death, with the effect that the issue of old age was moved to the sidelines. As Deutscher puts it, Beauvoir's frequent discussions of old age "are often subsumed by commentators under the general category of a preoccupation with death" (Deutscher 2003, 292). In an interview with Madeleine Gobeil in 1965 Beauvoir said, for example: "I've always been haunted by the passing of time and by the fact that death keeps closing in on us. For me, the problem of time is linked up with that of death, with the thought that we inevitably draw closer and closer to it, with the horror of decay" (Beauvoir 1965b). Obviously, for a very long time death as a predominating philosophical *topos* did not allow for any further differentiation; discussions about mortality, for example, were dominated by discussions about death—age and aging were seen as being merely transitory in meaning. Beauvoir's own reflections on aging in terms of the approaching limiting point of death give rise to such reductive interpretations of her work. However, as Deutscher rightly points out, "her interest in age is not reducible to this understanding" (Deutscher 2003, 292)—and, as we might add, it is not reducible at all. At a prominent place in her book *The Second Sex*, Beauvoir draws a philosophical distinction between these two. From a phenomenological point of view, death and aging have different meanings for us. While we do have a certain understanding of death, being aware of our human mortality, as Beauvoir believes, there is no such implicit knowledge or latent expectation with respect to age. And while death may come at any single moment, on the contrary, "no one ever becomes old in a single instant" (Beau-

---

6 One of the few laudable exceptions of this time, however, is the volume *The Other Within Us*, edited by Marilyn Pearsall in 1997, whose articles refer to the double discourse of women and aging in *The Second Sex* and *The Coming of Age* (Pearsall 1997).

voir 1996, 4). In order to do justice to the issue of age and to reflect upon aging in itself, the difference between the phenomenon of death and the phenomenon of age should be kept in mind. Although in many cases they cannot be separated, the separation of age from death would allow for a broader theoretical access to the specificities of age and aging.

The Beauvoir reception in feminist philosophy of the last thirty years was focused around a couple of predominating issues. This domination can be taken as another reason for the neglect of Beauvoir's study on age. First, in the 1980s, US-scholars and in particular Margaret A. Simons, with her pioneering work on Beauvoir, started to free Beauvoir's philosophical contribution from the overwhelming occupation of Sartre's existential philosophy, arguing that Beauvoir's philosophy was not an appendage to Sartre's existentialism but that she was an independent philosopher in her own right (Simons 1986). Debra Bergoffen's landmark work *The Philosophy of Simone de Beauvoir* also aimed at reading Beauvoir as a philosopher, situating her within the philosophical tradition (Bergoffen 1997).[7] At the same time, under the influence of post-structural philosophy, the focus shifted from Beauvoir's original philosophical contribution to the issues of gender identity and the construction of gender and gender identity. While for a long time Beauvoir's theoretical approach to gender equality had gone more or less unnoticed by post-structuralist feminists precisely because of her equality-based approach, feminist theorists eventually began to see Beauvoir as a partner in post-structuralist interpretations of gender, despite the fact that she was a representative of so-called "equality feminism." Surprisingly, some scholars have even argued that Beauvoir was a kind of a forerunner of post-structuralist gender theory. In an early article Judith Butler argued that Beauvoir's thesis on "becoming a woman" could at least partly be understood as an approach of "cultural construction" and thus shared some key insights in poststructuralist gender theory. While she remains critical of Beauvoir's existentialist theory of "choice," Butler nevertheless offers a reinterpretation of Beauvoir which places her closer to post-structuralism. In particular, Butler argues that Beauvoir's view of the body as a "situation" "certainly lays the groundwork" (Butler 1986, 47) for post-structuralist approaches such as those provided by Monique Wittig and Michel Foucault. Soon afterwards, from the late 1990s onwards, scholars with a phenomenological background began to pay attention to the phenomenological implications of Simone de Beauvoir's work. Various at-

---

7 The debate on the relationship between Sartre and Beauvoir is still going on, as can be seen from a collection of articles on the "philosophical and literary relationship between Simone de Beauvoir and Jean-Paul Sartre," edited by Christine Daigle and Jacob Golomb, who consider this question a "thorny" one (Daigle and Golomb 2009, 1).

tempts aimed at exploring the phenomenological roots and influences of Husserl, Sartre, Merleau-Ponty, Levinas, and even Heidegger, in Beauvoir's philosophical work. To mention only a few, Sara Heinämaa, for example, emphasized the Husserlian background of Beauvoir's feminist philosophy, arguing that her "discussion of femininity and sexual difference is phenomenological in its aims and its methods" (Heinämaa 2003, xii). Others like Sonia Kruks and many after her, however, underlined the influence of Merleau-Ponty on Beauvoir's existential feminism in her *Situation and Human Existence* (1990).[8] That even Heidegger's existential phenomenology plays a role in Beauvoir's work was first made visible by Eva Gothlin (Lundgren-Gothlin 1996). In her book *The Philosophy of Simone de Beauvoir*, Debra Bergoffen offered another brilliant interpretation of Beauvoir's background in phenomenology, concentrating on the "muted voice" of her philosophical studies (Bergoffen 1997). The volume *The Existential Phenomenology of Simone de Beauvoir*, edited by Wendy O'Brien and Lester Embree (2001), is a prime example of the new interest in Beauvoir's phenomenological background. Coincidently, the new theoretical approach of "feminist phenomenology" finally entered the academic scene at exactly the same time.[9] It appears that in the past the time had not yet come for a shift from the issue of gender to the issue of age (or reflections upon their intersections). Perhaps Luce Irigaray was right in saying that "each age has one issue to think through, and only one" (Irigaray 1993, 5). Indeed, maybe the twentieth century was the age when "gender" required all the attention feminists could raise, in order to strengthen not only a political awareness of gender issues but also to fight for the institutional foundation and establishment of what later became Women's and Gender Studies. Consequently, due to this theoretical and political preoccupation, age could not really move into the center of feminist concerns. One wonders if age might in fact be one of the key issues of the twenty-first century.

---

8 For an overview of the influence of Merleau-Ponty on Beauvoir, see Stoller 2010, ch. 4.

9 The first edited volumes that were exclusively dedicated to feminist phenomenology are *Phänomenologie und Geschlechterdifferenz*, edited by Silvia Stoller and Helmuth Vetter (Stoller and Vetter 1997) in German, followed by *Feminist Phenomenology*, edited by Linda Fisher and Lester Embree (Fisher and Embree 2000) in English, and another volume in German and English, *Feministische Phänomenologie und Hermeneutik*, edited by Silvia Stoller, Veronica Vasterling, and Linda Fisher (Stoller, Vasterling, and Fisher 2005) that newly added feminist hermeneutics to the already existing feminist phenomenology. Meanwhile, these volumes have been followed by special issues on "Feminist Phenomenology" in the *Continental Philosophy Review* 41/1 (2010), edited by Sara Heinämaa and Lanei Rodemeyer, and another one on "Feminist Phenomenology" in *Janus Head* 13 (1), a special issue edited by Eva-Maria Simms and Beata Stawarska, for the Winter/Spring 2013.

Last but not least, as Beauvoir herself emphatically argued in her introduction of *The Coming of Age*, it is individual and societal resistance against any broader theoretization of age that is responsible for the lack of consideration of the issue. People tend to evade aspects that distress them, and society looks upon old age, Beauvoir argues, "as a kind of shameful secret that it is unseemly to mention" (1996, 1). If there was a general denial of age in Western societies, why should the sciences be free of it? Indeed, in a somewhat provocative tone, Kathleen Woodward argues that *The Coming of Age* was ignored by "mainstream readers, feminists, and even scholars of Beauvoir herself" because "ageism is entrenched within feminism itself" (Woodward 1999b, xi). She points out that "ageism" cannot only be found within feminism but also in academics (Woodward 1999b, xi).

However, it should not go unnoticed that despite this general neglect of Beauvoir's *The Coming of Age* in feminist philosophy, some exceptional works have been published since the late 1980s. Among those exceptions is a short chapter on "Old Age, Death and Depression" (Moi 1994, 236–43) in Toril Moi's intellectual portrayal of Beauvoir's life and work, as well as Debra Bergoffen's inclusion of Beauvoir's philosophy of age in her important study *The Philosophy of Simone de Beauvoir* (Bergoffen 1997). In the 1980s scholars began to link sexuality to age. Elaine Marks, for example, argues that sexuality and aging are interrelated throughout Beauvoir's writings. She proposes that in Beauvoir's works, "sexuality emerges through the discourses on aging and that the uncontrollable body in decline is a body manifesting its sexuality" (Marks 1986, 183). Also, it is not the first time that somebody noted the phenomenological background of Beauvoir's *The Coming of Age*. Sarah Clark Miller argues that Beauvoir's essay on age "is a work of phenomenology, one which continues the research begun by Edmund Husserl and thereafter refined by such authors as Maurice Merleau-Ponty" (Clark Miller 2001, 128) and that her book in fact offers a "phenomenology of old age" (Clark Miller 2001, 145). Outside the narrow academic space of philosophy, though not less "philosophical," extensive research on Beauvoir and age has been carried out by US literary critic Kathleen Woodward, the editor of the pivotal collection *Figuring Age* that aimed to "help to bring the subject of older women into visibility" (Woodward 1999b, xvi) and that is considered an important contribution to age studies. In her articles on Beauvoir, Woodward offers an illuminating psychoanalytic reading of her work on age by placing her autobiographical writings within the context of her theoretical work, arguing that her theoretical work is grounded in her personal experiences. Woodward's interpretation of Beauvoir is unique in that she points to Beauvoir's unconsciousness and reads the French philosopher not only as an intellectual but also as a person with emotions whose work can be interpreted as "a symptom of personal concerns and obsessions, as a *figure* on which she has both projected her subjectivity and displaced her anxieties" (Woodward 1988a, 91).[10] More recently, for example, Ursula Tidd of the University of Manchester has included a chapter on age in her biography of Simone de Beauvoir, entitled "The Death of the Other," in which she briefly discusses Beauvoir's essay on *The Coming of Age* (Tidd 2009; cf. Tidd 2004). Bethany Ladimer also takes notice of Beauvoir's reflections on age in her book on age and women writers (Ladimer 1999). Moreover, textbooks on aging and gerontology include passages from Beauvoir's essay (cf. Moody 2006)—just to name a few.

It seems that, at the turn to the twenty-first century, the time to address the question of aging in Beauvoir has finally come. Feminist philosophers in general as well as Beauvoir scholars in particular can no longer ignore the topics of age and aging, and remarkable new works have been published. The self-explanatory title of the edited volume *Age Matters*, published in 2006, is symptomatic of the recent trend in feminist sciences (Calasanti and Slevin 2006). In relation to Beauvoir, *The Cambridge Companion to Simone de Beauvoir*, edited by Claudia Card in 2003, can be regarded as a magnificent highlight. Although placed at the very end of the list of essays, it includes an article by Penelope Deutscher on Beauvoir's *The Coming of Age* (2003). Perhaps her extensive, valuable research on Beauvoir's work on age and the elderly are exemplary for this positive turn in the field of feminist philosophy, which includes the focus on Beauvoir's philosophical reflections on age and aging in her essay *The Coming of Age*. Last but not least, this present collection of articles in English can be viewed as another weighty token of a turn in the same direction.

Beauvoir's Long-Lasting Interest in Age

Although Beauvoir published *The Coming of Age* at the advanced age of 72, this does not mean that she started to reflect upon age and aging only late in her career. In fact, considering her autobiographical writings, it becomes clear that this topic shaped her life and work from the very beginnings. As Debra Bergoffen has shown, aging has always been an integral part of her reflections on finitude. The question of finitude is raised early in her novel *All Men are Mortal* (*Tous les hommes sont mortels*, 1946), the story of a man called Fosca and his desire for

---

10 Also see Woodward 1988b, 1993, 1999a and 1999b. I would like to thank Kathleen Woodward for personally introducing me to her research at the Hypatia 25th Anniversary Conference in Seattle 2009.

immortality. Later, in *A Very Easy Death* (*Une mort très douce*, 1964), Beauvoir imposingly describes the dying and death of her mother. Finally, finitude is also a topic in *The Coming of Age* (*La Vieillesse*, 1970). In addition, Beauvoir did not stop focusing on age and aging after her philosophical study on age. Eleven years after her book on old age, she published her reminiscences in *Adieux* (*La cérémonie des adieux*, 1981), an impressive realistic and unadorned account of Sartre's last ten years which were determined by his illness and bodily decline, followed by a number of interviews she had conducted with him in 1974. One must assume that her preoccupation with illnesses, along with the decline and death of her friends and family members, only encouraged her to think more deeply about age and aging.

Thus, it should not go unnoticed that Beauvoir did not only have a purely theoretical interest in the issue of age. Indeed, aging was one of the experiences that had strongly influenced Beauvoir's life. She was only 36 when a sudden experience of aging and being old threatened her, as the illuminating epilogue of her autobiography *Force of Circumstance* (*La force des choses*, 1963) tells us: "Since 1944, the most important, the most irreparable thing that has happened to me is that ... I have grown old" (Beauvoir 1965a, 653). The experience of the passing of time and of becoming old, even as a young woman, remained a constitutive element throughout her life. "I've always been keenly aware of the passing of time. I've always thought that I was old. Even when I was twelve [sic!], I thought it was awful to be thirty, I felt that something was lost" (Beauvoir 1965b). Several other first-hand documents, such as an interview with the German feminist Alice Schwarzer conducted with Beauvoir in 1978 on the eve of her seventieth birthday about old age and her book *The Coming of Age*, confirm her deep concern with age. It was a "real shock," she said, when in her fifties she heard young women saying: "Oh well, Simone de Beauvoir is an old woman" (Schwarzer 1984, 83). This was a key event in Beauvoir's life that she mentions several times in her work and that she also refers to in *The Coming of Age* (cf. Beauvoir 1996, 288). Although I believe that her personal motivation should not be overemphasized so as not to diminish the intellectual achievement of her book, it is not wrong to say that it is some of both worlds that motivated Beauvoir to write *The Coming of Age* or a little of both: something personal and something intellectual. This is evident in her autobiography *All Said and Done*, a work she started to write immediately after her book on the aged: "But the reason why I made up my mind to embark upon this book was that I needed to understand a state that is my own, and to understand it in its implication for mankind as a whole" (Beauvoir 1993, 130). Indeed, Beauvoir was personally attached to her own experience of becoming old, but at the same time she wanted to dedicate her personal experiences—in line with her intellectual capacity—to the future philosophical research on age.

New Perspectives on Beauvoir's
The Coming of Age

Topically, the articles collected in this volume cover three main issues which are crucial with respect to an investigation of Beauvoir's study on age: gender, ethics, and time. Therefore, the book is divided into three parts. The first part is dedicated to the interrelation of age and gender. This should not come as a surprise. One wonders how the author of *The Second Sex* treats age in *The Coming of Age*. It is also of primary interest how, if at all, Beauvoir herself related age to gender in her main works *The Second Sex* and *The Coming of Age*. If women and the aged are the "other," to put it in Beauvoir's own terms, widely marginalized and oppressed in our society (Western societies as well as non-Western societies), then what implications does this have for aged women? Feminist theorists in the past increasingly emphasized the intersection of age and gender; in general, they share the opinion that age and gender must be conceptually related to each other in order to fully elaborate the mutual impact one has on the other.[11] Did Beauvoir herself sufficiently allow for a theorization of the intersection of gender and age? (Penelope Deutscher) Moreover, did she continue with her negative account of female bodily experience in *The Second Sex* when she addressed the aged in *The Coming of Age?* How did Beauvoir deal with the myth of femininity and the myth of old age? (Gail Weiss) Finally, how do habits constitute the life of the aged, and how can they be described positively, from a phenomenological perspective? (Helen Fielding)

The second part highlights the ethical and political implications of Beauvoir's *The Coming of Age*. Since Beauvoir herself understood her essay on old age as social criticism, sharply accusing Western societies of their ignorance towards aging and of their shameful treatment of old people, the issue of politics and social change remains a topic of importance. However, Beauvoir's pitiless criticism of the atrocious treatment of the elderly in Western societies goes hand in hand with her demand for radical existential ethics to acknowledge age in our lives. For this reason the articles turn towards the ethical implications of Beauvoir's reflections on age. First, one may want to know whose works influenced Beauvoir in her reflections on aging. If Sartre's influence on Beauvoir in

---

11 Cf. Krekula 2007, Maierhofer 2000, and Sontag 1997.

general cannot be denied, then in what ways did he influence *The Coming of Age?* (Sonia Kruks) What idea of otherness underlies Beauvoir's thesis that the aged are the "other"? (Linda Fisher) May we speak of a dignity of finitude when finitude along with physical decline is an essential characteristic of the life of the aged? (Debra Bergoffen) How is it possible for the aged individual to live so as to affirm the "joy of existence"? (Dorothea Olkowski)

Since it does not make sense to speak about age and aging without addressing the issue of time, the third and final part addresses age and time. Time is the ultimate factor of one's own experience of age. Without time and, more particularly, without the passing of time with all its predominant consequences, whatever they are, age would not be an issue at all. It is here that the unique phenomenological time theory comes into play.[12] In various ways, the articles in this section process the meaning of time in Beauvoir's age theory. They provide a profound phenomenological analysis on aging and death (Sara Heinämaa); they confront Beauvoir's own analysis of age and aging with phenomenological time theories (Silvia Stoller), and they finally open the door for alternative time concepts that promise to overcome certain failures which can be found in Beauvoir's essay (Christina Schües).

The articles included in this book are also completed by comments. The comments illustrate or delve deeper into the issues and theories brought up in the articles, or even go beyond them to develop further reflections. The comments thus contribute to a more productive and lively confrontation with the topic of this volume. In the following, articles and comments will be summarized and contextualized while considering the key issues outlined above.

Age and Gender

In light of Beauvoir's inestimable contribution to feminist philosophy, the question of how she relates gender to age becomes primary. How she connects gender and age is also of primary interest if her essay on *The Coming of Age* becomes the focus of research. Although it is not entirely true that Beauvoir scholars have neglected to take age into consideration along with the ways in which age and gender are related to each other in Beauvoir's work, both in *The Second Sex* and in *The Coming of Age*, research has only just begun to explore this dimension— mainly due to *Penelope Deutscher's* research in the last years. In her opening ar-

---

12 For more on feminist phenomenology with respect to the issue of time, see the recently edited volume *Time in Feminist Phenomenology* (Schües, Olkowski, and Fielding 2011).

ticle, Deutscher focuses on the relationship between *The Second Sex* and *The Coming of Age* in order to reconstruct the complex relations of sex and age in these two classic works. While it cannot seriously be denied that Beauvoir, at least partly, considers old age in her main work *The Second Sex* and sex in *The Coming of Age*, Deutscher argues that Simone de Beauvoir neglected, in both works, to discuss at any real length the experiences of "very aged women" (29). In *The Second Sex* Beauvoir refers to women not older than in their mid-sixties, and in *The Coming of Age* she states that aging is not as much a problem for women as it is for men and in so doing once again downplays, as Deutscher argues, the "perspective of aged women" (30). According to Deutscher's detailed analysis, one comes to the conclusion that Beauvoir's work suffers from the same failure that generations of age researchers are guilty of, namely neglecting the *very aged* among the aged. Moreover, in order to fully understand the meaning of age and aging for the very old, both women and men, in Beauvoir's work, it is indispensible, Deutscher argues, to read *The Coming of Age* in line with *The Second Sex*. Put differently, one cannot grasp the meaning of age and aging and the relation of sex and gender in *The Coming of Age* without considering Beauvoir's *The Second Sex*. In her comment, *Ulrike Kadi* refers to Deutscher's basic claim that Beauvoir neglected very aged women and calls our attention to two "exceptions." By a first step, she reminds the reader of a small chapter on "The Hundred-Year-Olds," included as an appendix in *The Coming of Age*, in which Beauvoir alludes to an inquiry from a French doctor about centenarians (most of them women), published in 1959. Second, Kadi stresses the role Beauvoir herself plays in her considerations of old age, insofar as her personal anxieties and her reflections upon human finitude at least indirectly express her engagement with very old women. Both articles raise the awareness for the imperative to take the advanced elderly into consideration and to distinguish between different stages of old age.

While Penelope Deutscher's primary interest is to relate Beauvoir's great essays on sex and age to each other, *Gail Weiss* emphasizes another highly important connection. She reflects upon two powerful myths which are addressed in *The Second Sex* and *The Coming of Age:* the "myth of femininity" and the "myth of old age." Beauvoir's vigorous efforts to deconstruct persistent and often contradictory myths in Western cultures and societies, whether they imply femininity or age, thereby come to the forefront in her illuminating reading of Beauvoir. At the same time, Weiss directs us to one of Beauvoir's key ideas in her entire social philosophy and perhaps to her most challenging idea of all, the idea that myths are responsible for the construction of women and old people as "the Other" with a capital O (Beauvoir 1989, 143). Weiss' contribution to this debate consists of her critical exploration of how these two "myths continue to operate in full force as women age" (48), arguing that elderly women are judged both according to the norms of femininity and according to the norms of age. In order to demonstrate this relationship, she first turns to Oscar Wilde's famous novel *The Portrait of Dorian Gray*, a depiction of a character who suffers tremendously from his process of aging. He sees himself Narcissus-like in a painter's portrait presenting him at the height of his youth and beauty—for Weiss an exemplary illustration of the "feminine" obsession with youth and beauty on the one hand and of the alienating effects of aging on the other. She then turns to Beauvoir's thesis that "old age is primarily a male problem" (Beauvoir 1996, 217) since, according to Beauvoir, retired men have more to lose than women by being cut off from the social, economic, and symbolic recognition they enjoyed while part of the working world. This view has been the object of serious feminist criticism and concern, and Gail Weiss adds that, in light of Beauvoir's description of the disadvantage of men at this point in life, the situation of elderly women becomes obscured. Moreover, she argues that the specific vulnerability of older women must be judged in a broader cultural context. Therefore, in her final passage, she returns to the myth of femininity, arguing that, contrary to men's life, there are cultural images of youth and beauty which have a negative impact on the experiences of women at an advanced age. Put differently, it is because of the "powerful myth of femininity" (62) that elderly women disproportionally (and because of their gendered identity) suffer from the aging process. In her article Gail Weiss puts a finger on the "coupling" of the myth of femininity with the myth of aging and thus makes visible the role the intersection of gender and age plays for women—perhaps even better than Beauvoir herself could or intended to do. *Anja Weiberg* expounds on Gail Weiss' article by taking up the central question of why Beauvoir in *The Coming of Age* failed to discuss the issue of age from a gender perspective at length, or put differently, why she, by and large, did not take the "myth of woman" sufficiently into consideration in order to explore the various effects age and aging have on women, that is, elderly women. She suggests that Beauvoir did not simply fail to adequately reflect upon the meaning of femininity for elderly women but that she was not interested in differentiating between women and men. In Weiberg's opinion, it is Beauvoir's general interest in aged people as a social group—independent of their sex or gender—that made her indifferent to a gender-related analysis. She concludes that Beauvoir, as the author of *The Coming of Age*, "is not primarily a feminist but an advocate for the aged" (67). This opens up the debate of whether or not Beauvoir did willfully, with good reason perhaps, refuse a closer examination of the relation of age and gender in her essay *The Coming of Age*.

For Simone de Beauvoir, being old means being condemned, neither to freedom, nor to meaning, but rather to boredom. Such boredom often characterizes the daily life of elderly people and it is clearly of negative nature. In her article, *Helen A. Fielding* focuses on significant passages in *The Coming of Age* in the chapter "Old Age and Everyday Life" (Beauvoir 1996, 448–504) in which Beauvoir deals with the question of how the aged live their daily lives and how they manage to deal with their situation, arguing that, because of their indifference to the present and the boredom they are condemned to, the elderly take refuge in habit. However, in her illuminating reading of Beauvoir's considerations of habit and the role it plays for the elderly, Fielding discovers a habit in Beauvoir's description that is of a different kind. Along with Beauvoir, she argues that habits can take on a "kind of poetry" (Beauvoir 1996, 468) which allows for promising modifications of the present. This is the point where phenomenology comes into play. In providing a phenomenological account of habitual existence and in reference to Merleau-Ponty's concept of the phenomenal body and the bodily existence, Fielding demonstrates how habits not only consist of unproductive automatic repetitions of the past but that they are indeed a "kind of doing" (70). The "poetical habit" as Fielding calls it in reference to Beauvoir, is not merely passivity but rather "active passivity" whereas emphasis is put on the active moment in the state of the so-called passivity. Moreover, in following Merleau-Ponty, she argues that habits are a way of keeping oneself engaged with the world. They provide the elderly with a sort of "ontological security" (Beauvoir 1996, 469), they hold them in the world, and as such represent an active inhabiting of space and time, a way of structuring the lives of the elderly. In putting emphasis on the constitutive role of the *habitus* in the world, Fielding sets the stage for a reinterpretation of the more negative account of habit as an unproductive act of repetition. Put differently, she allows for a transformation of the negative account into a positive account of habit, and in as much as she highlights the existential meaning of the habitual lives of the elderly, she contributes to the ethical and social acknowledgment of the specific life of the elderly. In her response to Helen Fielding, *Kristin Rodier* asks if what Beauvoir and Fielding described as poetical habit is "particular to the aged" (83). Indeed, she doubts that the outlined structure of habit is constitutive for the elderly only. In relating the experiences of the aged with those of the middle-aged, she contributes to a future discussion of how the habits of elderly people—respectively elderly women—at different ages differ from each other, if at all. Thus, Rodier's comment allows for a reconsideration of habitual life which not only characterizes the life of the elderly people but everybody's life in general. Certainly, what future researchers will continually need to address is the question of how to distinguish between the habits of the elderly and those of younger people.

Age and Ethics

Since the 1980s much has been said about the relation between Beauvoir and Sartre. Beauvoir researchers have explored Sartre's influence on Beauvoir's work, and they have also concentrated on her own individual contribution to the issues at stake. However, most of the time, *The Coming of Age* has remained untouched, and the same could be said about the influence of Sartre's philosophy on Beauvoir's study of old age. Generally ignored for a long time, *The Coming of Age* has never been at the center of such an investigation. *Sonia Kruks* puts things right in her article.[13] She relates Sartre's *Critique of Dialectical Reason*, originally published in1960, to Beauvoir's *The Coming of Age*, published ten years later, and examines how, in *The Coming of Age*, Beauvoir appropriated selected "materialist" elements of Sartre's *Critique*, including such notions as "exis" (another name for the Greek *hexis*) and the "practico-inert." She fills the unfortunate gap and thus eminently contributes to the subject of the relation between Beauvoir and Sartre through the inclusion of Beauvoir's *The Coming of Age*. She argues that Beauvoir, in a creative way, integrates these notions into her own work in order to develop a "dialectical account of old age as at once a materially constituted social reality and an embodied and individually lived experience" (100). This means that Beauvoir not only employs materialist aspects from Sartre's *Critique of Dialectical Reason*, as Kruks clearly demonstrates, but that she also transforms them. Like Fielding before her, Kruks turns toward a discussion of Beauvoir's reflections on habits, arguing that she does not fully embrace Sartre's pessimism documented in his *Critique of Dialectical Reason*, since in her opinion some habits can take on a form of meaningful existential value for the aged. Although habits remain forms of the "practico-inert" as described by Sartre, for Beauvoir they are far from his characterization as a "'demonic' force" (100). In her comment on Kruks, *Elisabeth Schäfer* opens up with a discussion of the limitedness of old age, arguing that contrary to Beauvoir the experience of limitedness is not restricted to aged people. Although, strictly speaking, only old people can have the experience of being old, Schäfer insists that due to the very irreversibility of time, young people can also share the experience of limitedness, even though this kind of experience is mostly of an unconscious nature. Interestingly, in her comment Schäfer poses a question that before had been raised by Kristin Rodier with respect to habits, namely whether what

---

13 In her recent book *Simone de Beauvoir and the Politics of Ambiguity*, Kruks has included a chapter on "The Coming of Age: Aversion" in which she demonstrates that the oppression of old age in Beauvoir's essay on old age is typified by aversion (Kruks 2012, 81–89).

Beauvoir ascribes to the elderly is really restricted only to old age. This may certainly stimulate future research on Beauvoir and her characterization of old age as singling out traits typical of the elderly. Moreover, Schäfer doubts—in accordance with Beauvoir and Kruks—that the practical existence of habits is reserved for the elderly only in that they refer to a life-long past. Instead, since habits are a way of organizing one's own daily life, regardless of age, they also relegate to the future and thus can be called a future-directed "project" in Beauvoir's sense of existentialism.

In order to do justice to Beauvoir's phenomenological philosophy of the aged, research on her theoretical background is indispensible. Sonia Kruks' work on Beauvoir's reference to and reinterpretation of Sartre's *Critique of Dialectical Reason* is such a contribution. Likewise, the interpretation of Beauvoir's thesis that the aged is the Other constitutes another, essential step towards Beauvoir's *The Coming of Age*. *Linda Fisher*, who has dedicated her life-long intellectual work in feminist phenomenology to the issue of alterity, in her article applies Beauvoir's thesis of the otherness to old age. Her illuminating interpretation of the otherness of the aged reveals two different kinds of otherness that should be taken into consideration: the otherness in economic terms, and a more "fundamental" (111) otherness that cannot be restricted to an economic otherness inherent in Beauvoir's description of the aged as the other. As Fisher argues, this fundamental otherness is one that already resides in one's own self. Reading Beauvoir's study as a "phenomenology of the lived experience of old age and aging" (112), she turns toward one's own experience of age, thus following Beauvoir in her description of the aged seen from the inside—"as lived experience of old age" (112) which, according to Beauvoir, collides with the outside perspective. As such, the old person is not just the Other seen from the outside by someone else, but the Other from within one's own self, which means "I am Other to myself" (113). Consequently, the alterity of old age already "resides within us" as Fisher claims with reference to Beauvoir's narration of Buddha. However, the process of otherness that takes place here can only be understood from these two perspectives, rather, it is a result of a constituting intertwining of the inside and outside perspectives. This leads her to an analysis of the sources of human resistance against becoming old: the fear of decline. As it turns out, it is the fear of decline rather than the fear of old age that actually constitutes the process of othering. It is precisely Beauvoir's treatment of age under the perspective of physical decline that has provoked scholarly criticism in the past, and *Veronica Vasterling*, too, calls attention to this point. In her response to Fisher, she asks whether today it is not Alzheimer's and dementia, that is to say mental decline, which sparks fear in one's life. In addition, in a more general sense, she contests the universal identification of old age with negative imagery, and reminds us of positive images of age in other cultures. Although this is clearly what Beauvoir herself did in her essay at length, a general investigation of the cultural meanings of age and aging will always have to acknowledge the diversity of cultural interpretations, while the interpretation of age as physical decline is only one of them.

Whereas Fisher concentrates on the aspect of the physical decline of the aged, *Debra Bergoffen* starts with the issue of decline but focuses on the experience of finitude as another essential aspect of Beauvoir's reflections on age and aging. Given that the lives of the aged are characterized by physical decline, illness, and the loss of bodily "I cans," a term Bergoffen takes from phenomenology, then what ethical implications does this have? In particular, how is the experience of aging related to the issue of "human dignity"? In her critical reading of Beauvoir she accuses her of unreflectively reproducing the idealizations of youth and work in *The Coming of Age*, arguing that her existentialist concepts of "project" and "transcendence" among others can be held responsible for it. However, as Bergoffen shows, in *All Men Are Mortal* Beauvoir shifts to an alternative interpretation of the ideologies of youth. There, finitude is not conceived as a curse but as an "ontological necessity" and thus the very "anchor of our humanity" (135) or, in Beauvoir's own terms, "a delusion" since it is precisely finitude that makes us human—a finitude that, strictly speaking, does not only belong to the aged but also characterizes the lives of the young, as Bergoffen claims. The perspective that Bergoffen opens up in her article consists of an "inter-generational dialogue" between the young and the old. This is a dialogue in which each side learns a lesson from the other: namely, that "the aged save the young from the tyranny of their illusions," while "the young save the old from the power of their habits" (139). Only if such a dialogue takes place, there can be real dignity for both. In her comment, *Gertrude Postl* starts where Bergoffen closed her reflections—her demand for an inter-generational dialogue. Bergoffen doubts that such a fruitful encounter can take place between the generations, since the two generational groups have experiences that are essentially different: the experience of the young "differs significantly from those of the old" (144). In particular, Postl insists that the experience of the loss of the "I can" of the aged is a hindrance for a mutual encounter between the generations since, in her view, more is required from the old than from the young. Moreover, Postl assumes that Bergoffen's considerations about the "dignity of finitude" are actually based on the idea of equality while, in fact, there is a difference. Thus, taking Postl's comment into serious consideration, is seems that the very fact of conflicting views—on the one hand, finitude is a human condition, and, on the other, there are different experiences of finitude—needs further exploration.

Although this book concentrates on Beauvoir's *The Coming of Age*, in order to understand Beauvoir's theory of the aged, it seems necessary to include works other than her seminal essay on age and aging. In her article, *Dorothea Olkowski* finds it helpful to engage with Beauvoir's early novel *She Came to Stay* which serves as a framework for addressing the question of how the joy of existence can be realized even in aging years. She introduces the concept of the "clinamen" which was first used by the Roman philosopher Lucretius. It was also used by Simone de Beauvoir and Jean-Paul Sartre and later on in Michel Serres' philosophy, in order to argue that the joy of existence can only be realized by abandoning the individualistic notion of the human being. In particular, Olkowski argues that, for Beauvoir, old age is not merely an individual task but a matter of inter-subjective relations, and further, that it is not a matter of nature, that is, an issue of physical decline, but rather it is of ethical nature. Finally, in her interpretation of Beauvoir, Olkowski maintains that only a "logic of ambiguity" (155) can guarantee the joy of existence in old age. Such logic does not negate the past while it remains open to the future at the same time. In her comment, *Annemie Halsema* positively highlights Olkowski's reflections on nature. Yet she believes that the relation of nature and ethics needs to be further elaborated in order to get into the essence of Beauvoir's theory of the aged. Finally it seems as if they both agree on this point and that future readings of Beauvoir's *The Coming of Age* should concentrate on this issue.

Age and Time

Age and aging cannot be interpreted without addressing time, since aging is linked to a temporal process. From the perspective of Beauvoir's existentialist account, aging cannot seriously be talked about without including the experience of becoming old. For this reason, the following three essays aim to explore the concept of time in Beauvoir's philosophical account of age. It is not a coincidence that phenomenology will play a key role in the interpretation of time and age in Beauvoir's essay. This is because classical phenomenologists from Husserl onwards, among them Martin Heidegger, Max Scheler, Henri Bergson, Maurice Merleau-Ponty, Emmanuel Levinas, and others, have all dedicated their work to the exploration of time from a phenomenological perspective. Moreover, Beauvoir's own reflections on time in *The Coming of Age* are infused with phenomenology, inasmuch as, in the second part of her book, she preferably relates to age and aging as a lived experience. At the very outset of Part III, *Sara Heinämaa* reads Beauvoir within the methodological framework of classical phenomenology, arguing that Beauvoir's own discourse on age rests on phenomenological concepts such as the concept of lived experience. She illuminates the "phenomenon" of age in outlining three philosophical ideas that can be found in Beauvoir's philosophical investigation of age and offers a thoughtful phenomenological reading of her characterization of age as an experience. First, aging is not a gradual process but rather a "sudden event," and as a form of metamorphosis it fundamentally changes one's way of being in the world. Second, while aging has an effect on one's way of life, this does not mean that it shapes the person in her/his entirety. Rather it is only the other in one's self that gets old. Paradoxically, according to Beauvoir, age cannot be experienced by the aged subject itself but only through the perception of others. Consequently, it is the double being of the embodied subject—being for ourselves and being for others—that contributes to the experience of being old. Third, the metamorphosis of aging coincides with a radical change in the temporal form of experience, which means that aging has an effect on the temporal horizons of the past and the future. While the future slowly closes for the aged, the past becomes loaded with a heavy weight. At the end, Heinämaa refers to Beauvoir's late dialogue with Sartre in *Adieux* in order to demonstrate how Beauvoir differs from her phenomenological contemporaries, since contrary to Sartre, Merleau-Ponty, and Levinas Beauvoir believes that the temporality of the aged is not inherent in humanity. *Bonnie Mann* puts Heinämaa's phenomenological reading of Beauvoir into a broader context, asking about her relation to the tradition of classical phenomenology. She claims that Beauvoir transforms classical phenomenology. In Mann's opinion, Beauvoir not only holds a critical attitude to the methodology of the phenomenological reduction, she also doubts that Beauvoir believes in "pure" experiences. In addition, contrary to Heinämaa, Mann asserts that Beauvoir's first part of *The Coming of Age*, with its focus on the empirical, social, and political, is as important as the second part dealing with the experience of age. It is Beauvoir's acknowledgment of social and political injustices that makes Beauvoir's phenomenology an approach in feminist phenomenology. In her own concluding words: "Beauvoir's phenomenology is *feminist* precisely insofar as it revisions classical phenomenology" (193). Inasmuch as Heinämaa and Mann put emphasis on the phenomenological implications of Beauvoir's work, their contributions in this volume allow for further investigations in feminist phenomenology.

Silvia Stoller links Beauvoir's considerations on age and aging to another classical phenomenologist, namely to Maurice Merleau-Ponty, and explores two different views on the experience of age and time that can be found both in Beauvoir's *The Coming of Age* and in Merleau-Ponty's *Phenomenology of Perception.* While the former calls upon us to "recognize ourselves in this old man or in that old woman," the latter claims that "in old age a man is still in contact with his youth." Obviously, their claims move in different directions: Beauvoir relates to the other in the social world (in German: *Fremdbezug*), Merleau-Ponty relates to oneself (in German: *Selbstbezug*); one is directed toward the future, the other toward the past. In order to support a gerontological ethics based on these two French phenomenologists, Stoller finally argues that a double reference to the future and the past, the inward (the Self) and the outward perspective (the Other), is required. Put differently, a phenomenology of age and aging that exclusively concentrates either on the past or on the future can only be half the story. In her response, *Marieke Borren* adds that the outline of a phenomenologically based gerontological ethics must be complemented by a "critical *social* theory of old age alongside an ethics of existence" (213) because of the impact social visions of old age have on the experience of age. Thus, though implicitly, Borren seems to favor Beauvoir's social criticism in her *Coming of Age* against a purely phenomenological account of the issue of age and aging. This also raises the question, as Bonnie Mann comments on Sara Heinämaa's work, of how to theoretically link Beauvoir's second part of *The Coming of Age*, entitled "The Being-in-the-World," to part one, entitled "Old Age Seen from Without," and establish it as a future research task.

Finally, *Christina Schües* offers an in-depth analysis of the time experience provided by classical phenomenology and, in so doing, regards phenomenology as a theoretical source for a comprehensive understanding of the experience of time and age. Her starting point, however, is Beauvoir's rather pessimistic view on age and aging which basically rests upon a certain time concept. According to Beauvoir, the elderly (as opposed to younger people) have a "limited future and a frozen past" (Beauvoir 1996, 378). If one does not want to follow her fundamental pessimism of age, then what would an alternative theory look like and how could Beauvoir's own account be transformed? Schües responds to this question by introducing an alternative account of time, that is, a time concept that manifests itself in a revalorization the present. She claims that the notion of "order of time," which she closely relates to the notion of "*Gestalt*," originally introduced by *Gestalt* theorists at the beginning of the twentieth century, may offer such an alternative. Considering aging a "temporal *Gestalt*," Schües argues, allows us to reconsider the age of the young and that of the old according to their own appropriate time order. Thus, contrary to Beauvoir, it is not the future that serves as a source of optimism, and it is not the past that counts as a source of pessimism. Rather, the source of optimism is inherent in each individual's order of time. Since everybody is allowed to live their own "order of time," a sort of humanity can take place in one's age-life. It seems then that the future of age must not depart from Beauvoir's future-centered account but must instead go beyond it. *Beata Stawarska* agrees with Schües in her hope for a "more authentic engagement with time" (232) that is supposed to be offered by a presence-centered account of time. Yet she doubts that the emphasis on the present comes without problems. In fact, she fears that, due to the focus on the present, the promising inter-generational perspective could end in a "uni-generational perspective on old age" (232) which would shirk ethical responsibility between the generations. It seems though, from the perspective of Christina Schües, that the emphasis on the present is the very condition for an ethical responsibility between the generations as well. However, future research on the issue of age and time will certainly delve deeper into the question of how the different classical philosophical time orders of the past, the present and the future, relate to each other; moreover, as Christina Schües and Beata Stawarska so clearly demonstrate, what this means with respect to the issue of ethical responsibility.

As we mentioned at the very beginning, in the introduction of her book *The Coming of Age* Beauvoir calls for shattering the silence on age and aging, and in her last sentence she addresses her future readers: "I call upon my readers to help me in doing so" (Beauvoir 1996, 7). This call has not lost its importance. The authors of this volume aim to analyze Beauvoir's work in three different respects: with regard to gender, ethics, and time. They have opened up a debate around Beauvoir's *The Coming of Age*, but it is hoped that this is just the beginning of a committed and ongoing debate of this rich text. Once this study has achieved the acknowledgment that it truly deserves, this will certainly also encourage future Beauvoir research and finally contribute to the issue at stake, the crucial issue of aging in our times.

References

Adamowski, T. H. 1987. Death, old age, and femininity: Simone de Beauvoir and the politics of *La Vieillesse*. In *Critical essays on Simone de Beauvoir*, ed. Elaine Marks. Boston, Massachusetts: G. H. Hall & Co., 110–15.

Alison, Martin. 2011. Old age and the other-within: Beauvoir's representation of ageing in *La vieillesse. Forum for Modern Language Studies* 47 (2): 126–36.

Bailey, Alison, Chris Cuomo, eds. 2008. *The feminist philosophy reader.* Boston, Massachusetts: McGraw-Hill.

Beauvoir, Simone de. 1955. *All men are mortal.* Trans. L. M. Friedman. Cleveland, Ohio: World Publishing (originally published as *Tous les hommes sont mortels.* Paris: Gallimard 1946).

Beauvoir, Simone de. 1965a. *The force of circumstance.* Trans. Richard Howard. New York: G. P. Putnam's Sons (originally published as *La force des choses.* Paris: Gallimard 1963).

Beauvoir, Simone de. 1965b. The Art of Fiction No. 35: Interviewed by Madeleine Gobeil. *The Paris Review* 35 (Spring-Summer), http://www.theparisreview.org/interviews/4444/the-art-of-fiction-no-35-simone-de-beauvoir (accessed July 30, 2013).

Beauvoir, Simone de. 1966. *A very easy death.* Trans. Patrick O'Brian. New York: Putnam (originally published as *Une mort très douce.* Paris: Gallimard 1964).

Beauvoir, Simone de. 1984. *Adieux: A farewell to Sartre.* Trans. Patrick O'Brian. New York: Pantheon (originally published as *La cérémonie des adieux.* Paris: Gallimard 1981).

Beauvoir, Simone de. 1989. *The second sex.* Trans. H. M. Parshley. New York: Vintage Books (originally published as *Le deuxième sexe.* Paris: Gallimard 1949).

Beauvoir, Simone de. 1993. *All said and done.* Trans. Patrick O'Brian. New York: Paragon House (originally published as *Tout compte fait.* Paris: Gallimard 1972).

Beauvoir, Simone de. 1996. *The coming of age.* Trans. Patrick O'Brian. New York: W.W. Norton & Company (originally published as *La vieillesse.* Paris: Gallimard 1970).

Beauvoir, Simone de. 2012. A walk through the land of old age: A documentary film by Marianne Ahrne, Simone de Beauvoir, Pépe Angel, and Bertrand Hurault, directed by Marianne Ahrne. In *Simone de Beauvoir: Political writings*, ed. Margaret A. Simons and Marybeth Timmermann. Urbana, Chicago, and Springfield: University of Illinois Press, 339–63.

Bergoffen, Debra. 1997. *The philosophy of Simone de Beauvoir: Gendered phenomenologies, erotic generosities.* Albany: State University of New York Press.

Bergoffen, Debra. 2004. Simone de Beauvoir. In *Stanford encyclopedia of philosophy*, first published August 17, 2004, 25 pages, http://plato.stanford.edu/entries/beauvoir/ (accessed August 13, 2013).

Butler, Judith. 1986. Sex and gender in Simone de Beauvoir's *Second Sex. Yale French Studies* 72: 35–49.

Card, Claudia, ed. 2003. *The Cambridge companion to Simone de Beauvoir.* Cambridge: Cambridge University Press.

Calasanti, Toni, Kathleen F. Slevin, eds. 2006. *Age matters: Realigning feminist thinking.* New York, London: Routledge.

Daigle, Christine, Jacob Golomb, eds. 2009. *Beauvoir and Sartre: The riddle of influence.* Bloomington: Indiana University Press.

Davis, Oliver. 2006a. *Age rage and going gentle: Stories of the senescent subject in twentieth-century French writing.* Amsterdam, New York: Rodopi.

Davis, Oliver. 2006b. Interview with Marianne Ahrne, director of "Promenade au pays de la vieillesse". In *Age rage and going gentle: Stories of the senescent subject in twentieth-century French writing.* Amsterdam, New York: Rodopi, 197–204.

Davis, Oliver. 2012. Introduction. In *Simone de Beauvoir: Political writings*, ed. Margaret A. Simons and Marybeth Timmermann. Urbana, Chicago, and Springfield: University of Illinois Press, 331–38.

Deutscher, Penelope. 1999. Bodies, lost and found: Simone de Beauvoir from *The Second Sex* to *Old Age. Radical philosophy* 96 (July/August 1999): 6–16.

Deutscher, Penelope. 2003. Beauvoir's *Old Age.* In *The Cambridge companion to Simone de Beauvoir*, ed. Claudia Card. Cambridge: Cambridge University Press, 286–304.

Deutscher, Penelope. 2008. *The philosophy of Simone de Beauvoir: Ambiguity, conversation, resistance.* Cambridge: Cambridge University Press.

Fisher, Linda, Lester Embree, eds. 2000. *Feminist phenomenology.* Dordrecht: Kluwer.

Gerassi, John. 1976. Simone de Beauvoir: *The Second Sex* 25 years later. *Society* 13 (2) (January/February): 79–85.

Heinämaa, Sara. 2003. *Toward a phenomenology of sexual difference: Husserl, Merleau-Ponty, Beauvoir.* Lanham: Rowman & Littlefield.

Irigaray, Luce. 1993. *An ethics of sexual difference.* Trans. Carolyn Burke and Gillian C. Gill. Ithaca, New York: Cornell University Press.

Krekula, Clary. 2007. The intersection of age and gender: Reworking gender theory and social gerontology. *Current Sociology* 55 (2): 155–71.

Kruks, Sonia. 2012. *Simone de Beauvoir and the politics of ambiguity.* Oxford: Oxford University Press.

Ladimer, Bethany. 1999. *Colette, Beauvoir, and Duras: Age and women writers.* Gainesville: The University Press of Florida.

Lundgren-Gothlin, Eva. 1996. *Sex and existence: Simone de Beauvoir's "The Second Sex."* London: Athlone Press.

Maierhofer, Roberta. 2000. Simone de Beauvoir and the graying of American feminism. *Journal of Aging and Identity* 5 (2): 67–77.

Marks, Elaine. 1986. Transgressing the (in)cont(in)ent boundaries: The body in decline author (s). *Yale French Studies* 72: 181–200.

Miller, Sarah Clark. 2001. The lived experience of doubling: Simone de Beauvoir's phenomenology of old age. In *The existential phenomenology of Simone de Beauvoir*, ed. Wendy O'Brian and Lester Embree. Dordrecht: Kluwer Academic Publisher, 127–47.

Moi, Toril. 1994. *Simone de Beauvoir: The making of an intellectual woman.* Oxford: Blackwell.

Moody, Harry R. 2006. *Aging: Concepts and controversies*, 5th ed. Thousand Oaks: Sage.

Mussett, Shannon M. 2006. Ageing and existentialism: Simone de Beauvoir and the limits of freedom. In *Death and anti-death*, vol. 4: *Twenty years after De Beauvoir, thirty years after Heidegger*, ed. Charles Tandy. Stanford, Palo Alto: Ria University Press, 231–55.

O'Brian, Wendy, Lester Embree, eds. 2001. *The existential phenomenology of Simone de Beauvoir.* Dordrecht, Boston, London: Kluwer.

Pearsall, Marilyn. 1997. Introduction. In *The other within us: Feminist explorations of women and aging*, ed. Marilyn Pearsall. Boulder, CO: Westview Press, 1–16.

Schües, Christina, Dorothea E. Olkowski, and Helen A. Fielding, eds. 2011. *Time in feminist phenomenology.* Bloomington, Indianapolis: Indiana University Press.

Schwarzer, Alice. 1984. "Women have less far to fall." In *After* The second sex: *Conversations with Simone de Beauvoir.* Trans. Marianne Howarth. New York: Pantheon Books, 81–93.

Simons, Margaret A. 1986. Beauvoir and Sartre: The philosophical relationship. *Yale French Studies* 72: 165–79.

Simons, Margaret A., ed. 2006. *The philosophy of Simone de Beauvoir: Critical essays.* Bloomington, Indianapolis: Indiana University Press.

Sontag, Susan. 1997. The double standard of aging. In *The other within us: Feminist explorations of women and aging*, ed. Marilyn Pearsall. Boulder, CO: Westview Press, 19–24.

Stoller, Silvia. 2010. *Existenz—Differenz—Konstruktion. Phänomenologie der Geschlechtlichkeit bei Beauvoir, Irigaray und Butler.* Munich: Wilhelm Fink.

Stoller, Silvia, Helmuth Vetter, eds. 1997. *Phänomenologie und Geschlechterdifferenz.* Wien: WUV-Universitätsverlag.

Stoller, Silvia, Veronica Vasterling, and Linda Fisher, eds. 2005. *Feministische Phänomenologie und Hermeneutik.* Würzburg: Königshausen & Neumann.
Tidd, Ursula. 2004. *Simone de Beauvoir.* New York: Routledge.
Tidd, Ursula. 2009. *Simone de Beauvoir.* London: Reaktion Books.
Woodward, Kathleen. 1988a. Simone de Beauvoir: *Aging and its discontents.* In *Theory and practice of women's autobiographical writings,* ed. Shari Benstock. Chapel Hill: University of North Carolina Press, 90–113.
Woodward, Kathleen. 1988b. Reminiscence, identity, sentimentality: Simone de Beauvoir and the life review. In *Twenty-five years of the life review: Theoretical and practical considerations,* ed. Robert Disch. New York: Haworth Press, 25–46.
Woodward, Kathleen. 1993. Simone de Beauvoir: Prospects for the future of older women. In *Changing perceptions of aging and the aged,* ed. Dena Shenk and W. Andrew Achenbaum. Special issue of *Generations* 17 (2) (Spring/Summer 1993): 23–26.
Woodward, Kathleen, ed. 1999a. *Figuring age: Women, bodies, generations.* Bloomington, Indianapolis: Indiana University Press.
Woodward, Kathleen. 1999b. Introduction. *Figuring age: Women, bodies, generations,* ed. Kathleen Woodward. Bloomington, Indianapolis: Indiana University Press, ix–xxix.

Part One: **Age and Gender**

Penelope Deutscher

The Sex of Age and the Age of Sex

The Compressions of Life

> *I myself am the future dwelling-place of old age.*
> —Simone de Beauvoir

What should we make of the fact that Simone de Beauvoir, in her two large-scale works of 1949 and 1970, the former an analysis of women as the second sex, and the latter of old age as alterity, neglected to discuss at any real length the experiences of very aged women?

In *The Second Sex* "woman," and "sex" were embedded in a cluster of Beauvoir's compressed terms when a complex network of ideas was brought to the questions: are there really women ("Y-a-t il même des femmes?"), and what is a woman ("Qu-est-ce qu'une femme?"). A similar compression is instituted from the early pages of *The Coming of Age*. Beauvoir, we learn, had been told repeatedly that old age did not exist. She agrees that it is not easy to define. It is, as she had earlier said of femininity, a complex network of biological, existential, social, and intersubjective, physiological, psychological, and historical aspects, such that "[a]n analytical description of the various aspects ... is therefore not enough: each reacts upon all the others and is at the same time affected by them, and it is in the indeterminate [*indéfini*] flow of this circular process that old age must be understood" (Beauvoir 1996, 9, translation modified). Beauvoir shows how layers of complexity are enfolded within these terms, "woman" and "old age," moreover, these layers are not necessarily consistent.

The Second Sex is also a book about time, and although this is not its main intent, it can be seen as expressing the near inseparability of the processes through which we are sexed and the processes through which we are aged. One could use its material to derive a suggestion that there is no sex (and thus, no "second sex") without the changing specificities of age. Beauvoir's depictions of sex are consistently related to the transitions of aging, differentiating the shocked experiences of the young and the old. Such differentiations are seen in the structural division of the *Formation* and *Situation* sections of Book II into the categories: "Childhood," "The Young Girl," "Sexual Initiation," and later "From Maturity to Old Age." We learn of the different ways in which young girls and boys acquire meanings for sexual difference, and of the gendered and temporal differentiations between lively exuberance and trying to please. The relationship to such modes is different for girls and boys of two, five, twelve and sixteen. What it means to try (or indeed to refuse) to please, whom one expects to please (or whom one will need to resist), and how, are different for these ages, as is the consequent meaning for one's subjective and bodily existence. One can compare, for example, Beauvoir's depiction of the different experiences and meanings for shame in puberty, and for some early sexual experiences, of perceptions of femininity or sexuality in terms of sexual exposure, awkwardness or risk, or pleasure and discovery, and the conflicted self-divisions of sexual and of maternal or paternal life. One can also compare Beauvoir's complex accounts of the interrelation between femininity, maternity and the specific forms of work to which women have historically had more access; and the different relationships to work, sex and maternity, of young adult women, and women in their fifties and sixties.

On the other hand, *The Coming of Age* prompts us to notice more than we might otherwise, the occlusion of the very aged woman in *The Second Sex*. Despite the promising title of one section of the latter, "From Maturity to Old Age," the work does not refer to the experiences of women older than their mid sixties, and gives its greatest attention to puberty, initial sexual experience, middle age, and menopause. When Beauvoir turned to a reflection specifically on old age some twenty years later after *The Second Sex* one might have expected that she would particularly take care to remedy the omission. Instead, the peculiarities of the work include not only that it again downplays the perspective of aged women, but also that it makes just one reference to *The Second Sex*. Moreover, with its few mentions of the diaries and correspondence of Virginia Woolf, Mme. de Sévigné, Juliette Drouet and Lou Andreas-Salomé, *The Coming of Age* is strongly disproportionate in its discussion of male writers on the topic. Further, Beauvoir states several times that aging is a particular problem for men. Thus it is not surprising to find the work assessed, as it is by Oliver Davis, as "overwhelmingly concerned with the situation of older men" (Davis 2006, 49).

The most generous way to understand the preference given to the perspective of certain men in the work is to view it as a means through which Beauvoir stresses that aging may be profoundly different for men and women. We can derive from this a suggestion which, while locatable in the substance of the work, also runs counter to the construction of *The Coming of Age:* that we will not be able to write well about old age if we abstract it from the differentiations of sex. As a result, one becomes curious to see whether and how a more articulated relationship between *The Second Sex* and *The Coming of Age* can be reconstructed.

I turn, first, to Beauvoir's explicit statements concerning the particular problem that old age is said to constitute for men. While she claims that it is "obvious" that "what we have here is a man's problem" (Beauvoir 1996, 89), this should not, she qualifies, be understood as holding true for every individual experience. Though she does not make reference to her earlier work, she had described some women's anguished response to aging in *The Second Sex* (1989, 575–76).[1] Nonetheless, in *The Coming of Age* she says that "when there is speculation upon the subject, it is considered primarily in terms of men" (1996, 89). And, although she seems to regret, or perhaps apologize for the fact that the documents on which she draws do give prominence to aging as a dilemma for men, she subsequently goes on to state: "we live in a male world," and "old age is primarily a male problem" (217).

Beauvoir gives various reasons. In the west, the majority of men have traditionally been more engaged in the public and work sphere, whereas women have typically worked more in the home, or have identified their interests somewhat more with the family. Perhaps women's interests and connections have been more diverse, and their sense of value and identification less wholly tied up with the public sphere, even when they have held paid positions. Thus, although many women may react very badly to aging, they may, nonetheless, eventually adapt better than men (1996, 261). Those whose activities have been more in the home, could find they are more strongly connected with family and personal friendships. Domestic spaces and relations may be more strongly a source of emotional connection, and are in any case traditionally the domain of women's special authority (261). Whether or not women have been in a situation of paid employment which ends, reaching age of retirement may, for these reasons, not be experienced as quite so dramatic a change as that of a man's retirement (262). By contrast, it may be that "suddenly flung from the active into the inactive category" (261), "retirement brings a radical break into a man's life; he is entirely cut off from his past and he has to adapt himself to a new status" (262). In such cases, relations may change drastically between the man and the woman: she may assume "a greater consequence ["prend alors le dessus," 279] than her husband" (279), feel a kind of superiority, even revenge (279).[2] She is said to be usually "less sensitive" to the appearance of a male partner (347) than is he to hers, and moreover her sexuality may be "less affected by age" than his (346).[3]

---

1 In the same chapter ("From Maturity to Old Age"), though her description is largely negative, Beauvoir also states that for some women aging can be a relief and a release from the expectations of femininity (1989, 583). She suggests not just that various women experience age differently, but also that aging is commonly a contradictory experience, both shocking and a relief, both progressive and abrupt, offering new reliefs and new possibilities for disappointment, and so on.

2 Beauvoir had earlier described some aspects of this scenario in *The Second Sex* (see Beauvoir 1989, 595).

3 Cf.: "[b]iologiquement, la sexualité de la femme est moins atteinte par la vieillesse" (1970, 367). See 1996, 321 for her discussion of the psychic attachment to the penis, and the "narcis-

For these and other reasons, although she certainly claims that "every individual age brings with it a dreaded decline" ["entraîne une dégradation," 47], and, moreover, that from the perspective of the ways in which we are culturally sexed, aging "is in complete conflict with the manly or womanly ideal" (40), she also claims, in a section that discusses a number of cultures yet seems to want to make of this a general point, that: "Old age does not have the same meaning nor the same consequences for men and for women. For the women it presents one particular advantage: after the menopause the woman is no longer sexed"[4] (84, translation modified).

With respects to each of the above points made above, and despite Beauvoir not mentioning the earlier work in the later work, it is in the context of the sex differentiations, and more specifically the othering of women described in *The Second Sex*, that we can best understand the dilemma faced by the man, as depicted by Beauvoir in *The Coming of Age.* We can not understand what Beauvoir takes many men to be losing, unless we understand what she otherwise takes them to possess. For this reason, it is all the more striking that Beauvoir does not discuss the possibilities of reading the works together, nor discuss aged women in *The Second Sex*, nor *The Second Sex* in *The Coming of Age*. Still the content of the works prompts us to read them together. Our capacity to do so seems not greatly impoverished by Beauvoir not having undertaken this. Even without authorial metastatement the two works enter into a sufficiently resistant and questioning relationship with each other.[5]

With respect to Beauvoir's claim that aging is in "complete conflict with the manly or womanly ideal" (40), certainly she depicts men as losing much of what has distinguished them from women. She does not state that men undergo a kind of feminization (in the context of the shared and contested meanings for masculinity and femininity) so much as describe them losing much of what has identified them as men in relation to women.

For example, they lose earning potential in a domestic arrangement where (in the conventional lives largely described by Beauvoir) this was often what had distinguished them from their wives and daughters. Because women had been traditionally associated with physical frailty and lesser strength, it is signif-

---

sistic traumatism" that may attach to the perception of "dysfunction," and on this see also Davis (2006, 54).

4 Cf. "La vieillesse n'a pas le même sens ni les même conséquences pour les hommes et pour les femmes. Elle présente pour celles-ci un avantage particulier: après la ménopause, la femme n'est plus sexuée" (1970, 93).

5 Richer possibilities still for an integrated reference to sex, gender and aging arise if one refers also to her autobiographies, letters and fiction.

icant that men may, in aging, lose muscular strength, vigour, and some forms of related physicality that have often served to differentiate men from women. Moreover, where women had traditionally been associated with more socially embarrassing, less controllable, "leaky" bodies, in the words of Margrit Shildrick (1997), men's aging bodies may be considered to come more into proximity with a kind of embodiment from which masculinity is conventionally distanced. Thinking of these traditional ways of differentiating the sexes, Beauvoir could plausibly argue that some men become more distanced, in aging, from what is associated with masculinity. For these and other reasons, the gender implications are different for men and women. She does not deny (and she had previously argued) that for women whose value as feminine is specifically associated with their looks and youthful sexuality, aging may be especially shocking. Nonetheless, she claims that, in a different sense, the transition of aging, particularly (but not only) as it may relate to retirement is more radical for men. So in relation to her argument that "[T]he aged, considered as social categories, have never influenced the progress of the world" (Beauvoir 1996, 88–89), she wrote about the impact of culturally significant sex difference on this phenomenon as follows:

> So long as the aged man retains some efficiency he remains an integral part of the community and he is not distinguished from it—he is an elderly adult male. When he loses his powers he takes on the appearance of *another*; he then becomes, and to a far more radical extent than a woman, a mere object. She is necessary to society whereas he is of no worth at all. (Beauvoir 1996, 89)

Without being feminized, men may be de-masculinized, moreover, she seems also to be arguing that they are differently de-humanized.[6] Furthermore, it would seem that both the de-feminization that aging women (in the context of social meanings for valued femininity) may undergo, and, the possible de-humanization, are different for women. Men's de-masculinization is not like women's de-feminization. Men are losing, according to this argument, what has distinguished them from women quite differently from the ways in which women may be losing what has distinguished them from men. Amongst the many reasons: consider that men have been associated with having a number of qualities women are taken, by traditional juxtaposition, to lack. We can make much more sense of the claim that men lose what they have been taken to have, than that

---

6 In this respect, consider her comments in the conclusion, in which she takes up the question of what is generally presupposed to make a "man" a "man," a question for which one can only partly substitute the question of what makes a "human" a "human."

women lose what they have, in any case, been taken to lack. Certainly, to nuance these descriptions one would require extensively differentiated readings of the way in which sex intersects with age. Beauvoir is quite clear on this general point, however much she gives the focus of her writerly attention to the dilemmas faced, as she depicts them, by men. She describes the differentials of power and hierarchy for men and women, young, middle-aged and aged, stressing the differences between a perceived loss of authority and status for those who, in relation to women, are considered to have possessed authority and status, versus a possible loss of femininity (according to the conventions) by those, who *as* feminine, have never been (by her argument) particularly entitled:

> The societies that have a history are ruled by the men: the women, both young and old, may perfectly well lay claim to authority in private, but in public life their status is always the same—that of perpetual minors. The masculine state, on the contrary, changes with the passage of time: the young man becomes an adult, a citizen, and the adult an old man. ... The movement from one group to the next may amount to a promotion or to a fall. (90)

Even phrased in this way, and even as a point about their public life, something nonetheless seems missing here in the depiction of what the passage of time means for femininity. Beauvoir stresses eloquently in *The Second Sex* that femininity has a special relationship to its own transience and jeopardy. We are not born, but rather become women but—never definitively so. She describes the changeable status of femininity, and its temporal intricacies: the changes brought by the passing of time, and more interesting still, the anticipations of such passing of time. Think of her memorable description of the young girl who looks forward passionately to the adult woman she will become, and of the adult woman who does not forget the young girl. Of gender, it is also true, according to Beauvoir's descriptions, that no time is ever its own time, but also the retention of past times and the anticipation, often passionate of impending times. Because of recollection, habit, expectation, and collective meaning, we are transversed by a number of different, and dehiscent times for gender. Its awkward, acquired and changeable habits also mean that one is never "of" or "in" one's own time. One's gendered habits are or become inappropriate, alienated or awkward, bodies may change faster (or more slowly) than do our bodily expectations. Psychically and bodily we live in the past and in various anticipated futures, some dreaded, some the objection of intense aspiration. Beauvoir stresses such differentiations of time, identity, change, attachment and alienation for the sexes.

Thus just as, as I have suggested, *The Coming of Age* can be used to resist some of the formulations and omissions of *The Second Sex*, so too can the earlier work be used to resist some of the formulations of *The Coming of Age*. Beauvoir's own work allows for a reconsideration of her remarks that aging is *the* problem of men, and that the masculine state is particularly to be associated with drastic social and physical changes to sexual difference as it interconnects with the passage of time. Instead, an analysis of the specific forms of temporality she associates with both sexes would be more appropriate, and the resources for such an analysis are offered in her own work. Thus the different works by Beauvoir enter into an interesting relationship—one could also characterize it as auto-resistant relationship—as we contemplate these tacit conversations between them.

This indicates how an analysis of aging should take place through an understanding of how it is inflected by sex difference. Consider that, where *The Second Sex* argues so famously that women is the other, *The Coming of Age* argues that in fact, men undergo a becoming object more radical than do women. How might we recalculate the proposals of *The Second Sex* in terms of Beauvoir's later description of men's eventual de-masculinization, de-humanization, perhaps even a "stronger" marginalization? What does this mean for the more famous arguments made by Beauvoir concerning women? How much of what has distinguished men and women according to the descriptions of *The Second Sex* would have to be reconfigured by the reader through the lens of the proposals made in *The Coming of Age?*

The conceptual compression of a number of terms in both works becomes particularly clear once *The Coming of Age* is read with *The Second Sex*. Consider that one of the constants of Beauvoir's work was her own devaluation of lives that have become habitual in an uninventive sense. She does seem to consider life a falling away of its best possibilities if habits and "automatic reactions" have taken the place of invention (1996, 540). It seems that a form of ethical existence might include the capacity and willingness to resist the rigidifying of our automatic reactions, our lives of habit. In *The Coming of Age*, she spoke of what could counter this hardening of set ways:

> to go on pursuing ends that give our existence meaning—devotion to individuals, to groups or to causes, social, political, intellectual or creative work. ... [i]n old age we should wish still to have passions strong enough to prevent us turning in upon ourselves. One's life has value so long as one attributes value to the life of others, by means of love, friendship, indignation, compassion. (1996, 540–41)

In both of Beauvoir's major works, she associates this particular kind of capacity for interest with the best possibilities of life. The extent to which I am capable of being engagedly, and on some matters passionately interested, relates both to how I have previously lived (such habits will enhance or erode the likelihood of interested engagement), and to my current context, status and opportunities. In this sense, "interest" is rendered by her a politicized matter. Her view that "one's life has value so long as one attributes value to the life of others, by means of love, friendship, indignation, compassion" is also seen very widely elsewhere in Beauvoir's work (and it relates to her depreciation of dulled, repetitive lives). This capacity for a life of passionate engagement and interest is for Beauvoir a vital human value. For this reason she is able to speak in *The Coming of Age* of Lou Andreas-Salomé whose circumstances she describes as, in this respect, "favourable" (517) in terms of the independence of her existence, the multiple kinds of work in which she engaged. In her old age Andreas-Salomé is described by Beauvoir as "inquisitive, strong-willed, active, passionately in love with life" (518), generous, intelligent (519), widely visited, involved in multiple kinds of relationships, engaged in a kind of independent work she was able to pursue late into her life, and constantly stimulated (519). We could mark Lou Andreas-Salomé's old age, as it is depicted by Beauvoir, as a kind of ideal for how some might age.

By contrast, a phenomenon Beauvoir relates to structural oppression (both in relation to the othering of aging and the othering of femininity) is its capacity to dull affect, to weaken interest, to produce a particular quality of apathy and indifference, a phenomenon Beauvoir at one point associates specifically with a kind of melancholia: "loss of ego, loss of value, boredom, blocked future, powerlessness" (496). She also describes it more generally without restricting herself to the specifics of that terminology. It can also be thought of as a loss of eros in the broad sense described so well by Debra Bergoffen (1997). Both in *The Second Sex*, and in *The Coming of Age*, oppression and unequal recognition are described as having the potential to shrink perspective, and the scope and range of interests and to encourage a deadening repetitiveness of one's concerns.

When Beauvoir wrote, in *The Second Sex*, of the dreadful monotony of many women's lives, and wrote of retirement in *The Coming of Age* that even "if he keeps his health and his clarity of mind, the retired man is nevertheless the victim of that terrible curse, boredom" (Beauvoir 1996, 541), she was again thinking of the phenomenon of boredom in social and political terms. This kind of apathy was deemed by her unhealthy: it endangers "physical and intellectual balance" 1996, 541)[7] and certainly she considered that it could be toxic to embodiment and subjectivity.

Here, a term—repetition—enfolds a richly dense problematics. Devaluing a boring and repetitive life, she brings complexity to the questions of when and why reiterated memories, repetitive tasks, the many habits in our lives, which may (as she does not deny) be the source of great satisfaction and pleasure,

---

7 "compromet ce qui lui reste d'équilibre physique et morale" (1970, 568).

may amount instead to the kind of negative repetition connected to shrunken perspective, constrained possibilities, dulled affect, disinterest, disvalue and disregard. She did so in order to protest the oppressed conditions she connected to the phenomenon. In referring to repetition as she does often, showing how it interrelates with social, political, intersubjective and institutional matters of value, recognition, history, and inequality, it could be said that the term enfolds an elaborate problematics concerning what makes repetition repetition?[8]

The interest in repetition offers one more reason why *The Second Sex* is as much about time, as about sex. Beauvoir relies, in both her 1949 and her 1970 works, on the definition of subjects as ek-static. But, as she stresses in *The Coming of Age*, we live time in different kinds of way according to its formations and contours as the bodily space of shared and contested social meanings. Meanings for youth, aging and generational difference, and their relation to sex, come from the other, and dislocate us as much as they consolidate us. Because of the ways in which aging and generational embodiment are differentially meaningful for us, we are this sense also, always subjects of time. I also suggested that if we go back to *The Second Sex*, we will find very few "women"—instead, one finds the carefully differentiated discussion of young girls, pubescent teenagers, middle aged women, menopausal women. Insofar as Beauvoir's tendency, often without laboring the point, is to differentiate sex into multiple ages, we are, to whatever extent that we are sexed, in this differentiated sense also "in time": always sexes bearing collective and contested meanings for the ages of sex. But insofar as repetition can be thought of as a relation to time, and is rendered by Beauvoir, in another of these gestures of compression, both politicized and an ethical matter, politics and ethics are also matters concerning the quality of our relation to time, and time's instantiations of us. A compressed term in Beauvoir's work, the question of time takes us to the question of life.

In the conclusions to both *The Second Sex* and *The Coming of Age*, Beauvoir tentatively explores her relationship to Marxism. In the concluding chapter of *The Second Sex*, she mentions the Soviet Revolution and its promise of a world in which women were to be "raised and trained" like men, to "work under the same conditions and the same wages" (Beauvoir 1989, 724). In this context marriage was to be a free agreement, and maternity "voluntary" and better supported by the state. In mentioning, skeptically, this vision, Beauvoir asks: "But is it enough to change laws, institutions, customs, public opinion, and the

---

8 This is a question taken up further in Deutscher 2008.

whole social context, for men and women to become truly equal" (725).[9] "We must not believe, certainly, that a change in woman's economic condition alone is enough to transform her" (725). After another reference to Marx, she concludes the work with a case made for an ethics for which she has spoken intermittently throughout the work, one addressed to a reign of *liberté* not reducible to economic relations, and, moreover one in which *fraternité*, would be affirmed as refracted through differentiations between men and women.

Some twenty years later, Beauvoir seemed to end *The Coming of Age* with a less equivocal commitment to the need for radical economic reorganization. In its conclusion, the lower status of many after retirement is said to arise from contexts in which value is measured in terms of earning capacity and wealth. This contributes to the complex social and historical factors, greatly relating to value and perception, with which "biological facts" are intertwined. Because her discussion of those social and historical factors, in the concluding chapter, is dominated by the economic considerations, it may be tempting to think of the two works as concluding in extremely different ways. *The Second Sex* concludes with the reminder that while economic reorganization is vital, it is in no way sufficient, while *The Coming of Age* seems to conclude with the point that wealth and economic productivity are so overriding as ways of understanding value, that we cannot hope to alleviate the alterity of aging unless we reorganize economic relationships radically. Her concern with human interaction is presented—in this concluding chapter—as a concern with economically inflected human interaction.

So consider Beauvoir's view, proposed in the last pages of *The Coming of Age*, that "it is the whole human that must be remade, it is the whole relationship between humans that must be recast" (1996, 543, translation modified). Such a statement, in the context of *The Second Sex*, would intertwine with the reminder we have already seen, that economic solutions could never be sufficient. But in the context of *The Coming of Age*, her point is that the relationship between humans intertwines so thoroughly with economic solutions, that to revise these *would* be to revise our impoverished relationship to the human as a brute material, to value as related to profit and productivity. A significant alteration to economic solutions would significantly alter the way we relate to each other in every sense, including to our own aging.

---

9 "Mais suffit-il de changer les lois, les institutions, les mœurs, l'opinion et tout le contexte sociale pour que les femmes et hommes deviennent vraiment des semblables?" (Beauvoir 1949, II, 569).

For this reason, "economics" should also be considered one of the more highly compressed terms in Beauvoir's work. We would have to add to the complexity of answers Beauvoir brings to such apparently simple questions as: What is it to be a woman? What is aging? What makes repetition repetition? What makes boredom boredom? These are some further questions apparently of interest to her. What are (for Beauvoir) "economic" relationships? The density of her answer to the question is such that we effectively see Beauvoir suggesting that economics is "life." Although it seems a substantial difference in stress to that with which *The Second Sex* ends, the elaborate layers and relations she enfolds into her critical terms mean that in the end, the two works may not be that opposed in their conclusions.

For example, we surely miss the scope of her point if we take her to be suggesting that life is reducible to economics. We may do better justice to her proposals by concentrating on the way in which she is enlarging the scope of economics to something as broadly construed as "life," rather than reducing the latter to the apparently narrower conceptual constraints of the former. Certainly, a radical change to economic relations would, as she conceives these, be a radical change to life. We see this both in her definitions of aging, and, as I conclude by suggesting, of life.

To see how this is formulated, consider the question that she poses in the introduction of *The Coming of Age:* What is aging? "[W]hat does growing old mean? The notion is bound up with that of change" (1996, 11).[10] At this point, the question, takes her directly to the question: What is life? Accordingly, she gives an answer also to the question: What is life? "[L]ife is an unstable system in which balance is continually lost and continually recovered ... Change is the law of life" (11).

By contrast, as she presents it, inertia is like death. She famously describes non-literal forms of inertia in *The Second Sex* and in *The Coming of Age.* The former includes, the justly beloved passage in which Beauvoir depicts the housewife endlessly re-circulating dust, inertia and frozen time as she sweeps, for the dust will only have to be swept again tomorrow. The latter describes the contraction of a world, and one's possible future, to the space of four walls. But why might one find oneself in this form of what she thinks of as inertia? In *The Coming of Age,* she blames and criticizes the tendency to perceive the human as material, as means to an end, and individual value in terms of exchange value, profitability or financial worth. This particularly aggravates the perception of many aged subjects who no longer undertake paid work as less fully human. The per-

---

10 "[q]u'est-ce que vieillir? Cette idée est liée à celle de changement" (17).

ception and self-perception as less fully human interconnects with the experiences of inertia, disinterest, and withdrawal from the world. A world less interested in us, is a world in which it is very much harder for us to be interested.

What does this mean for Beauvoir's arguments concerning political change? To seriously resist the rendering other of the aged, would require more than a change in attitudes to "old age." One would need to change relationships not only to aging throughout life, but also to more general perceptions of human worth in terms of exchange value and economic worth. On her view, the whole framework for the identification of the human would have to be remade, and the relationships between humans in their entirety "would have to be recast" (543). For, where life is associated with the acquisition of value, and value with recognition, to be unprofitable is to lack recognition as interesting and valuable, life may be experienced as, in addition to impoverished, as duller, less interesting, pointless, affectless, amounting to an experience of one's life as deadening.

Beauvoir thus takes as an ideal, both for women, and for the experience of advanced aging, the life of affect and interest. Notice that this is not because she is, in particular, a philosopher of affect, nor less of "interest," nor of "vitality," still less of economics, but because she was a philosopher who, at her most interesting, stressed the dense compression, interrelation and enfolding of these matters with each other. This is the philosopher who also reminded us in *The Coming of Age* that "sexuality, vitality and activity are indissolubly linked" (350). For Beauvoir, value was interest, economics was recognition, respect and opportunities were also sexuality and vitality, and so on.

The solutions she proposed reflected her attention to the shared and contested values and lived meaning for existence. Some are perceived as existing a time which is posterior to their greatest economic profitability, and thereby presupposed as less than human, Beauvoir's solution is, of course, anything but simple: "The answer is simple: one would always have to have been treated as human" (542, translation modified).[11]

Beauvoir envisaged the possibility of not treating humans primarily as so much raw material, with useby dates tacitly amounting to sub-humanity. Thus, to return to the conclusion of *The Coming of Age*, changes to the conditions of the aged (laws, pensions, health benefits, right to work) could not be sufficient, nor indeed changes in "our" attitudes towards the aged or aging. What was required was a more radical—arguably an impossible—transformation of general attitudes towards a human body, an individual, the basis of capacities, worth,

---

11 Cf.: "La réponse est simple: il faudrait qu'il ait toujours été traité en homme" (568).

not to mention the basis for our mutual interest. For we must, as Beauvoir concludes the work, change life, *changer la vie*. Oliver Davis reminds us that this citation from Rimbaud, also cited by Sartre in *What is Literature?* (Sartre 1950, 138) was an expression used in May 1968, only two years before Beauvoir's work appeared (Davis 2006, 40). Reinforcement for this reminder comes from Beauvoir's reference in this same passage to the youth who "dreads this machine that is about to seize hold of him, and sometimes ... tries to defend himself by throwing half-bricks"[12] (1996, 543). Yet, there is also much in *The Coming of Age* to suggest that, for Beauvoir, life had become a broader, and a highly compressed term. To change life would be to change what life is, how it is conceptualized—to stress the perpetuity of change, transformation, and generational transformation, rather than our displacing change (often understood as degradation) away from the perception of the normal and valuable adult. For this reason, Beauvoir imagines a possible time in which there could be old age without "degradation" (543) for the perception of degradation arises in context, and in relations to aims or projects in terms of which the changes of aging may appear as degradation.

To change life would also mean that one would not deny the perpetual transformations inevitable through embodied temporal existence. Beauvoir imagined the possibility of living more constantly in relation to the idea that "I myself am the future dwelling-place of old age" (1). To re-modulate our understanding of humans in terms of value would be to modulate the relation to life. What is a human not understood in terms of material and productivity? It would mean, Beauvoir argued, a different conceptualization of the relationship between a human vitality, sex, time and life.

References

Beauvoir, Simone de. 1949. *Le deuxième sexe*. Paris: Gallimard.
Beauvoir, Simone de. 1989. *The second sex*. Trans. H. M. Parshley. New York: Vintage.
Beauvoir, Simone de. 1970. *La vieillesse*. Paris: Éditions Gallimard.
Beauvoir, Simone de. 1996. *The coming of age*. Trans. Patrick O'Brian. New York and London: W. W. Norton & Company.
Bergoffen, Debra B. 1997. *The philosophy of Simone de Beauvoir: Gendered phenomenologies, erotic generosities*. Albany: State University of New York Press.
Davis, Oliver. 2006. *Age rage and going gently: Stories of the senescent subject in twentieth-century French writing*. Amsterdam and New York: Rodopi.

---

12 "Le jeune redoute cette machine qui va le happer, il essaie parfois de se défendre à coups de pavé" (569).

Deutscher, Penelope. 2008. *The philosophy of Simone de Beauvoir: Ambiguity, conversion, resistance*. Cambridge: Cambridge University Press.

Sartre, Jean-Paul. 1950. *What is literature?* Trans. Bernard Frechtman. London: Methuen.

Sartre, Jean-Paul. 1963. *Saint Genet: Actor and martyr*. Trans. Bernard Frechtman. New York: New American Library.

Shildrick, Margrit. 1997. *Leaky bodies and boundaries: Feminism, postmodernism and (bio) ethics*. London: Routledge.

Ulrike Kadi
Gender, Age, and Passivity

Comment on Penelope Deutscher

Penelope Deutscher points out that in *The Coming of Age* the experiences of very aged women were neglected. This omission is also found in Beauvoir's earlier book *The Second Sex*. Deutscher assumes an internal relationship of the arguments in both books, which leads her to a benevolent interpretation of Beauvoir's point of view: for men aging is accompanied by loss, which is not the case for women. But as Deutscher shows, there is a contradiction between Beauvoir's awareness of woman as the other in *The Second Sex* and Beauvoir's claim that aging men are objectified in a more radical sense than women. Although Deutscher all in all seems to be right as to Beauvoir's omission, I will point out two exceptions. In addition to the one intersection Deutscher found, I will then suggest another link between *The Coming of Age* and *The Second Sex* which might solve the apparent contradiction between Beauvoir's treatment of objectification of men and of women.

First, we must note that there is one section where Beauvoir does indeed focus on advanced age. In the appendix of *The Coming of Age* there is a short chapter about 100-years-old people (Beauvoir 1996, 544–45); most of them are female. Beauvoir describes them as living in the countryside close to their children or in nursing homes, looking meager but downright robust. All of them sleep well. They are occupied with reading, knitting or walking around. Beauvoir finds them remarkable. And in fact, in Beauvoir's book they are a remarkable exception because their very existence seems to lend them legitimacy. These old people seem to be satisfied, plodding along as they do, and do not feel the need to be creative. To overcome their misery they apparently need not engage in writing, politics, art or other intellectual pursuits. That is my first remark: Including these very old women means including the unspectacular. I assume Beauvoir did not consider the experiences of very old women in detail because there are only very few women like Lou Andreas-Salomé who fit into the ambitious categories which intrigue Beauvoir.

Second, I think we have to concede that *The Coming of Age* is—to a considerable amount—an account of the experiences of a certain aged woman, namely of Beauvoir herself. Of course, she was not very old. She was 62 when *The Coming of Age* was published. But she was a post-menopausal woman and she was dealing with the problems of age very intensively. I sensed hints of an underlying anxiety gleaming in certain passages of the book: moments when Beauvoir might have felt uneasy facing the limitedness of life and tried to diminish these feelings. An example of this is the passage where she explains why death does not touch her the way it did before (Beauvoir 1996, 444–45). She claims she has become used to absence: absence of the past, absence of her dead friends, absence of so many parts of the world she will never see again. As to the experiences of aged women, it might be useful to follow the traces of Beauvoir's own feelings towards age which shine through in *The Coming of Age* (which of course is—from a philosophical point of view—a difficult if not impossible task, since it implies a psychological approach to the author's persona).

However, we cannot ignore the fact that women are left out when it comes to some crucial arguments of *The Coming of Age*, which leads to my third point: a hidden link between the two books which might help to understand Beauvoir's special interest in male aging. A little vignette from my daily work as a psychiatric trainee might help to draw further conclusions: Recently, a seventy-one years-old man was admitted to my hospital department on the recommendation of a staff member of a victims' organization. The patient himself was not dealing with any serious psychological problems. But his daughter was addicted to alcohol. While being drunk she had attacked her father. Consequently, the police had forbidden the daughter to enter her father's apartment for a period of ten days. In Austria, for example, this type of restraining order (*Wegweisung*) is usually implemented to keep violent people away from their spouses, partners or children. Since it is usually men, not women, who are ordered to stay away from their homes—all the police documents about this restraining order refer to men. And the leaflet about self-defense handed out by the victims' organization assumes that the victim is a woman. My patient, the old man, the father, had an enormous problem reading this material and finding himself being referred to as a woman. It was an even bigger problem than being beaten by his daughter or being the father of a daughter who is an alcohol addict. In the end, he allowed his daughter to return home after only two days, just to avoid dealing with all the papers humiliating by referring to him as a woman. I wonder if there are any parallel or comparable experiences concerning aged women when being referred to as belonging to the male sex.

Of course, in order to grasp the difference between the aging of men and of women we must take into account the meaning of being male or female. Deutscher proposes to consider the concepts "in the context of the shared and contested meanings for masculinity and femininity" (32). According to Sigmund Freud, activity and passivity fit best albeit not fully to name the cultural ascribed qualities of the sexes (Freud 1933, 115). As Deutscher quotes Beauvoir, sexuality, vitality and activity have to be seen as being closely linked. Passivity seems to be missing in this chain, which is not surprising bearing in mind the function of passivity in Beauvoir's thinking. Being passive means being alienated, being lost, being subjected to someone else's will (Beauvoir 1989, xxvii), sticking to the realm of immanence. It is the bodily perceived "horror of carnality" (Heinämaa 2003, 131) culture has attached to the female body by way of male projection. Beauvoir describes the difficulties girls encounter if they try to rid themselves of this ascribed passivity (Beauvoir 1989, 298). The very old woman, on the other hand, can overcome the experience of being passive: having been subjected to her husband and having been a victim of her children during her earlier life—old age enables her to feel liberated (Beauvoir 1996, 488).

I suggest we consider *The Coming of Age* and *The Second Sex* as being linked via the problem of passivity which is—as a culturally bound development—a threat for women earlier in their lives than for men, who have to face this dilemma more intensively as they grow old. This might explain why Beauvoir has no need to go deeper into the experiences of aging women, since passivity is not the main problem of this period of a woman's life. Viewed from this angle, the contradiction between the woman as the other in *The Second Sex* and the man being objectified in a radical way in *The Coming of Age* vanishes. Both states are consequences of differently gendered positions towards passivity.

Hence it becomes easier to understand my patient's reaction: being literally feminized as an aging man, he must face a double dose of passivity, which is obviously too much for him.

References

Beauvoir, Simone de. 1989. *The second sex.* Trans. H. M. Parshley. New York: Vintage.
Beauvoir, Simone de. 1996. *The coming of age.* Trans. Patrick O'Brian. New York and London: W. W. Norton & Company.
Freud, Sigmund. 1933. New introductory lectures: Femininity. In: Sigmund Freud, *The standard edition of the complete works of Sigmund Freud*, ed. James Strachey in collaboration with Anna Freud. London: The Hogart Press and the Institute of Psychoanalysis 1953–74, vol. XXII, 112–35.
Heinämaa, Sara. 2003. *Toward a phenomenology of sexual difference: Husserl, Merleau-Ponty, Beauvoir.* Oxford: Rowman & Littlefield.

Gail Weiss
The Myth of Woman Meets
the Myth of Old Age

An Alienating Encounter with the Aging Female Body

In actuality, of course, women appear under various aspects; but each of the myths built up around the subject of woman is intended to sum her up in toto; each aspires to be unique. In consequence, a number of incompatible myths exist, and men tarry musing before the strange incoherencies manifested by the idea of Femininity.
—Simone de Beauvoir

In this well-known passage from *The Second Sex* (1989, 253–54), Beauvoir emphasizes that there is not one but many myths about women that tend to circulate in any given society. While some might argue that the coexistence of multiple myths of women is not necessarily a bad thing since their very plurality could serve to lessen the coercive power of any one of them, nonetheless, it is never the case that women are free to pick the myth that best suits them or even to refuse the influence of any mythical view of women altogether. As Beauvoir painstakingly demonstrates both in *The Second Sex* and in *The Coming of Age*, where she critically examines myths of femininity and myths of old age respectively, the omnipresence of incompatible myths, each with its own prescriptive standards for women, makes it impossible simply to ignore them since, even if one personally rejects mythic ideals for placing unrealistic and even impossible demands upon women, society continues to judge individual women according to their conflicting standards. Moreover, even if one chooses to live up to the stringent demands associated with a particular myth, and is rewarded with the general social approbation that comes from doing so, the presence of several *incompatible* myths of women, makes it virtually inevitable that success in embodying one will lead to failure in embodying another.

In this essay, I will focus on the specific gendered tensions that emerge when elderly women are pressured to remain loyal both to the myth(s) of femininity and the myth(s) of old age that are operative in their community.[1] While it

---

1 Although I will often refer to the myth of woman and the myth of old age in the singular throughout this essay, the reader should bear in mind, in keeping with my opening comments above, that there are usually not one but several myths about women that hold sway within any given community. When using the singular, I am referring not necessarily to any single myth, but rather the collective force of all the myths as they are expressed in a set of accepted societal norms for how women should comport themselves on a day-to-day basis. I am not interested in

may be tempting to regard the myth of woman as applying solely to younger women because of its overwhelming identification of beauty with youth, and to see it as eventually supplanted by the myth of old age for elderly women, I argue that both myths continue to operate in full force as women age, thereby intensifying the sense of failure older women may experience insofar as they are expected to meet the demands of two incompatible and internally contradictory myths simultaneously.

The Case Against Myths

Insofar as the myth of femininity offers us an image of a thin, beautiful, young, graceful, seductive, and nurturing woman, it might seem to have an advantage over the myth of old age where the image of the ugly old hag immediately comes to mind as the feminine woman's very negative counterpart. To the extent that old women are perceived to be beautiful in early twenty-first century Western visual media, their beauty is almost always associated with their miraculous ability to retain the youthful face and expression associated with the myth of femininity, that is, with their success in expressing what Beauvoir calls the "Eternal Feminine"[2] (Beauvoir 1989, 294). While there are literary examples of lovely older women whose beauty is directly associated with weather-beaten, wise, lined faces, these images rarely appear in a positive light in the cinema or on television!

Whether a particular myth offers a flattering or unflattering image of women does not make it more or less palatable for Beauvoir. She emphatically rejects mythical understandings of any human being for any reason, asserting that "To discard the myths is not to destroy all dramatic relation between the sexes, it is not to deny the significance authentically revealed to man through feminine reality; it is not to do away with poetry, love, adventure, happiness,

---

teasing out the subtle distinctions that differentiate one myth from another in this investigation, though this would be a fascinating project in its own right; rather, I want to focus on how the myths, despite their incompatibilities, function together in a hegemonic fashion to shape how elderly women in particular are judged by their societies and almost inevitably found wanting. I use the terms "myth of woman" and "myth of femininity" interchangeably in this essay.

2 The desire to attain this "nirvana" is succinctly expressed in the title of the Bruce Springsteen hit song, "Forever Young."

dreaming. It is simply to ask that behavior, sentiment, passion be founded upon the truth"[3] (261).

One of the main concerns Beauvoir has about myths, whether positive or negative is that, over time, they tend to take on a life of their own that is independent of reality even if they originated in concrete situations. This leads, Beauvoir suggests, to a growing separation between a myth and the reality to which it is applied. What makes this split so problematic is that, even when it greatly diverges from reality, the myth continues to function as a model for what human beings should be trying to achieve in their real lives, that is, it retains its normative force and alleged universality. The result, as Beauvoir ironically observes in reference to the myth of woman, is that when the myth is found to be in tension with reality, it is the former that tends to prevail and the latter that is rejected. In her words,

> As against the dispersed, contingent, and multiple existences of actual women, mythical thought opposes the Eternal Feminine, unique and changeless. If the definition provided for this concept is contradicted by the behavior of flesh-and-blood women, it is the latter who are wrong: we are told not that Femininity is a false entity, but that the women concerned are not feminine. (253)

One of the main reasons why myths are almost guaranteed to fail in being helpful guides for behavior, Beauvoir suggests, is because through their repetition they become congealed, static entities, lacking the fluidity that is the existentialist's hallmark of the changing temporal and spatial rhythms that characterize actual human existence. As in *The Ethics of Ambiguity*, where she rejects grounding ethics in absolute values that would apply universally to all people, it is the totalizing quality of both the myth of femininity and the myth of old age that Beauvoir views as especially pernicious; each myth identifies the essence of woman with the embodiment of a fixed (though, in point of fact, culturally and historically variable) set of physical, psychical, and social attributes. Since, for both she and Sartre, a human being is a for-itself who "is what it is not and is not what it is" any attempt to embody the ideal qualities associated with one myth, much less multiple myths that are in tension with one another, will be doomed to failure. As she notes, "An existent is nothing other than what he does; the possible does not extend beyond the real, essence does not precede

---

3 The correspondence Beauvoir is establishing here between truth and reality on the one hand, and myths and falsehood on the other hand, may be seen as begging the question. See my "Are Myths Indispensable: Reflections on Myth and Reality in Beauvoir's *The Second Sex*" for an extended discussion of this issue.

existence: in pure subjectivity, the human being *is not anything*. He is to be measured by his acts" (257).

If each of these totalizing myths function as societal ideals for how women should comport themselves in their daily lives, how is it possible for any woman to live up to one myth without violating its tenets to fulfill another? Moreover, Beauvoir reveals internal tensions within the myths themselves such that even if a woman only embraced a single myth and tried to embody its prescriptions and prohibitions to the best of her ability, she will inevitably fail in the attempt to live its competing demands in a coherent manner. While she concentrates, in *The Second Sex*, on the oppressive effects of the myth of woman both on women who attempt to adhere to it and on women who reject it, and while she offers an in-depth study of not one but many myths concerning old age (and elderly women in particular) in *The Coming of Age*, she does not ever provide a sustained analysis of how these two incompatible, internally inconsistent myths can and do function together to sharply distinguish the experiences of elderly women and elderly men, often intensifying the sense of alienation and even disgust that the former feel toward their aging bodies and that younger women and men often feel toward them as well. And yet, I would argue, the work she has done in both *The Second Sex* and *The Coming of Age*, demands that we explore critically how these myths operate together, by focusing upon some of the unique challenges faced by elderly women as they are simultaneously judged according to the norms of femininity idealized by their culture as well as the norms that govern their society's view of the elderly.

Paradoxes of Old Age

Even if one has never read Beauvoir's *The Second Sex*, it is not hard to conjure up the hegemonic norms associated with the myth of femininity, at least as it functions within one's own culture. Indeed, with our contemporary global communications network, one need do no more than turn on one's television or computer to be bombarded with idealized images of femininity. The reigning conceptions Beauvoir identifies with the myth of old age are arguably less obvious even though they potentially apply to every elderly human being, and perhaps this is why she herself felt compelled, as she moved into her 60's to devote a full-length cross-cultural, historical study to them.[4] Like the myth of femininity,

---

4 Beauvoir's own advancing age, she suggests at the outset of *The Coming of Age*, led to her growing realization of the lack of social, political, economic, physical, and psychical resources

the myth of old age is also gendered, racialized, and directly impacted by one's social class in very interesting ways that Beauvoir explores in depth. Given both, its unisex *and* sex-specific qualities, the myth of old age seems to have a broader reach than the myth of femininity, applying to men as well as to women. Yet, the antipathy that most cultures express toward the aging process creates a major disincentive for understanding the experience of old age. It seems that, as far as old age is concerned, the familiar adage "out of sight, out of mind" tends to hold sway, unless the issue is absolutely unavoidable (e. g., having to deal with aging parents). Insofar as the experience of old age is usually perceived to be undesirable, and even abject, it may not seem so curious that this topic has been under-theorized and this population under-served.[5] Indeed, as noted earlier, while the expression "the myth of femininity" immediately conjures up all sorts of culturally recognizable images, it is less evident what the myth of old age even refers to, and so it is important to clarify what Beauvoir means when she uses the expression and to illuminate some of the specific existential tensions that are its by-products.

As I am especially interested in the social, psychic, and corporeal effects of the specific gendered myths that differentiate elderly women's experiences of their own aging bodies and of the aging process more generally from that of their male counterparts, it may seem strange to turn now to the description of an elderly man offered by Oscar Wilde's title character in his famous late nineteenth century novel, *The Portrait of Dorian Gray*, however, I think this is a fascinating transgressive example of the devastating effects of a stereotypically feminine obsession with preserving one's youthful good looks, precisely because it is expressed through a male protagonist. Not only does Wilde's description of Dorian's horror of old age (as registered in his growing antipathy toward his aging self-portrait), provide an exemplary illustration of the uncomfortable mixture of identification and alienation that characterizes what Beauvoir calls the paradox of old age, but Wilde's novel reveals how a preoccupation with one's aging

---

available to elderly people to understand their newfound identities as "senior citizens"; this clearly served as a powerful motivation for her critical analysis of the existential significance accorded to the final years of an individual human life. Since 60 is typically identified in first world nations in the late twentieth and early twenty-first century as the very beginning of old age, it is not surprising that Beauvoir's attention turned at this time in her life to this particular topic. Indeed, though I do not have room to develop this point here, I would argue that in all of her writing (both fictional and non-fictional, literary and philosophical), her central preoccupations can be traced to the issues that are most concretely impacting her own existence and/or that of her compatriots (see Beauvoir 1997, 73).

5 Beauvoir herself comments on the lack of accurate data regarding the experience of old age and cites it as a motivation for researching and writing *The Coming of Age*.

body is coded as a feminine, narcissistic concern that is capable of being experienced by males as well as females. It is crucial to remember, however, that even though men and women can and do share this "feminine" (over)concern with the bodily changes that mark the aging process, what Sandra Lee Bartky calls the "social disabilities of old age" are always experienced differently by men and women; these social disabilities are influenced not only by one's own sexual and gender identifications but also by society's judgment of how appropriately or inappropriately one's sexuality and gender are expressed (Bartky 1999, 69).[6]

At the outset of Wilde's novel, Dorian Gray has his portrait painted by his friend Basil Hallward. The portrait is, by all accounts, a resounding success. It depicts Dorian in the full flower of his youth (he is a young man of twenty) and Dorian himself, just like Narcissus viewing his image in the water beneath him, is overcome by the sight of his own beauty.[7] In a famous, fateful passage, Dorian makes a Faustian pact with the devil, without even realizing that this is what he has done. He wishes aloud that he will always look exactly like the portrait, that is, that he will retain his present youthful beauty forever:

> "How sad it is!" murmured Dorian Gray, with his eyes still fixed upon his own portrait. "How sad it is! I shall grow old, and horrible, and dreadful. But this picture will remain always young. It will never be older than this particular day in June ... If it were only the other way! If it were I who was to be always young, and the picture that was to grow old! For that—for that—I would give everything! Yes, there is nothing in the whole world I would not give! I would give my soul for that! (Wilde 1992, 29)

---

6 This is not to suggest that one's sexuality and gender are the only or even always the most significant influences upon the aging experience for other aspects of one's identity such as one's race, class, health, religion, and national identity also play central roles in how the elderly are viewed and how they view themselves. To take just one example, the fact that they were both men did not guarantee any great commonality between the experience of an elderly black male slave and his aged white master during the antebellum period in the United States. While it is evident, simply by virtue of individual bodily differences, that no two people will experience the aging process in exactly the same way, the almost universal tendency throughout history to value men more for their intellectual achievements and women for the youthful beauty of their bodies, makes it virtually impossible for most elderly women to remain unaffected by the societal association of a loss of youth with a loss of one's femininity. Of course there are many different ways women can resist such an identification, however, as Beauvoir persuasively demonstrates in *The Coming of Age*, the internalization of such negative gendered stereotypes encourages a disidentification both with one's own and with others' aging female bodies.

7 Indeed, Lord Henry Wotton, who becomes Dorian's closest friend and supporter, refers to Dorian as a Narcissus before he has even met him, based on the beauty of the portrait alone.

Basil gives Dorian the portrait as a gift and it becomes Dorian's most prized possession until he discovers, to his absolute astonishment, that while his own visage remains unchanged, the face in the portrait magically alters, expressing the cruelty and selfishness that Dorian increasingly exhibits in his relations with his lovers and friends. Moreover, while his own body remains miraculously unaffected by time throughout the many years that follow, making him an even greater figure of admiration and envy to his social peers, the figure in the portrait registers his actual age as well as his character. Horrified, Dorian recognizes that his earlier wish is indeed coming to pass:

> Hour by hour, and week by week, the thing upon the canvas was growing old. It might escape the hideousness of sin, but the hideousness of age was in store for it. The cheeks would become hollow or flaccid. Yellow crow's-feet would creep round the fading eyes and make them horrible. The hair would lose its brightness, the mouth would gape or droop, would be foolish or gross, as the mouths of old men are. There would be the wrinkled throat, the cold, blue-veined hands, the twisted body, that he remembered in the grandfather who had been so stern to him in his boyhood. The picture had to be concealed. There was no help for it. (Wilde 1992, 138–39)

While Dorian is disturbed by the way the portrait eerily registers the growing corruption of his soul as he pursues his narcissistic pleasures without regard for the feelings and welfare of others, it is clear from the above passage that it is the "hideousness" of age itself that is his greatest object of fear. We can make sense of this deepest fear, I suggest, through Beauvoir's rich analysis of how the reality of old age threatens one of our most cherished fantasies, namely, the hope that human beings can somehow escape the biological, psychological, social, and even economic effects of their own mortality. Dorian's desperate attempts to hide the moral disintegration and physical deterioration incarnated in the portrait from all other human beings at all costs also reveals the power of what Diana Tietjens Meyers calls the "facial legibility postulate," namely, the all too human tendency to closely link a person's "inner" (i.e., moral) nature with their external visage such that an aesthetically displeasing face is interpreted as a visible sign of the moral ugliness that allegedly resides within (Meyers 1999, 30). Indeed, one of the reasons Dorian is able to persist virtually unabated in his terrible treatment of lovers, friends, and strangers throughout his adult life is that almost no one gazing upon his beautiful face can truly imagine that someone who appears to so perfectly embody the innocence of youth can actually be guilty of the horrible deeds he is rumored to have committed.

Aging Others/Ageless Selves

Beauvoir observes, "Since it is the Other within us who is old, it is natural that the revelation of our age should come to us from outside—from others. We do not accept it willingly" (Beauvoir 1996, 288). To say that "it is the Other within us who is old" suggests that human beings tend to profoundly disidentify on a subjective level with the aging process that is occurring in and through our bodies. Insofar as the facial legibility postulate operates in a largely unconscious yet ongoing way, positing a direct link between a time-altered face and an undesirable moral character, there are powerful motivations, it would seem, for people to refuse to acknowledge, much less accept, the embodied effects of the aging process even when the evidence of these latter are no more than a mirror away. However, Beauvoir offers several other compelling reasons throughout *The Coming of Age* for the rejection of one's aging body as an essential part of one's identity. There are two, in particular, that I will be focusing on. First, she argues that there is an important sense in which consciousness itself is subjectively experienced as ageless (283–84). Even though one's mental capacities are undoubtedly affected by the aging process in a manner that may be perceptible to oneself as well as to others (e. g., one's memory might become less reliable than in the past), nonetheless, the sense of oneself flowing through time that Henri Bergson calls one's *durée*, continues uninterruptedly throughout one's life, thereby enabling the illusion that one is remaining untouched by time.[8] Secondly, Beauvoir maintains that not only do most human beings tend to persist in the illusion that they are ageless, but we also "see those who are close to us *sub specie aeternitatis*, and the discovery of their ageing is also a painful blow" (288). Given that the effects of the aging process are inscribed upon our bodies and corporeally experienced, it is striking that so many of us nonetheless experience aging from an alienated perspective, that is, as an insight that comes to us from others and not from ourselves.

Since Dorian's portrait literally incarnates this (abject) Other, it is not so surprising that he places his aging doppelgänger under lock and key so that no one else can see it and witness his degradation. However, even when the portrait is safely hidden from all viewers behind a tapestry in a locked room in the attic of his house, he is always anxious that his secret will be discovered by others. By the end of the story, the portrait itself has become Dorian's mortal enemy. In a

---

8 To the extent that psychotics experience serious disruptions in their *durée*, they present an exceptional case that would presumably result in a significantly different experience of the aging process.

final act of self-destruction, he stabs the repulsive self that is revealed in the portrait, seeking to vanquish its mocking countenance once and for all. His servants, hearing a cry and a thud, but finding the door locked and unyielding as they attempt to force it open, climb to the roof and enter the locked attic room through the balcony. And, the narrator tells us:

> When they entered they found, hanging upon the wall, a splendid portrait of their master as they had last seen him, in all the wonder of his exquisite youth and beauty. Lying on the floor was a dead man, in evening dress, with a knife in his heart. He was withered, wrinkled, and loathsome of visage. It was not till they had examined the rings that they recognised who it was. (Wilde 1992, 254)

In the eternal "battle" between youth and age, as Wilde depicts it, youth will always prevail. But, both he and Beauvoir seem to be asking, at what price? In his zeal to retain his youth and beauty at all costs, Dorian loses himself in the process. Indeed, he ends up dying alone, a pariah in the very community to which he has belonged his whole life, envied and despised in equal measure.

Beauvoir tells us that "old age exposes the failure of our entire civilization" (Beauvoir 1996, 543). This is not because of an inherent failure in the elderly themselves, she maintains, but rather is due to the failure of specific societies to value the unique knowledge, skills, history, and experience that their aged members individually and collectively offer. And, she argues, in a passage that applies as much to Dorian Gray as to society at large, "by the way in which a society behaves towards its old people it uncovers the naked, and often carefully hidden, truth about its real principles and aims" (87).

Re-Situating Age

Beauvoir offers what is today commonly referred to as an "intersectional" account of the combined influence of biological, social, psychological, and economic factors in establishing the significance and value of the experience of old age. In her words, "the various factors that define the old person's state influence one another, as I have pointed out: none has its real meaning except in its relationship with the others" (Beauvoir 1996, 279). Despite the fact that she believes that all of these factors work together and cannot be understood apart from one another, she also makes a strong case for the ability of financial status to outweigh all the others, because, she asserts, one's economic class is what distinguishes those who have the resources to enjoy the benefits old age can offer (e.g., retirement from the work force and a corresponding increase in leisure time), from those who are condemned to suffer from all of its privations (e. g., who are forced to continue working even as they are no longer as physically fit and therefore less able to produce at the same level as they could when they were younger). For the menial laborer, she declares, "Once the worker has grown old he no longer has any place on earth because in fact he was never given one. No place: but he had no time to realize it. When he does discover the truth he falls into a kind of bewildered despair" (274). Before the 19th century, she informs us, those who were poor did not even live to old age; however, by the mid-twentieth century, she states, "'old and poor' is almost a tautology" (275).

Beauvoir articulates her intersectional perspective right at the outset of *The Coming of Age* when she proclaims in her preface that: "man never lives in a state of nature: in his old age, as at every other period of his life, his status is imposed upon him by the society to which he belongs" (9). And, although she repeatedly acknowledges that there are many factors that influence how a society views its aged population, she is clear that ultimately the respect and care elderly people receive is almost always a direct function of how well-off that society is, and how many resources it is willing to devote to supporting its oldest members.

According to Beauvoir, all aged workers share a "twofold requirement" that can and should be facilitated by their society no matter when or where they live: "to rest and to live decently" (267). Yet, it is also clear that comparatively few old people in the world today actually have this dual requirement met in their daily lives. Indeed, pragmatically speaking, this dual requirement has functioned more as an attractive ideal that is unattainable for the majority of people in the world today, despite the plethora of "How to Enjoy your Retirement" manuals that are increasingly being published in the United States for the benefit of the "Baby-Boomer" generation born after World War II in the 1940s to 1960s. Thus, despite the deathly confrontation between youth and old age depicted by Oscar Wilde, and despite the less dramatic tensions between the younger and older generations that Beauvoir also acknowledges are a common feature of virtually every known society, she stresses that economics almost always plays the leading role in establishing the possibilities (and lack of possibilities) available to the elderly in any given society. Accordingly, she asserts, "Far more than the conflict between the generations, it was the class struggle that gave the notion of old age its ambivalence" (215).

What is the ambivalence of old age that Beauvoir is invoking here? And, what contribution does the gender of the aged person make in heightening (or even lessening) the ambivalence she may experience in relation to her own aging body as well as the ambivalence that characterizes how she is responded to by others? In a particularly striking passage, Beauvoir argues that "we live in a male world and ... old age is primarily a male problem ..." (217). Given that the aging process is experienced by all human beings regardless of their gender (though men's and women's bodily differences guarantee that the aging process will not affect them in exactly the same way), it may appear strange to hear Beauvoir refer to old age as "primarily a male problem." What can this mean? Her answer, I would argue, takes us to the heart of the question of how one's gender impacts how society regards one's aging person, and this, in turn, influences how one views the aging bodies of others as well as how one views and lives one's own aging body.

Beauvoir has much to say about the ambivalence of old age throughout *The Coming of Age*. Some of the claims she makes about old age reflect her more general view that human existence itself is ambiguous insofar as no one factor alone determines the meaning of any given experience. While, as I have noted, she maintains that biological, psychological, social, and economic factors cannot be understood apart from one another in any person's life, she also argues that each has a unique role to play in co-constituting the significance of that person's situation at any given point in time. As we just saw, however, Beauvoir also suggests that a person's economic class plays an especially powerful role because it affects the other aspects of one's experience in such a profound way. For instance, if one is elderly and has a bad fall, but does not have adequate health coverage and does not have the independent finances to pay for good medical care, then this lack of funding will have serious physiological, psychological, and even social effects in one's life. Indeed, here is one area where gender differences in the quality of life enjoyed by the elderly tend to be especially striking insofar as, in countries without universal health care like the U.S., those who have not been in the work force (e. g., stay-at-home housewives) or who have not received health insurance while they were working (e. g., part-time workers), or who have been working illegally and hence have never received health insurance (e. g., non-documented immigrants), are at a distinct disadvantage compared to their male counterparts who had stable full-time jobs throughout their adult lives. Old age has been viewed primarily as a "male problem," according to Beauvoir, precisely because the transition of these "breadwinners" who have functioned as heads of their households into retirees is so dramatic, requiring a radical change in their primary identity. The "problem" she identifies is that society expects these men simply to step aside and let the younger generation take over their positions and their power, without providing a new role and a new set of responsibilities for them.

Interestingly, Beauvoir argues that it is precisely because so many women have not received their primary identities through their professional occupations but rather through their families and domestic lives that the transition to old age can be easier for them than for their male counterparts. In her words:

In the immense majority of cases, being suddenly flung from the active into the inactive category, being classed as old, and undergoing a frightening drop in income and standard of living is a tragedy that has serious psychological and spiritual consequences. It is men who feel the effect most. Women live longer, and it is the very aged solitary women who make up the most underprivileged stratum of the population; yet generally speaking the elderly woman adapts herself to her state better than her husband. She is the person who runs the home, and in this her position is the same as that of the peasants and craftsmen of former times—for her too, work and life merge into one another. No decree from without suddenly cuts her activity short. It does grow less from the time her grown-up children leave the home, and this crisis, which often happens quite early in life, often disturbs her very badly; but still she does not see herself thrown into total idleness, and her role of grandmother brings her fresh possibilities. (261– 62)

Although this hetero-normative account of gender differences presupposes that most elderly women are wives, mothers, and grandmothers and so leaves out of account women (homosexual, bisexual, and heterosexual) who never married or who married and don't have children, Beauvoir's larger point is that even though elderly women live longer, almost always with less financial resources at their disposal than elderly men, and so tend to be economically worse-off, they tend to "fare better," that is, they tend to live more satisfying lives precisely because their former occupation and the identity associated with it, was never as sharply separated from their personal lives as it has traditionally been for men.[9] Paradoxically, then, married men who have had the luxury of not having to be directly involved in the running of their households, can end up at loose ends because they have no real role to play in the domestic sphere to which their retired status has relegated them. For this reason, as Beauvoir observes, elderly men are often viewed as a "nuisance" by their elderly wives who now have to contend with the additional burden of having these men at home and underfoot as they go about their ordinary domestic labors.[10] The man's retirement, she

---

9 This is true not only for housewives who may never have held a job outside the home but also for working wives and mothers who even today continue to take on the lion's share of the housework and childrearing responsibilities even when they work as many hours (and in some cases even more hours) as their male partners. For the very reason that most women are forced to contend with both domestic and professional responsibilities throughout their working lives, the transition out of the workforce does not represent such a break with their former identity because, I would argue, it was never a singular identity to begin with.

10 Indeed, a March 25, 2003 article in the *New York Times* describes the rising divorce rate in Japan among the middle-aged and elderly as noteworthy not only because divorce is still fairly uncommon in Japan but also because middle-aged and elderly women are increasingly the ones seeking divorces from their husbands. The wives' discontent was directly tied to the husbands' lack of assistance in the domestic sphere and the women's refusal to continue to accept the status quo.

notes, often "brings a radical break into a man's life; he is entirely cut off from his past and he has to adapt himself to a new status;" his wife, it should be noted, is usually the one who bears the brunt of this rupture, and who must help him find ways to establish a new identity that reflects his altered situation for, if she does not, she too must suffer the consequences! (262)

By emphasizing the unique difficulties men with active professional lives face when they retire, however, we run the danger of painting too rosy a picture of their female counterparts. Even though Beauvoir acknowledges that the balance of power between a couple may shift upon retirement, with the elderly woman becoming "the ruling partner" and the elderly man functioning "as a submissive being in the background, dominated by his wife" (262), it is also crucial to recognize the other cultural forces at work that place elderly women in an especially vulnerable position vis-à-vis society as a whole. More specifically, in the discussion that follows, I would like to turn to the challenges that the myth of femininity, described by Beauvoir in *The Second Sex*, continues to pose for elderly women who contravene its primary defining characteristic, namely, youthful beauty.

Revisiting the Myth of Femininity

If Oscar Wilde's *The Picture of Dorian Gray* had been the story of a woman who sought to retain her youth and loveliness at all costs, it never would have caused the sensation that greeted its 1890 publication in England. For, to the extent that women's main "accomplishments" have traditionally been associated not with their mental or professional achievements but with their corporeal endowments, that is, with how they *look* rather than what they have *done*, being obsessed with retaining the very qualities that give one social recognition and value seems quite natural.[11] Thus, despite the fact that the original Narcissus was male, it is women, not men, who have always been identified as quintessentially narcissistic creatures.[12] *The Picture of Dorian Gray* is a transgressive novel then, not merely because it portrayed Dorian's choice of male as well as female lovers

---

11 I am placing "accomplishments" in scare quotes here because, although the efforts required to cultivate one's beauty can be very time-consuming (e. g., spending hours on one's makeup, hair, jewelry, and clothing whether a woman does these things for herself or has them done for her by others), a woman is supposed to be (or at least look!) *naturally* beautiful and this means that her beauty is supposed to appear effortless and hence not be an "accomplishment" at all.
12 Freud's discussion of women's narcissism in "Three Essays on the Theory of Sexuality" and "On Narcissism" especially come to mind here.

to its Victorian readers in such matter-of-fact terms, but also because Dorian's early despair over the prospect of losing his beautiful youthful countenance is supposed to be a woman's abiding preoccupation, not a man's.

In *The Second Sex*, as mentioned earlier, Beauvoir argues that the myth of woman is internally inconsistent insofar as some of the characteristics most closely associated with it are in serious tension with one another. For this reason, she declares, rather unexpectedly citing Kierkegaard, no woman can actually embody all of the qualities associated with the myth at any given point in time:

> "To be a woman," says Kierkegaard in *Stages on the Road of Life*, "Is something so strange, so confused, so complicated, that no one predicate comes near expressing it and ... the multiple predicates that one would like to use are so contradictory that only a woman could put up with it." (Beauvoir 1989, 143)

Although there are many contradictions one may point to such as the impossibility of being dainty and fragile and hauling children, vacuum cleaners, and groceries around on a daily basis, or of being emotional and submissive and, at the same time, running a complicated household and raising children to be responsible adults, the contradiction I would like to focus on is the demand to remain attractive throughout one's life when beauty itself has historically been associated almost exclusively with youth. And, while women of color have actively campaigned for broadening the Western cultural aesthetic so that non-Eurocentric forms of beauty are increasingly being recognized (even if they are not yet seen as equally desirable and therefore not given equal value within Western cultures), less work has been done to dismantle the strong coupling of youth and beauty.

The challenge of retaining one's beauty even as one ages when beauty is so closely tied to being young (or at least youthful in appearance), is compounded, moreover, when one more closely examines the ambivalent manner in which human beings experience the aging process. In *The Coming of Age*, Beauvoir applies Sartre's concept of an "unrealizable" to the existential experience of old age, arguing that even though one may indeed be an elderly person, no human being ever coincides exactly with this particular identity. In her autobiography, *The Story I Tell Myself*, Hazel Barnes portrays the unrealizability of old age depicted by Beauvoir and Sartre as follows:

> Sartre, and Beauvoir, too, insisted that age is an "unrealizable," that is, I am old for others, not for myself. I think they are mostly right. To be sure, I cannot grasp my total situation objectively. What I am overflows the category of being an old person just as my being is never wholly expressed or confined in being a woman or an American. With respect to

age as with any other aspect of my facticity, my understanding of it is colored by the reactions of others. (Barnes 1997, 285)

Just as Sartre's famous waiter from *Being and Nothingness* is always "more" than a waiter since he has other facets to his identity outside of his job (even if his patrons treat him as if he is merely a waiter and nothing more), so too, the elderly person is always more than the sum of the years she has been alive. "It is impossible," Beauvoir maintains, "for us to experience what we are for others in the for-itself mode: the unrealizable is 'my being seen from without which bounds all my choices and which constitutes their reverse aspect'" (Beauvoir 1996, 291). Indeed, it is precisely because my identity as an elderly person is "unrealizable" from my subjective perspective that I can be surprised by viewing the tangible signs of my age that are objectively revealed by my body in the mirror. Moreover, I do not require a mirror to register the "marks" the aging process has inscribed on my body since others (especially those who haven't seen me for a long period of time) are often eager to function as such a mirror in my stead, just as Inez offers to serve as Estelle's mirror in Sartre's play *No Exit*.

Despite maintaining that old age is subjectively unrealizable for the one who embodies it, Beauvoir also argues in the passage above that the fact that others can grasp an identity that is unrealizable to me does in fact serve to constrain my choices. That is, even if I never coincide completely with the existential project that is my aging body, this project has an impact on all the other projects I may or may not pursue. And, to the extent that her body has always been seen as women's most prized project (in the sense of offering the greatest social and economic rewards to those who are most successful in making their bodies the objects of others' admiring regard), and to the extent that this project has been viewed as most successful not when a woman has maximized her body's motor potentialities, as Iris Marion Young has observed in "Throwing Like a Girl" (2005), but rather when she has succeeded in captivating the desiring male gaze, the constraints that elderly women face in coming to terms with the meaning of the aging process are indeed formidable. In Beauvoir's words,

> Since, as men see it, a woman's purpose in life is to be an erotic object, when she grows old and ugly she loses the place allotted to her in society: she becomes a *monstrum* that excites revulsion and even dread. Just as we see it in certain primitive nations, she takes on a supernatural character when she falls outside the human state: she is a witch, a dangerously powerful sorceress. (Beauvoir 1996, 122–23)

The "normal abnormality" that Beauvoir identifies with old age thus takes on a peculiar character for elderly women, creating unique challenges that they face in coming to terms with the aging process that are not shared by elderly men

(286).[13] Since, as Beauvoir observes in *The Second Sex*, to be seen as a successful man has not traditionally been a function of one's looks (since these latter are tied to the immanence of one's body and the body is associated with women more than men) but rather with one's cognitive accomplishments (one's transcendent activities that have the power to transform and not merely maintain the world of one's concern), the societal devaluation of the elderly male is not as directly connected with changes in his physical appearance but with changes in the professional, economic, and social contribution he makes to society.

In conclusion, the unrealizability and ambivalence of old age for women, is intensified, I would argue, by their being forced to grapple at every turn with the powerful myth of femininity that equates old age with ugliness, and that refuses to separate beauty from youth. Insofar as their bodies continue to be a primary determinant of the value they are accorded in society, it is inevitable that the coupling of the myth of femininity with the myth of aging, only enhances women's alienation from the corporeal effects of the aging process that is unfolding in their bodies and in their lives as a whole. If, as Beauvoir suggests, an old person is viewed by her society as "no more than a corpse under suspended sentence," it should be no surprise that myths of somehow transcending the aging process, or using its unrealizability to deny that it is even happening to oneself, or, increasingly, using medical technologies to "reverse" the effects of the aging process are becoming ever more popular (217). Indeed, given these ongoing pressures, as Hazel Barnes observes, "The cliché 'You are only as old as you feel' is less reassuring as you reflect on it. And if we are to shift to the question of attitude, it may be equally true that you are as old as others make you feel" (Barnes 1997, 284).

For women, in particular, this collapse of hard-and-fast distinctions between self-regard and other-regard is especially fraught because the myth of old age is haunted by the ever-present, contradictory myth of femininity. Though one might plausibly argue that elderly men must continue to contend with the predominant myth of masculinity operative in their culture, and that this latter also equates attractiveness with youth (or lat least youthful vigor), men's bodies tend to be identified in almost every mythical understanding of masculinity, if not as vehicles of/for transcendence (e.g. Hercules), then at least not as obstacles to it. What a man *does* has almost always been regarded as more important than how a man *looks* and the same cannot be said for a woman.

---

13 This does not mean that elderly men may not face pressures to present an attractive, youthful appearance to the world; the point is that the pressure to do so tends not to be so great for them precisely because their physical appearance (movie stars aside!) is not held to be the most important part of their identity.

Although Beauvoir maintains that "It is unusual for old people to have guilt-complexes: their age serves them as an excuse and as an alibi; and it does away with competition in their calling" she also claims that the price for this freedom from guilt is quite high: "their individual inferiorities are forgiven because they are looked upon as definitively inferior beings; they no longer have anything to lose because they have already lost everything. They are freed from their guilt-complexes: for most of them the price is a bitter feeling of decay" (Beauvoir 1996, 462). I am not as sure as Beauvoir that old people are ever truly able to leave their guilt-complexes behind. One of the guilt-complexes that I am arguing women retain throughout their lives, is the one that comes from failing to live up to the demanding dictates of the myth of femininity. To be seen as having relinquished this guilt-complex means that a woman has committed the unpardonable sin: she has "let herself go."

The universality and inevitability of the aging process guarantee that it cannot be bypassed, as Wilde dramatically illustrates, except through an early death. In Dorian Gray's case, his own humanity slowly perished even as his youthful body lived on. The rest of us, age-defying "remedies" aside, are not so (un)lucky. To deconstruct the entangled myths of femininity, masculinity, and old age that make the lives of elderly people seem tragic and debased, requires that we give up a cherished set of illusions that, Beauvoir argues, have done way more harm than good. Re-valuing the aging human (and non-human) body would, as Wilde realizes, require a new Dorian, and therefore a new picture of Dorian Gray. Such a creative, and ultimately open-ended project cannot be pursued individually; to be successful it must be a communal undertaking that affirms the possibilities, and not merely the limits, of the dynamic, aging bodies that are the mark of our humanity.

References

Barnes, Hazel E. 1997. *The story I tell myself: A venture in existentialist autobiography.* Chicago: The University of Chicago Press.

Bartky, Sandra Lee. 1999. Unplanned obsolescence: Some reflections on aging. In *Mother time: Women, aging, and ethics*, ed. Margaret Urban Walker. Lanham: Rowman & Littlefield Publishers, Inc., 61–74.

Beauvoir, Simone de. 1989. *The second sex.* Trans. H. M. Parshley. New York: Vintage Books.

Beauvoir, Simone de. 1996. *The coming of age.* Trans. Patrick O'Brian. New York and London: W. W. Norton & Company.

Beauvoir, Simone de. 1997. *The ethics of ambiguity.* Trans. Bernard Frechtman. Secaucus, NJ: Citadel Press.

Bergson, Henri. 1955. *An introduction to metaphysics*. Trans. T. E. Hulme. New York: Macmillan Publishing Co.

French, Howard. 2003. As Japan's women move up, many are moving out. *The New York Times*, March 25, 2003. Accessed through www.nytimes.com: October 24, 2008.

Freud, Sigmund. 1914. On narcissism: An introduction. In *The standard edition of the complete psychological works of Sigmund Freud*, vol. 14, trans. under the editorship of James Strachey in collaboration with Anna Freud. London: Hogarth Press, 67–104.

Freud, Sigmund. 2000. *Three essays on the theory of sexuality*. Ed. and trans. James Strachey. New York: Basic Books.

Kierkegaard, Søren. 1988. *Stages on life's way*. Ed. and trans. Howard V. Hong and Edna H. Hong. Princeton: Princeton University Press.

Meyers, Diana Tietjens. 1999. *Miroir, mémoire, mirage:* Appearance, aging, and women. In *Mother time: Women, aging, and ethics*, ed. Margaret Urban Walker. Lanham: Rowman & Littlefield Publishers, Inc., 23–41.

Sartre, Jean-Paul. 1982. *Critique of dialectical reason*. Trans. Alan Sheridan-Smith. London: Verso.

Sartre, Jean-Paul. 1984. *Being and nothingness*. Trans. Hazel E. Barnes. New York: Washington Square Press.

Sartre, Jean-Paul. 1976. No exit. In *No exit and three other plays*. Trans. Stuart Gilbert. New York: Vintage Books, 1–47.

Weiss, Gail. Are myths indispensable: Reflections on myth and reality in Beauvoir's *The Second Sex*. In *Ethical ambiguities in Beauvoir and Merleau-Ponty* (manuscript in progress).

Wilde, Oscar. 1992. *The picture of Dorian Gray*. New York: The Modern Library.

Young, Iris Marion. 2005. Throwing like a girl: A phenomenology of feminine body comportment, motility, and spatiality. In *On female body experience: "Throwing like a girl" and other essays*. Oxford: Oxford University Press, 27–45.

Anja Weiberg
Age as a Problem for Both Sexes

Comment on Gail Weiss

In her essay, Gail Weiss emphasizes the significance of a synthesis of the so-called myths of femininity and of old age as, in her view, older women are confronted with both of them. I think that an investigation on the possibly subsisting norms of femininity which constrain women even at an advanced age is an important and meritorious project. It is the more surprising to find that Simone de Beauvoir as the author of *The Second Sex* does not undertake any such investigation in her book on aging. Although she describes a number of gender-specifics concerning the living or handling of one's own age, most of the features, problems, discriminations, and (few) prospects or advantages constituting the theme of this book relate to both sexes. In my reading of Beauvoir, the latter are the aspects she is particularly interested in. To substantiate this view, I will address some topics from Weiss' essay.

(1) Nearly all of the passages where Beauvoir generally speaks of the woman as an erotic object which loses its place in society as soon as she starts growing old may be found in her chapter "Old age in historical societies." For example, the cited quote articulating the view of the older woman as a "*monstrum*" (Beauvoir 1996, 123) refers to the time of the Romans, to the time of poets like Horace and Ovid and *their* descriptions of old women. In the chapter "Old age in present-day society," however, such descriptions cannot be found at all, or at least not to this extent of generalization. In her time, in Beauvoir's opinion the most severe disadvantages of elderly women are that they have more difficulties in finding jobs, that they have less money, and that they live longer, yet more isolated, and on a much smaller income. The status of an erotic object, however, comes up only in the context of one aspect of the life of the elderly—their sexuality (346–50).

(2) Another of those rare passages in Beauvoir's book on aging, where she explicitly refers to the subject of femininity, is embedded in the context of age as the "unrealizable." Here she writes:

> There is nothing that obliges us in our hearts to recognize ourselves in the frightening image that others provide us with. That is why it is possible to reject that image verbally and to refuse it by means of our behaviour ... This is a usual choice with some women who have staked everything on their femininity and for whom age means being entirely out of the running. They try to deceive the rest of the world by means of their clothes,

make-up and behaviour; but above all they make a hysterical attempt at convincing themselves that they are not affected by the universal law. (Beauvoir 1996, 294–95)

This remark is interesting, above all because Beauvoir does not even come close to mentioning an "imposed status" or "dependency." The change of appearance as such entails that the Other will identify us as old, and as her many examples prove this seems to come as a shock to men and women alike.

(3) As Gail Weiss describes, Beauvoir thinks that for two reasons women do not have to face an equally sharp break when getting older: first, because they do not have to construct a new primary identity, and second, because they do not need to master a sudden and grave loss of power—because most of them never had power in their lives, to begin with. And I think that Beauvoir speaks earnestly when she sees a considerable advantage (though nearly the only one) for women in this when getting old, an advantage exactly deriving from the earlier discrimination, which is proven, among others, by the following remark: "Age does not bring women down from such a height; there are more things they can still do; and not being so embittered, so demanding, they 'uncommit' themselves less" (475).

(4) It seems to me that in Beauvoir's view older wives are not primarily in the position of suffering from their husbands' retirement-induced confusion but rather that they are very conscious about their newly achieved power and use it successfully. When she describes the (cited) development that the wife becomes "the ruling partner" while the husband turns into "a submissive being in the background," at the same time she describes this development as "the normal evolution of the average couple" (262), not as a rarity. Moreover, she quotes from interviews how women feel disturbed by their husbands' staying at home, and time and again ask them to go for walks. And, finally, you may read the following remark in her book: "From one day to the next, domestic tyrants may become so timid that they no longer cut a slice of bread without asking permission. Others sink into hypochondria" (268).

To conclude: Weiss discusses "the specific gendered tensions that emerge when elderly women are pressured to remain loyal both to the myth(s) of femininity and the myth(s) of old age" (47). In order to do this she needs to combine the results of *The Second Sex* and *The Coming of Age*, since Simone de Beauvoir herself never linked one with the other. Accordingly, the question arises why Beauvoir did not give a prominent place to the norms of femininity in her book on aging. And to me it seems that in this book she is not primarily interested in the gender differences of the aging process. Rather, she is outraged by the way old people (as a social group) are dealt with—irrespective of their sex or gender. She is outraged by the fact that in her view old people have an even worse standing than the female sex or black people: "[W]omen are struggling for equality and the blacks are fighting against oppression; the aged have no weapons whatsoever, and their problems belong strictly to the active adults" (Beauvoir 1996, 89). For this reason, I believe, Beauvoir did not again address the myth of the woman but concentrated on the other aspects, namely the economic and social aspects, and our personal refusal to recognize our future selves in the old person we see on the street. In this book she is not primarily a feminist but an advocate for the aged.

Translated by David Wagner

References

Beauvoir, Simone de. 1996. *The coming of age.* Trans. Patrick O'Brian. New York and London: W. W. Norton & Company.

Helen A. Fielding
The Poetry of Habit
Beauvoir and Merleau-Ponty on Aging Embodiment

Introduction

As people age their actions often become entrenched—we might say they are not open to the new; they are less able to adapt; they are stuck in a rut. Indeed, in *The Coming of Age* (*La Vieillesse*) Simone de Beauvoir writes that to be old is to be condemned neither to freedom nor to meaning, but rather to boredom (Beauvoir 1996, 461; 486). While in many ways a very pessimistic account of aging, the text does provide promising moments where her descriptions do capture other possibilities for aged existence. In particular, I turn to Beauvoir's suggestion that habit can take on a "kind of poetry" since it merges past, present and future in a sense of eternity that the present moment now lacks with its limited futural horizon (468; 492). In this paper, I draw out, delineate, and further explore this phenomenological reconfiguration of the present that she gestures towards through a consideration of the intensification and modification of the present through habit. Drawing as well upon Merleau-Ponty's insights into the phenomenal body, I argue that poetical habit is an active passivity that allows for the spontaneity of the new out of the sedimentation of corporeal memory, and for the attentive perception of what appears in the present. To disrupt someone's habitual life is to unanchor that life from the world, from an identity shaped by repetition, by the constancy of a shared reality of things, that is, from the spatial-temporal process of inhabitation, and thus from her ability to engage with others and to disclose the world.

In her observations, Beauvoir for the most part provides bleak accounts of aging. Attempting to draw out its phenomenological essences, she relies primarily upon descriptions drawn from literature, history, correspondence, diaries and ethnography. In agreeing with Aristotle's insight that "'[l]ife resides in movement'," she concludes that life for the aged is too often curtailed; while actions that are geared towards accomplishment are those that can infuse our lives with purpose, curiosity, and delight, a life devoid of claims and specific aims is at risk of provoking indifference (459–60; 483); the temporal, and hence freedom, are collapsed since the aged confront "[A] limited future and a frozen past" (378; 400). They have either accomplished what they set out to do, or they have abandoned their projects. Nor do they feel in a position to take up new ventures; they know that time is against them. To learn new skills is difficult if not impossible, and the initiation of new projects is always threatened by the likely possibility that they will never be brought to completion; there is rarely enough time. Thus, the elderly are not as open to the new as are those whose lives extend before them. Yet, without the movement of accomplishment that our projects provide, existence becomes reduced to the cyclical rhythms of biological necessity. It is indeed aging, and not death, that contrasts with life (539; 565). The elderly are thus too often defined by being, an *exis*, rather than by doing, or *praxis* (217; 231).

Habit, however, can potentially allow for the continuation of a life's projects and passions precisely because it is the body's way of carrying the past along with it in the present in anticipation of the future. While habit can too easily become caught up in rigid stereotypical movements that are tied solely to the past and the known, as opposed to a future that is to come and must be awaited without expectation, what distinguishes habit as a "kind of poetry" is its continued attentiveness to new possibilities of disclosure, to an openness to creative encounters that cannot be determined in advance. It is this cultivated attentiveness that permits one to remain engaged in the world; withdrawal from the world is a refusal of the "passion" which belongs to the "human condition" (Beauvoir 1948, 42), but such engagement is only practicable for the aged if they are not beset by anxiety over daily survival and control of their environment. The question of habit is hence a social and ethical problem that should be addressed as such. Aging is, as Beauvoir points out, a biological fact, but as a biological fact it is open to the cultural meanings accorded to it and according to which it is shaped: it also persists as characteristically "*antiphysis*" (1996, 40; 47).

Habit as the Continued Movement of Existence

The habitual allows for the possibilities of the continued movement of existence because habit is a kind of doing rather than being (459; 483). Referring to bodily actions, social rituals and even attitudes, the habitual is not just any kind of doing. Habit comes from the Latin *habere* which means to have or to hold suggesting both possession and belonging (Carlisle 2006, 22). It also comes from the ancient Greek *hexis* which, from Aristotle, we understand as more suggestive of the characteristic actions and emotional reactions that a person cultivates over time rather than an emphasis on the actions themselves (Kent 2006, 224). Although inactivity leads to boredom, activity allows life to transcend itself, "moving towards given ends"; inactivity, by contrast, "falls back, dull and motionless, upon itself" (Beauvoir 1996, 459; 484). Sartre describes the experience of pure presence as one of nausea. While nausea and boredom are often also experienced by the young who do not yet have a hold upon the world, for them it is not a lack of desire or the absence of plans, however vague, that prevents them from pursuing certain aims, but rather parental or societal control (460; 484). For the aged, however, with no more claims being made upon them, either through circumstance or their own indifference, the hold the world has upon them is relinquished; detached from their projects, devoid of curiosity, they risk being reduced to mere presence (461; 486).

Ascribing sensor-motor memory, "in which recognition is a matter of action and not of thought" (362; 385), to automatic forms of behavior, Beauvoir takes habit as action to encompass what we understand as a form of "automatic reaction and routine" (467; 491). Henri Bergson distinguishes between habit as action corporeally learned and linked to usefulness, and memory-images which belong to thought (Bergson 1991, 80–88). But for Merleau-Ponty, the habitual is also more than this. The body is not an autonoman; it has its own way of taking up, interpreting and engaging with the world. For example, I learn to play the violin. The process takes place over a number of years and, in fact, if I keep playing, does not really end. Although the origin of the learning of each new musical skill generally becomes lost, if I put the instrument aside for a number of years, my fingers still know, if at first a little clumsily, how to find the notes. Or, I hear a piece and know I have at one time played it simply because I find myself counting out the rhythm of the time signature. Learning how to play the instrument is a progressive sedimentation of new possibilities, new ways of sensing out harmonies with my fingers, new rhythms that belong to the dash of the bow. If I begin to play an unfamiliar piece of music, I focus on new arrangements, but my fingers generally know the notes, and where they must be placed. My hands seem to have their own way of interpreting a new situation and taking it up. As I age and my technical proficiency diminishes, my playing seems to gain in a layer of feeling and understanding of which perhaps my youthful self was incapable, and the pleasure derived is more likely to come from simply being caught up in the music rather than from any anticipation of a future proficiency. But there is another possibility for delight, which comes in playing *with* others, which is not the same as playing *for* others as such. Playing a duet, or a quartet, for example, can have moments of a musical conversation amongst the players where the phrases unite in a kind of coherence that discloses the interactive space between the players. This coherence in the present can only be achieved through a habitually incorporated understanding of instrument and music that is directed towards completion of the piece. Of course, even for accomplished musicians, a precise completion is never guaranteed which is one of the charms of live performance, and one of the characteristics of habit; it is never an exact repetition.

In short, our body gives "to our life, [in Merleau-Ponty's words], the form of generality, and develops our personal acts into stable dispositional tendencies" (Merleau-Ponty 2003, 169; 171). These tendencies can become habits that Aristotle suggests are ones we can cultivate; thus, even if they become actions that seem automatic, they have still at one time been freely chosen and further developed. Moreover, such habits are not ones that once learnt are subsequently turned over to routine automation; rather, they are further deepened and cultivated. As the cognitive aspects of taking on a new habit move to the background, the affective, perceptual and motile regions, that is, the bodily, can be allowed to intensify. Nevertheless, though these aspects of the corporeal have interpretive possibilities other than those of cognitive reasoning, they still overlap and intertwine. Habits are not instincts; nor are they simply passive. Although actions are not linked to representations—we do not represent to ourselves the movements we shall make—still, "the body is our general medium for having a world" (Merleau-Ponty 2003, 169; 171). To possess the world is to inhabit it—to have a grip or a hold upon the world through the power of our corporeal being. Thus the acquisition of habit is not simply cognitive. It is rather the body's way of understanding the world that is not merely passive, but is also active, and it allows the body to find "anchorage in [as well as] perpetual movement towards a world". In fact, habit "has been cultivated when [the body] has absorbed a new meaning, and assimilated a fresh core of significance" (Merleau-Ponty 2003, 169; 171). Ascribing meaning, then, belongs not only to consciousness, but also to a body engaged with the world.

If this is so, then the aged have the potential of dwelling in a world that is steeped in meaning. Rather than being condemned to boredom, which is of course always a risk, aging also holds the potential of allowing for deepened understandings and more complex corporeal intuitions. If habit can be understood in terms of dispositional tendencies, then clearly at stake are the habits we develop over the course of our lives. Beauvoir concludes that it is unlikely we will develop new ways of being when we age, and further, our habits of being that manifest over the span of our lives will determine how we live when we are old. Thus, corporeal memory can hold someone in the world even as her cognitive capacities begin to diminish. She recounts the story of a woman whose memory was failing yet who was able to adapt herself to her surroundings by relying upon her habitual memory:

> She did not recognize people, but she was aware of the social category to which they belonged, and she treated the nurses, doctors, ward-maids and other patients in different ways. She knew she had lost her memory and it vexed her if there was any attempt to make her recall past events; but her judgment was sound, she was capable of discrimina-

tion, and she joked readily. She lived with neither past nor future, in a perpetual present. (Beauvoir 1996, 467; 491–2)

Clearly, then, a kind of corporeal memory allows habit to bestow "a certain quality upon the world and a certain charm to the passage of time" (469; 493). For this reason the elderly can experience deep loss when they forsake a habit—smoking, drinking coffee or wine, meeting with certain friends. For the young, for whom the future stretches before them, this loss is not so keenly felt; the elderly, however, suffer, for something of their lives has been torn away; they do not anticipate in the same way the formation of new habits and new rituals that hold them in and connect them to the world.

Habits, it would then seem, provide the elderly with a kind of ontological security. Since life is movement, then identity is not something we have but is rather secured through repetition providing the impression of a core stable being and a knowledge of who we are (Carlisle 2006, 29); accordingly, the loss of habit can be experienced as a loss of a sense of self (Beauvoir 1996, 469; 493). Often dependent upon others for the arrangement of their existence, the elderly can become anxious about losing a part of themselves. Moreover, even our possessions, Beauvoir explains, are solidified habits: a garden in which one walks each day, or a chair in which one sits every evening. These objects provide continuity through time. Against any grounding in a metaphysics of presence, we might phenomenologically understand objects as presencing into a finite appearance, of providing a sense of an ongoing shared reality that provides a kind of stability. Since existence for the aged is often curtailed in terms of doing, having can sometimes contribute to being. An attachment to money or objects is demonstrative of this tendency. Possessions help to secure for the elderly a sense of identity and a connection with the world which seems threatened by others "who claim to see [the elderly person] as nothing but an object" (470; 494). In short, habit is a kind of active inhabiting of space and time (Merleau-Ponty 2003, 161; 162). Thus to have familiar objects around one, as well as a familiar environment, allows for corporeal memory, the sedimentation of embodied identity; for having an active grip on the world can only come out of a passive generality that is through and through temporal (497; 489).

Habit has a Kind of Poetry

Although Merleau-Ponty's understanding of habit as disposition, as our general grip upon the world, seems to lie for Beauvoir on the side of the body as immanence rather than on that of the possibilities for transcendence, this is not necessarily the case. On the one hand, habit is always in danger of being or becoming a rigid and repetitive form of behavioral response that excludes any new possibilities for creative encounter. As Beauvoir describes:

> Playing cards every afternoon in a certain café with certain friends is a habit that in the first place was freely elected and its daily repetition has a meaning. But if the card-player is angry or upset because *his* table is occupied, it means a lifeless requirement has come into existence, one that prevents him from adapting himself to the situation. (468; 492)

In this description the habit has become inflexible, and the meaning of the game seems to exclude any other possibility other than its own repetition; it is tied to immanence, the fact that it has always taken place just so and must continue to do so. On the other hand, Beauvoir writes, a habit that is "thoroughly integrated" into someone's life "makes it richer, for habit has a kind of poetry" (468; 492). It would seem, then, that habit that is poetical entails an element of transcendence. Heidegger, in his phenomenological account of poetry provided in his lectures on thinking, describes it as one of the nine muses, as the child of *Mnemosyne*, of Memory (Heidegger 1968, 11; 7–8). Memory is mindful, he writes, and thus bears in mind that which needs to be thought and said; poetry allows for this disclosure, for this bringing forth of being, of that which is; it is a thinking back "toward the source," toward that which endures (11; 7–8). In other words, it discloses enduring essences or ways of being.

But the poetry of habit is a kind of corporeal mindfulness. Irigaray indeed reminds us that we do not in fact need words to remember—our bodies remember: "Your body says yesterday in what it wants today. If you think: yesterday I was, tomorrow I shall be, you think: I have died a little" (Irigaray 1985, 214; 213, translation modified). For Irigaray, then, the body has a capacity to remember and to bear its desires, its passions with it; hence, to rely on a cognitive account is "to store, count and capitalize" what is past. It is to anticipate death, whereas to focus on corporeality is to say, "here and now how we are moved" (214; 213). Though clearly Heidegger's account of poetry is itself a critique of Cartesian certitude since being, as that which is disclosed, can never be defined or counted upon, it still focuses on the disclosure of being rather than on that of individual beings. Alternatively, Irigaray emphasizes the corporeal and lived aspect of memory and existence that can be forgotten in Heidegger's phenomenological account of revealing through saying.

Undoubtedly there are habits, or ways of corporeally remembering to which people have become attached which no longer have any meaning or revelatory power—that do not disclose any aspect of existence. But there are also poetic habits that seem to provide for transcendence, for a hold upon the world that is not only disclosive but also an essential aspect of someone's identity, of who they are, and not what they are, and this identity is essentially corporeal, expressed in actions, gestures, emotions and desires.[1] Beauvoir refers to Sartre's distress when he decided to give up smoking because smoking belonged to his sense of self (1996, 468; 493). Habit can thus bring about a "crystallization," a "power of revealing the whole world to us" (468; 492–93).

Beauvoir offers the English habit of drinking tea every afternoon as example of the poetry of habit, or, as I would propose, of corporeal mindfulness. She suggests that the habitual participation in certain rituals can also allow for the repetition of a meaningful event whereby "the present moment is the past brought to life again, the future anticipated; [she] experience[s] both together in the for-itself mode" (468; 492). The habitual aspect of drinking tea each day at the same time, perhaps with others, allows then for an ekstatic connection to the past that is not cognitively remembered, yet allows one to remain connected to one's passions and commitments. Similarly, it opens up a future that is not defined by projects or goals but simply by the continued possibility of a joy and delight in existence. Moreover, perhaps the ritual of drinking tea might provide for moments of disclosure, of perhaps partaking in the company of friends or family, opening up a temporal space or boundary within which people can relate with one another and disclose who they are in perhaps even the small yet unpredictable ways that belong to everyday existence.

Alternatively, when I consciously throw myself back to an event in the past I am presented with a mere "skeleton" of the event since the moment remembered was lived as a present moment that was "rich in the future towards which it was hurrying" (366; 388). The for-itself does not coincide with being. Thus, the fullness of the present at which we aim can never be fulfilled, for a life is not something we can actually possess other than by living it (368; 390). In our conscious memories, then, this ekstatic non-coincidence of the present with what is cannot be recreated. Even to return to a certain place "I shall not find myself" since "my plans [...], my hopes and fears" escape me. Some event that took place is "fixed against that background like a butterfly pinned in a glass case ... relationships are numbed, paralysed. And I myself no longer expect anything at all" (366; 388).

For Beauvoir, then, habits that are stultifying, that prevent spontaneity and the embracing of new possibilities are, despite their link to activity, nevertheless, more on the side of being. There is always the risk of settling into patterns of behavior that protect the aged from the world, and in so doing reduce their ability

---

1 See Arendt 1958, 178.

to engage rather than enhance it. For habitual life not to become one that petrifies our existence, that "polishes time—you slip as you do on an over-waxed floor"[2]—habits must not only, for Beauvoir, be freely chosen, they must also be kept alive, integrated into our passionate engagement with the world, and remain open to rearticulation.

I would like to suggest that Merleau-Ponty's insights into the prereflective body actually allow us to take Beauvoir's understanding of habit as poetry further. For habit relies upon corporeal memory which is unreflective experience and which amounts to, in Merleau-Ponty's words, "a kind of original past, a past which has never been a present" (Merleau-Ponty 2003, 282; 280). Corporeal memory is evoked through action, through the intentional movement of the body. As Edward Casey points out, "the issue is not that of reopening the past but of carrying it forward into the future of eventual accomplishment." The past is carried forward in concrete action (Casey 1984, 294). Habit thus unites the past, present and future without fixing the past as a memory and without looking forward to a foreshortened future. In fact, habit can be a kind of self-affirmation of life rather than an awaiting for the unknown of death to approach (Carlisle 2006, 32). For this reason the diminishing of capacities that require us to give up certain habits provokes an even deeper loss than merely that of something that provided pleasure; for what is also lost is a little part of the self.

But here, even Casey's understanding of the body being carried forward into concrete action overlooks another aspect of corporeal memory that is not so much about the movement of doing but is rather expressed by being moved. For example, friendships too can share in this "poetry of habit" that the aged perhaps especially cherish since they in particular are habits that merge past, present and future, providing an eternity which is otherwise no longer to be found in the present (Beauvoir 1996, 468; 492). Thus, when a close friend dies, there is a sudden break with a shared past that perhaps did not need to be uttered and yet somehow provided a depth to ongoing relations and to one's very being. Indeed, our sense of self is reflected to us in our relations with others. Moreover, past events lose their reality when there is no one else to confirm their having taken place. Beauvoir describes her losses: "wiped out too my arguments with Merleau-Ponty in the gardens of the Luxembourg, at his home, at mine, at Saint-Tropez; gone those long talks with Giacometti and my visits to his studio." While her friends lived she did not need to reflect upon their shared past for it to remain alive. Yet, she writes: "In the 'monuments to the dead' that stud my history, it is I who am buried" (367; 389).

---

2 This quote is from Eugène Ionesco's *Journal en miettes* quoted in Beauvoir 1996, 376.

Engaging with the World

It is a biological and unavoidable fact that in aging our bodies deteriorate, and our capacities diminish. Though of course, as Beauvoir notes, the rate of diminishment can be countered and modified by the quality of the life lived. In her much earlier book, *The Ethics of Ambiguity*, she asserts that it is still the body through which we express our relationship to the world (1948, 41). This relationship, which is conveyed through both the ways we speak and our bodily comportment, is one of intelligence and sensitivity only if one remains corporeally attentive to other beings as well as to one's own bodily capacities; for this attentiveness, that can only be described as our engagement with the world, is exactly what allows us to "discover reasons for existing" (1948, 41). Thus, in old age, a withdrawal that can come with diminishing capacities leads invariably to indifference—it can be socially proscribed, or individually intended. To withdraw is to cease engaging with the world, turning the present into pure immanence, and the past into a weight that must be borne. The future is anticipated with dread, and one is condemned to inaction (1996, 496; 521). Habit can allow the aged to escape petrification but still ensconce them in a rigidity of stereotypical movements endlessly repeated (497; 522).

It would seem, then, that the danger of aging could be likened to becoming what Beauvoir, in her earlier work called the "sub-man" (1948, 42). The sub-man refuses engagement with the world. He rejects the "'passion' which is his human condition" and instead finds around him only an "insignificant and dull world" for which he feels no desire "to feel, to understand, to live." As his existence further diminishes he finds no reason to exist since reasons are generated through the engagement of existence itself. Bored, and fearful in a world with which he has no bonds, he feels powerless in face of present events and the future seems dark; his uncertainty only "reinforces his terror" (1948, 42–45).

Beauvoir's insights allow me to conclude that habit plays a subtle but crucial role in the lives of the elderly since it potentially holds them in the world. Thus, the ways that we socially provide for and allow for the habitual reflect upon the quality of life the elderly are allowed to experience, for this habitual life that emerges from corporeal sedimentations relies upon the smooth operation of the outside world. There is a necessity to keep things in place, and events require a kind of regularity. Yet Beauvoir suggests that the extreme reactions the elderly can have to the upset of their habitual lives emerges from an insecurity they experience, as the powerlessness to have any effect on others, to be unable to impose their will. Thus an entrenched habitual life protects them from this feeling of powerlessness that is ultimately the same as withdrawal since it implies the inability to effect change or engage with the world. What I am suggesting here is that the rigidity that seems to emerge in the habitual life of the elderly reflects upon the society in which they are embedded—a society that may fail to acknowledge and respect aging as a stage of life that is the destiny of all, though of course some may not live to fulfill it.

Beauvoir's concern is that the elderly not be reduced to their facticity whereby the world is for them silent. She questions how we are to allow for transcendence when the future with its goals and projects begins to close down. There are, for Beauvoir, as Debra Bergoffen explains, two moments of intentionality: "a moment that discloses being, and a moment that identifies the disclosing I with the being it discloses" (Bergoffen 1997, 76). In the first, there is an experience of the self as participating in the revelation of an intersubjective world and in the second there is an appropriation of the meanings disclosed, perhaps in an identification with a project or goal (76–77). As Bergoffen points out, there is no clear way to negotiate between disclosure, letting be, and the will to mastery in the establishment of projects. There is a joy or delight to be found in the desire to reveal but not control being, and to "introduce the desire for control undermines this desire's delight" (95). So when Beauvoir writes that it is "by the light of our projects that the world reveals itself," she gestures towards how the two moments of intentionality might work together (Beauvoir 1996, 451; 475). Our lives are directed by certain projects and goals, ones we cannot perhaps master; at the same time, these ways of approaching the world will also imbue the ways in which it becomes revealed to us through our engagement with it and with others. Thus, for Beauvoir, to preserve passion in living it is important to have projects and goals, but not necessarily ones that can be definitively controlled since joy can be achieved through letting be and allowing being to unfold.

Indeed, precisely because a future can no longer be anticipated as coming towards one, if permitted, the present moment, experienced as being moved, has the potential to be "a joy in still being", "in the very act of living" [*le seul fait de vivre*] in survival whereby you "'are no longer attached to anything and yet you are more sensitive to all'" (448; 472). Beauvoir quotes Claudel: "[y]ou must reach old age before you can understand the meaning—the splendid, absolute unchallengeable irreplaceable meaning of the word 'today'!" (448; 472). Thus, an engagement with the world does not have to be directly with things or with projects; this emphasis in "a joy in still being," in being more sensitive to the world suggests not so much a project as rather the fruition of the cultivation of perception and affection, of our corporeal ability to engage with and disclose the world, to let it be.

Nevertheless, since aging is something that we inevitably must endure—it belongs to our appearing and disappearing, our birth and our death which marks the boundaries of life that allow us to presence, to engage with the world and with others—it is not in itself an activity; this means, then, that only in the continued pursuit of those aims that provide meaning to our existence, "devotion to individuals, to groups or to causes, social, political, intellectual, or creative work," do our lives not become mere parodies of themselves (540; 567). And even if this devotion need not require individual will to mastery and control, which could, in some cases, be relinquished to the care of others, the devotion itself seems necessary. For this reason, we cannot suddenly acquire new projects, but rather must continue with those that have given our lives meaning in the past. Thus the continuation of these projects takes on the texture of habit, habit that belongs to the unique existence of each individual, and that is hence open to being shaped in new ways, yet resists a sudden break or unexpected reconfiguration; habit implies both a past and an ongoing future even if it is not necessarily the elderly person herself who will be there to see the project fulfilled. For this reason, hobbies are not sufficient for keeping the elderly engaged in the world. Hobbies neither disclose being nor are they projects with which the elderly person could herself identify. They do not involve actions or speech that reveal the agent (Arendt 1958, 118, 176).

Thus there is a problem when the elderly suddenly realize that they have been caught up in pursuits they did not themselves choose; they were too busy to realize this since they were, for example, taken up in a labor market that required from them a participation in a system whose meaning comes from the efficiency of the system itself. In other words, mere utility is not sufficient. It might give one a sense of purpose, of feeling needed, but it cannot be equated with the goals one sets for oneself. When utility is over, there might be left only rigid habits, or not even these. Alternatively, poetical habits evolve out of our projects and pursuits freely chosen and allow for the disclosure of meaning that is brought forth in our engagement with the world and with others. Only in the idleness of old age does this discrepancy between the two kinds of habit become apparent, and by then it is too late to seek out new projects. For this reason, she concludes, humans must always be treated as humans, and not "as so much material" (542; 568–69). Taking on the problem of old age cannot be isolated from rethinking the relationships among humans of all ages.

Conclusion

Accordingly, what might shift for the elderly is the emphasis on projects to that of disclosure, to the internal contemplation that overlaps with the world through the cultivation of attunement, and an attentiveness which is another kind of movement or being moved more subtly evoked. If life is to be understood as "perpetual change" rather than a "gradual death," as an "unstable system," one in which balance is both lost and restored, then it is lack of movement that equates with death: "[c]hange is the law of life" and aging is simply another kind of movement or change, if at that, an irreversible decline (11; 17). At the same time, even as corporeal capacities to adapt might have diminished, the body's own interpretive capacities to sense out the new in light of the old, to layer meaning against depth, have the possibility of becoming more complex. Though motility becomes reduced, and the active pursuit of projects might be laid aside, this does not mean that the aged are incapable of the cultivation of a joy of being that is supported by the habitual, inhabiting and habituated self.

Beauvoir's insights on ageing thus lead me to conclude that supporting the habitual lives of the elderly in a way that maintains the potential for their ongoing poetical possibilities is ethically significant. Beauvoir shows us how a life cannot be carved up into stages but is rather the emergence of a whole and that old age is as much about the particularities of that whole as any other stage. For this reason, her phenomenological descriptions of ageing have ethical implications for all stages of life. The ways we live from the beginning also determine the ways in which we will age. Moreover, the elderly cannot be expected to suddenly develop new lives, new habits, and new projects more fitting to their diminished capacities. Though habits can become rigid repetitions that tie the elderly to immanence, they can also draw upon a poetical corporeal potential that allows the elderly to remain engaged in a world that has not only a past but also a kind of future.

In elaborating upon what remains in Beauvoir a mere sketch of the possibilities of habit, I conclude that the habitual holds the poetical possibility of allowing one to be open to the unexpected and to creative encounters with the unknown, to the unpredictable that belongs to disclosure, but only if the person in question is not beset by anxiety over daily survival. The question of habit is thus a social and ethical problem that should be addressed as such. For Beauvoir, habits are less likely to be rigid and systematized, as well as lacking in meaning if they are freely chosen and not imposed by the utilitarian exigencies of an economic system to which they have been usefully adapted. What we could hope to achieve is a stage of life that possesses "its own balance" and provides "a wide range of possibilities open to the individual" (543; 569). Yet, I would add, that even habits that are part of the lived cultural texture of particular lives—customs and rituals, the tastes of particular foods, for example, that might sustain and support the identity of immigrants and those in exile—while not necessarily freely chosen, are indispensable to a sense of self. Thus the support of the elderly in their enduring projects, passions and daily lives has profound social implications—for this means we are responsible not only for supporting the aging but also for helping to provide a life worth habituating.

References

Arendt, Hannah. 1958. *The human condition.* Chicago: The University of Chicago Press.

Beauvoir, Simone de. 1948. *The ethics of ambiguity.* Trans. Bernard Frechtman. New York: Citadel Press.

Beauvoir, Simone de. 1996. *The coming of age.* Trans. Patrick O'Brian. New York: W. W. Norton & Company (originally published as *La vieillesse.* Paris: Éditions Gallimard 1970).

Bergson, Henri. 1991. *Matter and memory.* Trans. Nancy Margaret Paul. New York: Zone Books.

Carlisle, Clare. 2006. Creatures of habit: The problem and the practice of liberation. *Continental Philosophy Review* 38, 19–39.

Casey, Edward S. 1984. Habitual body and memory in Merleau-Ponty. *Man and World* 17, 279–97.

Heidegger, Martin. 1968. *What is called thinking?* Trans. J. Glenn Gray. New York: Harper & Row Publishers (originally published as *Was heißt Denken?* Tübingen: Max Niemeyer 1961).

Irigaray, Luce. 1985. *This sex which is not one.* Ithaca: Cornell University Press (originally published as *Ce sexe qui n'en est pas un.* Paris: Les Éditions de Minuit 1977).

Kent, Bonnie. 2006. Habits and virtues. In *Aquinas's Summa theologiae: Critical essays,* ed. Brian Davies. Lanham, MD: Rowman & Littlefield Publishers, 223–44.

Merleau-Ponty, Maurice. 2003. *Phenomenology of perception.* Trans. Colin Smith. New York: Routledge (originally published as *Phénoménologie de la perception.* Paris: Gallimard 1945).

Kristin Rodier
Are Poetic Habits Particular to the Aged?

Comment on Helen A. Fielding

In Helen Fielding's "The Poetry of Habit," she develops a view about habit in the life of an aged person that breaks away from what might be thought of as a standard existentialist reading of habit as a negative part of life (because it is "unfree"). Existence in general relies heavily upon habitual understanding of the world, and habitual actions in the world, but Beauvoir's claim in *The Coming of Age* (1996) is that this becomes especially so with the aged: they often experience rigidity in their habits that keep them ontologically secure, yet as a result they are less open to the new. With a Merleau-Pontian reading of habit, Fielding suggests that once the aged's cognitive attentiveness to the acquisition of habits fades into the background and the habit becomes corporeally sedimented, the past can be carried along into the present with the potential of an added layer of feeling or more complex corporeal intuitions. If indeed the aged can have these experiences we would be well motivated to further understand this potentiality of experience.

We are given the example of the violinist who may gain pleasure from getting caught up in the music—she plays for the pleasure of disclosure (cf. 71). The cognitive attentiveness needed to form new habits fades into the background and the bodily experience can then be intensified. This allows for the aged person to potentially experience with those habits which they have already corporeally sedimented new and fresh feeling. Added on to this are the poetical habits where the feeling is both intensified and the person remains open to reinscription, new sedimentations and the possibility of joy and delight. What remains unclear is what it takes to achieve these kinds of experiences, and whether or not they are, in the end, particular to the aged. It seems that the possibility of achieving these experiences is laid bare by Fielding's reading of habit, but if we go deeper into Merleau-Ponty we may find some help in understanding these ideas further.

In order to see what may be added to this account I believe we can draw an analogy to Merleau-Ponty's account of sexual significance. Merleau-Ponty claims that to be sexual we must open ourselves to sexual meanings and experiences by taking up a sexual attitude. The use of "attitude" is technical; we can understand Merleau-Ponty's use of it is as rooted in Gestalt psychology. An "attitude" is a *"capacity level of the total personality* in a specific plane of activity" (Goldstein and Scheerer 1941, 112). Each attitude furnishes the basis for all performances pertaining to a specific set of movements, gestures, and feelings. When we take up a sexual attitude towards something, the being of its sexual significance begins to exist for us: it gains a physiognomy (Merleau-Ponty 2002, 180). If we accept this extension of Merleau-Ponty's theory of embodiment, then what is left to be described is, perhaps, a poetical attitude. This attitude would allow us to project or create the possibility of the kinds of experiences and feelings (joy! delight!) that come from poetical habits. The difficulty arises when we really flesh-out this analogy. Most people will understand straightaway what Merleau-Ponty means by sexual significance because sexuality in its most general form is common to most humans, but more difficult to spot is just this experience that the idea of poetical habits affords us. The example of the woman playing the violin who does not play for a future proficiency, but remains open to new and deepened feeling, sounds like an experience I might want, but perhaps one that I might get caught-up in *trying* to have. I worry that I may not be able to have the cognitive fade into the background in the right way: if I try to play for the pure pleasure and spend the whole time worried about the calorie content of the yogurt I just ate it seems as though I'm not open in the right way—but how do I fix it? How do I get the first intuition so that I may repeat the experience, so that I may learn more and gain a greater ability to project the poetical attitude?

If this analogical worry holds, then we ought to wonder what it is about the poetical attitude that is particular to the habitual life of the elderly. Imagine the middle aged woman who took figure skating lessons as a youth who, for the first time in twenty years, has gone back on the ice to skate with her own children. She may remember how to skate backwards, she can stop and start with ease, yet her physical ability not being what it once was is standing in the way of performing the more detailed and creative moves of which her younger self was capable. Could she not skate for the deepened feeling? She does not anticipate her future ice skating the way the young do because her years of triple-lutzes and double-toe-loops are behind her. As in the case of the elderly, the action of the middle-aged woman is not aimed at a future proficiency, yet it seems that she can be open to new meanings in the poetical way described. This woman is not aged in the way Fielding or Beauvoir mean, but she seems to be equally capable of the poetical attitude and performing these actions now with her own children would provide ample opportunities for more complex corporeal intuitions and deepened meanings. Figure skating is, perhaps, not violin playing, but it also is not a hobby as Fielding defines it either.

Perhaps more determining than age is each individual's flexibility for taking up different attitudes towards their life and experiences. Further description of how we can bring the poetical attitude to the foreground of consciousness would be fruitful for reclaiming the joy and delight that the habitual body can afford us in experience.

References

Beauvoir, Simone de. 1996. *The coming of age.* Trans. Patrick O'Brian. New York and London: W. W. Norton & Company.
Goldstein, Kurt, and Martin Scheerer. 1941. Abstract and concrete behavior: An experimental study with special tests. *Psychological Monographs* 53 (2): 110–30.
Merleau-Ponty, Maurice. 2002. *Phenomenology of perception.* Trans. Colin Smith. New York: Routledge.

References

Part Two: **Age and Ethics**

Sonia Kruks

Beauvoir's *The Coming of Age* and Sartre's *Critique of Dialectical Reason*

The Material Mediations of Age as Lived Experience

In her late autobiographical volume, *All Said and Done*, Simone de Beauvoir described *The Coming of Age* as "the counterpart [*le symétrique*] of *The Second Sex*" (1993, 130, translation altered; 1972, 147). In the same work she also discussed *The Second Sex*, self-critically saying:

> if I were to write [it] today I should provide a materialist, not an idealist, theoretical foundation for the opposition between the Same and the Other. I should ground [*je fonderais*] the rejection and oppression of the Other not on the antagonism of consciousnesses, but on the economic basis of scarcity (1993, 448, translation altered; 1972, 497).

Similarly, in her earlier autobiographical volume, *Force of Circumstance*, Beauvoir had also said that she would now base the notion of the "Other" not on "the idealist struggle of consciousnesses," but on "scarcity and need" (1992, vol. I, 192, translation altered; 1963, 267). "As the basis," she wrote, "I would take a more materialist position in the first volume. I would base the notion of the *other* and the Manichaeism it implies not on the a priori and idealist struggle of consciousnesses, but on scarcity and need" (1992, vol. 1, 192, translation altered; 1963, vol. 1, 267).[1] Given Beauvoir's two claims: first, that *The Coming of Age* is the counterpart to *The Second Sex* and, second, that her earlier work lacked sufficient attention to "scarcity and need," I set out in this paper to examine the "materialist" aspects of *The Coming of Age*.

What is at issue here is Beauvoir's relationship not just to materialism but to Sartre's later work, for "scarcity" and "need" are shorthand for a particular kind of materialism: Sartre's. In 1960, almost mid-way in time between the initial French publication of *The Second Sex* in 1949 and of *The Coming of Age* in 1970, Sartre had published the first volume of his *Critique of Dialectical Reason*. Beauvoir gave this monumental work of Sartre's only the briefest mention in her

---

1 In French, Beauvoir refers to "la rareté et le besoin," that is, to "scarcity and need" (1963, vol. 1, 267). However, the English translation unfortunately renders this as "the facts of supply and demand"! There has been considerable discussion of the inadequacies of the English translations of *The Second Sex*, but many other translations, including those of the autobiographies and of *The Coming of Age*, are also flawed.

autobiography (1992, vol. 1, 220). However, elements of its conceptual apparatus play an important role in several of her own later works, including *The Coming of Age*.[2] In the *Critique of Dialectical Reason*, synthesizing his earlier phenomenology with a Marxist-inspired materialism, Sartre sets out systematically to investigate the foundational role of the forms of "humanly worked matter" that he calls the "practico-inert" in constituting social existence and experience. In what follows, I set out to show the ways in which the later Sartre's account of need and scarcity, and of how they shape and mediate social relations and experiences, significantly inform Beauvoir's account of old age. However, true to form, Beauvoir engages in only an ambiguous appropriation, for she creatively reworks aspects of Sartre's theoretical framework for her own ends.[3] I begin by introducing some of the key ideas that inform Sartre's *Critique of Dialectical Reason*, before showing how Beauvoir both employs and transforms them.

Need and Scarcity: The Emergence of Praxis, the Practico-Inert, and Reciprocity

In the *Critique of Dialectical Reason*, Sartre distinguishes between "need" [*le besoin*] and "scarcity" [*la rareté*]. "Need," he argues, is an *ontological* structure of human existence, for we cannot exist as a species unless we satisfy basic biological need. Need thus initiates what Sartre calls "praxis." "Praxis" is the term that Sartre now uses (borrowed from Marx) to describe those intentional human activities that transform the material world around us in order to satisfy need. "Need," however, includes not only our basic biological needs but also more complex social and cultural ones. Praxis, because it is intentional, must involve freedom. But, because praxis involves a *materially conditioned* freedom, the

---

2 Notably, she also draws on the *Critique of Dialectical Reason* quite extensively in the first chapter of *All Said and Done*, where she reflects on the question of what constitutes a life, here her own (1993, 1–113).
3 This far, the debate about the "Beauvoir-Sartre relationship" has focused on an earlier time-period: above all discussions have been about whether or how far Beauvoir is indebted to Sartre in her works up to and including *The Second Sex* (1949) and, conversely, how far Sartre is indebted to Beauvoir for some of the central ideas of *Being and Nothingness* (1943). Many, myself included, have argued that Beauvoir is an original philosopher in her own right, not a mere disciple of Sartre's, and I have also suggested elsewhere that Beauvoir played a significant role in Sartre's trajectory in the late 1940s and 1950s toward a more socially oriented and materialist theory (Kruks 2001, 49–51). Thus my focus here on what Beauvoir drew from Sartre's later work is intended to illuminate a specific moment in a complex on-going dialectic of mutual influence between them, and is not to intended to cast Beauvoir once again in the role of disciple.

"practical" subject of the *Critique of Dialectical Reason* differs significantly from the absolutely free consciousness that, in *Being and Nothingness*, Sartre had called being "for-itself." For, in order to implement the goals of praxis, we must also objectify ourselves, turning ourselves into the instruments necessary to arrive at the intended ends. We must make ourselves into the *material means* necessitated by our goals. Furthermore, our praxis produces material transformations, new material forms and objects, in the world—that is, new forms of the "practico-inert," and we become constrained by these forms of already-worked matter in which past praxis is congealed. For when we engage in praxis, Sartre argues, we "interiorize" the inertia that is a material quality of both the instruments and the products of our praxis. Ironically, it is thus our own praxis, as mediated by matter that "drains our freedom from us" and turns us into the hapless products of our own products. There is often a "demonic" quality to this dialectic, as Sartre presents it, in which our freedom may be reduced to no more than the ability to recognize the "destiny" that we have imposed upon ourselves. We discover, as he puts it, "necessity as the *destiny in exteriority of freedom*" (1976, 227).

"Scarcity," unlike "need," is not an ontological structure of human existence. However, it remains a universal fact of human history, at least this far. Consequently, says Sartre, we encounter each other as agents of praxis in competition for scarce resources; and thus we are for each other agents through whose mediations we most often experience our own praxis as yet further altered, or alienated. In the *Critique of Dialectical Reason*, human antagonism and reciprocity are not now enacted through "the look," or in the conflict of consciousnesses, as Sartre had argued in *Being and Nothingness* and Beauvoir in *The Second Sex*. Rather, they are said to emerge through the mediation of scarcity-conditioned praxis. In what Sartre calls relations of "seriality," we each discover we have become "other," through the materially mediated praxis of others. Such materially mediated praxis is, however, also the site for "reciprocity" among us. For it is in praxis that a reciprocal recognition of each other *as* intentional agents also takes place. This reciprocal recognition may take forms of positive solidarity, when the praxis of each supports and furthers that of the other. More frequently, however, what takes place is an "antagonistic" or what Sartre calls a "negative reciprocity," in which each of us recognizes the other as a practical agent, but as one whose praxis threatens to alienate our own. But even in cases of "negative reciprocity" a fundamental, albeit antagonistic, bond of mutual recognition remains, in which each is acknowledged to be an intentional and practical agent.

To turn now to Beauvoir's *The Coming of Age:* it is with this conceptual framework—of need and scarcity, of praxis, the practico-inert, and reciprocity

—in mind that we can make fuller sense of her insistently repeated claim, that the greatest scourge of the aged is their exclusion from *productive* activity. This exclusion is particularly harmful, she argues, in a capitalist society, where the worth of "men" is measured by their employment and income (1996, 263; 2005, 281).[4] Work, in a for profit-economy, is for most men *already* the site of a negative reciprocity, and of an alienated praxis in which their freedom is meaninglessly consumed. Thus, when they finally are granted the "leisure" of retirement few are capable of using it meaningfully. For, "yet more scandalous is the treatment that [society] inflicts upon the majority of men during their youth and maturity. It prefabricates the mutilated and miserable condition which is their lot in their final age" (541–42, translation altered; 2005, 568). Retirement initiates for most workers not only a condition of penury but also one that renders them the "Other," indeed the "sub-human," in the eyes of the still-active population.

In *The Second Sex*, it was through a reworking of Hegel's "mater-slave dialectic" that Beauvoir had approached the question of reciprocity. There, she wrote that: if, "following Hegel," we realize that "a fundamental hostility to any other consciousness is found in consciousness itself," then we can see how each "asserts itself as the essential" and constitutes the other "as inessential, as the object"—and we can also see how "the other consciousness has an opposing reciprocal claim" (2010, 7; 1988, vol. 1, 17). In *The Coming of Age*, by contrast, Beauvoir now accounts for the "otherness" of the aged by drawing on Sartre's account of reciprocity in the *Critique of Dialectical Reason*. She writes that the members of a society "are separated yet united by relations of reciprocity: individuals comprehend one another ... through the diversity of their praxis" (1996, 216, translation altered; 2005, 230). She then proceeds to summarize Sartre's account of how reciprocity arises when we encounter others as agents whose praxis alters the meaning and outcome of our own. She concurs that in such encounters—irrespective of whether others are recognized as antagonists or as allies—a reciprocal recognition takes place among *practical* subjects. But what, then, of those like the aged who do not engage in praxis? What of those who, effectively, are no longer practical subjects?

---

4 Beauvoir explicitly focuses on men throughout most of the book. Because men are overwhelmingly those in the work-force, those who are active in public life, and those who make history, she argues that they suffer the losses and exclusions of old age far more acutely than women do. See especially Beauvoir 1996, 89, 217, 261–62. By contrast—and in contradiction—to her discussions in *The Second Sex* of the crisis that aging often presents to women, she problematically argues here that the transition to old age is less difficult for women than men because they are already in the domestic, private sphere.

Exis

Here I must introduce another idea of Sartre's: that of "exis." Sartre uses the notion of "exis"—roughly the antonym, or opposite, of praxis—to characterize a condition of reification that is so extreme that new praxis is precluded.[5] Exis is most often the effect of an exterior condition: it is imposed through one's involuntary location in a particularly objectified social "collective," or "series." In such a condition, Sartre says, the *very being* of each person comes to be constituted by their membership in the unchosen, passively formed, "collective." In exis, the self becomes so fully constituted from without that the possibility of future praxis is profoundly foreclosed: one's selfhood comes to be defined above all by one's "being," and not by one's actions (1976, 255). But although exis is most often a condition that is socially imposed on the individual, it may also characterize the relationship of an individual to his or her *own* prior praxis, when the latter serves to reify the self and to block future praxis.

For Beauvoir, the notion of "exis" becomes pivotal in accounting for the condition of the elderly and especially for the disgust they arouse in others. Apart from a few exceptions, she writes:

> [t]he old man [*le vieillard*] ... doesn't *do* anything. He is defined by an *exis*, not a *praxis*. Time carries him toward an end—death—which is not his end, which is not intended [*qui n'est pas posée*] as a project. And this is why he appears to active individuals as a "foreign species" in which they don't recognize themselves. (1996, 217, translation altered; 2005, 231)

She continues, "I have said that old age inspires a biological repugnance; in a kind of self-defense one pushes it far away from oneself. But this rejection is possible only because the fundamental connection with all human undertakings is no longer at play in this case" (1996, 217, translation altered; 2005, 231).

Exis is the scourge of the aged, and it is the primary source of the "non-reciprocity" that marks their treatment by others. Furthermore, the social and economic dependence of the aged is more intense than that of any other subordinated group. For, from a practical perspective, they *alone* are wholly superfluous.[6] A dependent woman still offers her husband valuable services, and a child has fu-

---

5 McBride notes that Sartre is here adapting for his own uses the Aristotelian notion of exis (or, more properly transliterated, *hexis*). For Aristotle, *hexis*, meaning habit, is conceived as a desirable part of education; for Sartre it, of course, carries a far more negative connotation as the blockage of free praxis (McBride 1991, 121–22).

6 However, one should note, a similar designation may be inflicted upon—and interiorized by—some people with physical or mental disabilities.

ture potential. But, in a world that is shaped by scarcity, and that is continually created and recreated through praxis, the aged person has no value and he is not acknowledged as a subject. Instead, he is seen, says Beauvoir, as "a pure object and encumbrance, useless;" he is treated as a "nullity" [*en quantité négligeable*] (219, translation altered; 2005, 233).

However, although exis is pivotal in Beauvoir's account of the situation and experience of the aged, she avoids the reductionism to which Sartre tends in the *Critique of Dialectical Reason*. She extends her account of the dynamics of objectification beyond those developed by Sartre. For example, she insists that dynamics of non-reciprocity are mediated by other important social relations, such as familial ones, so that an old man's exis alone will not necessarily account for a son's hostility towards aged his father. Furthermore, she notes that, even in those rare cases where the aged do continue to engage in meaningful praxis, such vicissitudes as the death of loved ones, a sense of their own impending death and, perhaps above all, illness and failing physical powers may devastatingly undermine their zest for life. Thus, what may seem "in exteriority" to be an "ideal" old age may be experienced as devoid of joy or meaning. For example, Verdi composed major new works and continued to conduct until almost the end of his life, and he also received tremendous acclaim and public recognition until the end. Yet, Beauvoir observes, his letters reveal him to feel as pointless and sad as an old man who sits alone and does nothing (1996, 515–17). Similarly, Freud continued to make important contributions when old, yet felt full of weariness and ready for the end. "'I am as weary as it is natural to be after a hard-working life, and I think I have fairly earned my rest'," she quotes him as writing (521).[7] Thus, although Beauvoir's treatment of old age is always anchored in the notions of "praxis" as the site of reciprocity and "exis" as its negation, the phenomenological accounts she gives of old age still greatly exceed these notions.

In *The Second Sex*, Beauvoir had linked women's oppression with "immanence," writing that "every time transcendence lapses into immanence there is a degradation of existence into the in-itself, of freedom into facticity" (2010, 16, 1988, 31). But just as praxis now encompasses both, the project *and* its materialization, so exis now encompasses both immanence and *its* materialization. For the aged's lack of future praxis is powerfully associated with the domination

---

7 See Deutscher (2006) for an interesting discussion of this lack of zest, or "alacrity," in the aged. It is worth noting that there is a striking dissonance here between Beauvoir's approval (from her "exterior" perspective) of those individuals who continue to be so active and their accounts of the misery of their "lived experience," as reported in their letters, journals, and so forth that she cites. For more examples, see especially chapter 8 of *The Coming of Age*.

of the practico-inert, of various forms of reified or congealed prior praxis, over them. This domination comes from two directions, from both exterior and interior sources, and these will cohere and reinforce each other.

Initially, this domination most often comes from exterior, societal, sources. The onset of "old age" comes upon us from without, Beauvoir says. One arrives at the discovery that, without having chosen such an identity, one now belongs to the "social category," or series, of "the aged."[8] We will discover, through the words and actions of others that we now belong to the social category of those who, no longer having a useful social function, modern society designates as "pure objects"—as not worthy of respect (1996, 88). Until this point, we do not feel old "inside." For even if our bodies begin to suffer from various disabilities of age, such as rheumatism, we will not see these as symptoms of "old age" until through others we have interiorized and—as we must—"assumed" that condition. Until then, Beauvoir writes, "we fail to see that [such symptoms] represent a new status. We remain what we were, with the rheumatism as something additional" (285). The onset of old age takes place, then, within a practico-inert field that comprises wide-spread social practices, institutions, and discourses that shape old age in our society. "In our society the elderly person is marked as such by custom, by the behaviour of others and by the vocabulary itself: he must assume this reality" (291, translation altered; 2005, 309). With few exceptions, each isolated and each "the same," passively unified by social institutions and practices that serialize them in the category of "the aged," powerlessness is the common hallmark of those who are "old." Dispersed and excluded from public activities and public spaces, they lack the capacity for organized resistance.[9]

But, in addition, there are interior sources. For the practico-inert also constitutes the being of the aged through a lived, dialectical relationship with their own bodily decline, their shifting experiences of time, and their prior praxis. Thus, Beauvoir addresses aspects of the specific lived experience of old age that do not have analogues in the *Critique of Dialectical Reason*. In particular, Sartre gives no consideration in the *Critique* to the experience of discovering that one's *own body* presents an objective limit to one's praxis. Although Beauvoir insists in *The Coming of Age* that there is no purely natural body, that "for man the body itself is not pure nature" (1996, 12, translation altered; 2005, 18),

---

8 "Les vieillards" (2005, 493). Debra Bergoffen is incorrect in saying that Beauvoir "never speaks of the aged" (1997, 187), for Beauvoir is speaking in her own voice here. Both the terms "le vieillard" and "les vieillards" are used, but the singular form more commonly.

9 Again we see certain parallels here between the aged and women. For, Beauvoir writes in *The Second Sex* that women "do not say 'We'." Instead, they "live dispersed among men, tied ... to certain men—fathers or husbands—more closely than to other women" (2010, 8).

she still asserts that biological decay, physical and mental debility, and physical pain, are real facts that strongly contribute to the tendency of the elderly toward exis. "Biological decay [*dechéance biologique*]," she says, "brings with it the impossibility of transcendence, of becoming passionately concerned; it kills projects and … makes death acceptable" (443, translation altered; 2005, 468). Such decay is also intimately linked to the temporal aspects of old age: to the emergence of a temporal horizon that is "both short and closed" (373). This foreshortening increasingly precludes new projects and it locks the aged into a being that is constituted by their past praxis, that is, by forms of the practico-inert.

For all of us, Beauvoir writes, "The past defines my present situation." For active adults, however, although it circumscribes action, the past is also what enables an "opening to the future." For, "from the past I carry all the techniques my body has built up, the cultural tools I use, my knowledge and my ignorance, my relations with the other, my activities, my obligations. Everything that I have ever done has been taken back by it and become reified [*se chosifié*] under the form of the practico-inert" (372, translation altered; 2005, 395]. But, for the aged the practico-inert reifications of their former activity increasingly fail to provide an "opening to the future." For, Beauvoir continues, "the older we grow, the more heavily the burden of the practico-inert weighs upon us … Projects are frozen [*pétrifiés*] … an entire long life is fixed behind us, and it holds us captive" (373, translation altered; 2005, 395). The elderly person becomes frozen in the products of his prior praxis, and his being thus comes to be constituted from "without." Increasingly, then, he must "consent" to the condition of exis, for exterior and interior aspects fold into each other. They cohere dialectically to constitute the condition of old age, in what Beauvoir calls an "indeterminate movement [of] circularity." She writes: "an analytical description of the various aspects of old age is not therefore enough: each reacts upon the others and is at the same time affected by them, and it is in the indeterminate movement of this circularity that old age must be grasped" (9, translation altered; 2005, 15–16).

Beauvoir discusses, in particular, three sites where this circular constitution of old age takes place. They are: "interests," "habits," and "possessions."

Interests, Habits, Possessions

What Sartre, in the *Critique of Dialectical Reason*, calls "interest" is the identification of one's very *being* with things, with one's property. "Interest," he writes, "is a certain relation between man and thing in a social field. … to take the clearest example, real bourgeois property, the first moment of the process is the identification of the being of the owner with the ensemble of his property" (1976, 197).[10] In *The Coming of Age* Beauvoir extends Sartre's idea of "interest" to describe the entrapment of once-creative individuals such as scientists, writers, or artists in the products of their former praxis. Taking the example of her own prior creative work, she writes that, "for me, the practico-inert is the collection of books I have written, which now constitute my life-work [*mon œuvre*] outside of myself." She goes on to quote from the *Critique:* "'I am what I have done that escapes me in constituting me as an other'" and "Interest is 'being wholly-outside-oneself-in-a-thing in so far as it conditions praxis as a categorical imperative'" (1996, 372–73, translation altered; 2005, 395).[11] The meaning of my prior work is thrust upon me as "other" and exterior. However, when I choose to assume that meaning as my "interest," it is still *I* who will alienate, or reify, myself in it. Famous scientists, for example, rarely make further new discoveries when elderly, she explains, because they have established too much of an interest in their own prior work. They now have a "being-outside-themselves," an "ideological interest," that is the product of their earlier intellectual praxis. (391; 2005, 413). They will now obsessively defend their previous work; and by constituting it as their very being, they will block any further creativity, instead taking as self-evident what younger, fresher minds might question. Indeed, some are so alienated in their ideological interest that they may even falsify new experimental results that challenge their theories (390–95; esp. pp. 390–91).

But even for those of the elderly who do not develop such a strong interest in their prior praxis, the practico-inert still weighs exceptionally heavily. Beauvoir discusses the significance of "habit" here. Habit is the sedimentation of our life-long ways of acting, and it functions for the aged in several important ways. Many old people become very rigid in their habits, developing routines that they follow unswervingly and without reflection. "Habit," writes Beauvoir, is the past as it is "lived" (644). In a world that is changing with frightening rapidity, habit offers some protection from the threat of the new. It can also compensate for failing intellectual powers and for loss of memory (466–67). More profoundly, Beauvoir suggests that habit offers the aged [*le vieillard*] "a sort of ontological security" (469). For a life devoid of new projects, a life conditioned by exis, encounters the sickening void of "excess leisure" (467). She writes, "if existence does not transcend itself towards goals, if it falls back on itself

---

10 Beauvoir also describes such a relationship to real property in the person of the elderly miser. For him, money "is synonymous with power; it is a creative force and the old person magically identifies himself with it" (1996, 470, translation altered; 2005, 494).

11 The latter of the two quotes from the *Critique of Dialectical Reason* appears at page 197, however, Beauvoir slightly misquotes Sartre. I have not been able to locate the first quote.

inert, then it incites [*provoque*] the 'nausea' which Sartre has described" (459, translation altered; 2005, 484). But habits fill up time. They allow the aged person to evade the "anguishing" question "What shall I do?" for they ensure that "there is something to be done every moment of the day" (467).[12] Beauvoir also notes that habit extends into a relationship with one's daily possessions, for "the things that belong to us are, as it were, solidified habits." For example, the garden that I walk in every afternoon, or the armchair that "is waiting for me to sit in it every evening," are integrated into my habits (469).

Significantly, Beauvoir does not treat these attempts to escape into interest, habit, or possessions, as moral failures. They may be unsuccessful as strategies of defense against anxiety and misery, but they are not portrayed as instances of seriousness, bad faith, or complicity. Indeed, this earlier moral vocabulary is wholly lacking in her evaluations of the aged. Instead, her opprobrium is now reserved for the younger adults who refuse reciprocity to them.[13] Beauvoir's stance is generally one of sympathy for the aged, rather than judgment. She does not hold them responsible for their fall into exis: in comparison with her early "moral essays" and even *The Second Sex*, where woman's complicity in her oppression is a major theme, Beauvoir has significantly shifted her views on freedom. She now acknowledges that facticities such as a failing or diseased body, or subjection to pervasive practices of social objectification, may come to suffuse and delimit the ontological freedom that, in her early works, she had argued is "infinite" or indestructible.[14]

However, although Beauvoir now acknowledges that freedom may be constrained even to the point where it effectively comes to be suspended, she does not fully embrace the pessimism of Sartre's *Critique of Dialectical Reason*, in which the practico-inert relentlessly robs our actions of their intentions and meanings, forever stealing our freedom from us. Unlike the later Sartre, Beauvoir also argues that there may be an existential value to certain kinds of habit. Although the pivotal claim of *The Coming of Age* remains that the incapacity to engage in future-oriented praxis—an incapacity that may be at once organic and socially inflicted—is what makes of old age a condition of oppression and onto-

---

12 "What shall I do?" The question is, of course, posed by Beauvoir in her first philosophical essay, *Pyrrhus et Cinéas* (1944), in the opening dialogue between Pyrrhus and Cinéas about why one might set out to conquer the world. Beauvoir will argue in this essay that "doing"—here, free, transcendent, action—is what gives meaning to human existence.
13 Penelope Deutscher has also pointed out this shift (Deutscher 1999).
14 For example, in 1944, in *Pyrrhus et Cinéas*, she had written, "one can throw a man in prison, take him out of it, cut off an arm, lend him wings; but in all cases his freedom remains infinite" (86). She herself later criticized the "idealism" of such claims.

logical crisis, she also observes that the elderly may still sometimes enact a meaningful "disclosure of the world" through habit. For "the word habit has more than one meaning, and one must distinguish between them" (466).

Instead of constituting a fall into exis and creating nothing other than "impossibilities" habits may sometimes be profoundly meaningful, for they may involve an *intentional* "re-presenting" of the past (466). They may produce an "integration" in which a "reanimated past" and an "anticipated future" are drawn together (468, translation altered; 2005, 492). Then, they are lived, Beauvoir says, in the mode of the "for-itself." Such habits possess a heightened quality, which Beauvoir describes as a "kind of poetry" (468). For a ritual that is perfectly repeated daily (Beauvoir give as an example the English habit—alas now mainly defunct—of taking afternoon tea), may draw together in a "synthesis" that, while it is "fictive" (since it is not in actuality realized), is still profoundly meaningful. Habits, she continues, may produce "a *crystallization* which is analogous to what Stendhal describes with regard to love: *such* an object, *such* a possession, *such* an activity acquires the quality of *disclosing the entire world to us*" (468, translation altered; 2005, 492–93, emphases added). Here, the practico-inert is taken up in manner that does not drain away, but rather affirms, freedom. Moreover, fusing past, present, and future, the "poetry of habit" also offers the aged person a respite from the "enemy" of time, and "it provides him with that eternity which he no longer finds in the present moment" (468).

Debra Bergoffen has argued that, running throughout Beauvoir's works one may find what she calls a "muted voice," that conceives and values freedom not as a Sartrean "project" but rather as the "disclosure of being" (1997). It is such a voice that emerges here, in *The Coming of Age*, albeit in a somewhat different key than the one Bergoffen considers. For, although such habits may not ground the bonds of erotic generosity with other people that are Bergoffen's main concern, still, as forms of world-disclosure they may create a deeply affective bond with the world. They create, Beauvoir suggests, meaningful relations with the *things* of the world, both in their materiality and as on-going mediations between past and future. [15]

---

15 Bergoffen does briefly discuss *The Coming of Age* in her book, pointing to the continuation of erotic intentionality in the aged (1997, 188). However, my interest here is in this rather different, materially mediated, style of world-disclosure.

Beyond Sartre's Materialism

In conclusion, what is striking is how far Beauvoir has reworked aspects of Sartre's *Critique of Dialectical Reason*, even as *The Coming of Age* remains deeply and fruitfully anchored within its dialectics of need, praxis, and the practico-inert. In Beauvoir's hands the practico-inert has become a more supple and ambiguous notion than it is for Sartre. It is not only the "demonic" force that it is in the *Critique of Dialectical Reason*. Habits do, indeed, still remain forms of the practico-inert and that is why they do not achieve the "real" transcendence that lies in praxis. Yet, we have seen, they may also meaningfully meld the past with a future. In addition, Beauvoir brings to Sartre's framework another dimension of "materialism": a phenomenological account of embodiment that his work lacks.

Sartre examines "the" body as the generic site of "organic," material need and as the instrument for praxis. However, beyond the barest minimum necessary for survival, needs are specific to particular embodied selves, as are, most often, their styles of praxis. In the *Critique of Dialectical Reason*, Sartre is inattentive to the specificities of embodied lived experience and to how they, variously, emerge within concrete situations. Through her considerations of how the organic aspects of aging and the social situation of the aged interact, and by developing a phenomenological account of the specificities of old age as embodied lived experience, Beauvoir enhances Sartre's work as well as drawing from it. She does, indeed, now provide a fuller and more "materialist" grounding to the characterization of oppression and otherness than she had done in *The Second Sex*. However, she does so not do by sacrificing the focus on lived experience and the nuanced attention to the significations of embodied subjectivity that made her earlier book so remarkable. Rather, *The Coming of Age* offers a dialectical account of old age as at once a materially constituted social reality and an embodied and individually lived experience.

References

Beauvoir, Simone de. 1944. *Pyrrhus et Cinéas*. Paris: Gallimard.
Beauvoir, Simone de. 1992. *Force of circumstance*, vol. 1, trans. Richard Howard, introduction by Toril Moi. New York: Paragon House [*La force des choses*. Paris: Gallimard 1963].
Beauvoir, Simone de. 1993. *All said and done*. Trans. Patrick O'Brian, introduction by Toril Moi. New York: Paragon House [*Tout compte fait*. Paris: Gallimard 1972].
Beauvoir, Simone de. 1996. *The coming of age*. Trans. Patrick O'Brian. New York, London: W. W. Norton & Company [*La vieillesse*. Paris: Gallimard 2005 (1st ed. 1970)].

Beauvoir, Simone de. 2010. *The second sex.* Trans. Constance Borde and Sheila
    Malovany-Chevallier. New York: Knopf [*Le deuxième sexe.* Paris: Gallimard 1988 (1st
    ed. 1949)].
Bergoffen, Debra. 1997. *The philosophy of Simone de Beauvoir: Gendered phenomenologies,
    erotic generosities.* Albany, NY: State University of New York Press.
Deutscher, Penelope. 1999. Bodies, lost and found: Simone de Beauvoir from *The Second Sex*
    to *Old Age. Radical philosophy*, no. 96 (July–August): 6–16.
Deutscher, Penelope. 2006. La vieillesse: Simone de Beauvoir on corporeal time and the
    ethical quality of alacrity. In *Women making time*, ed. Elizabeth McMahon and Brigitta
    Olubas. Crawley, WA: University of Western Australia Press, 81–93.
Kruks, Sonia. 2001. *Retrieving experience: Subjectivity and recognition in feminist politics.*
    Ithaca: Cornell University Press.
McBride, William. 1991. *Sartre's political theory.* Bloomington: Indiana University Press.
Sartre, Jean-Paul. 1976. *Critique of dialectical reason*, vol. 1, trans. Alan Sheridan-Smith, ed.
    Jonathan Rée. London: New Left Books [*Critique de la raison dialectique*, tome 1, text
    established by Arlette Elkaïm-Sartre. Paris: Gallimard 1985 (1st ed. 1960)].

Elisabeth Schäfer
Habits Shifting Into Projects

Comment on Sonia Kruks

Being subjugated to the movement of time, which limits our lives, we are existentially confronted with the closure of our future. This is something that we cannot change, suspend or eject from the horizon of our lifetime-experiences.

In Sonia Kruks' "Material Mediations of Age as Lived Experience" age is focused on its very heart as a lived experience. Referring to Simone de Beauvoir's own commentary on her project of *The Coming of Age*, which is to be found in her late autobiographical volume *All Said and Done*, Kruks concentrates on a shift taking place within Beauvoir's thinking. Beauvoir herself described *The Coming of Age* as a "counterpart of *The Second Sex*" (Beauvoir 1993, 130). Given this description, it is Kruks' purpose to elaborate on how the shifting moments become evident. She aims at reading Beauvoir's late work as a *reworking* of Sartre's *Critique of Dialectical Reason*, and at revealing the shift in Beauvoir's work. She argues that Beauvoir significantly altered her thinking about freedom to such a great extent that she shifted the concept of transcendence—the subject's ability to engage itself—into projects. In the context of Beauvoir's late shifting of the concept of freedom and transcendence a new term becomes important: habit.

Starting out from this observation, I want to raise the question: Does the experience of time limiting our lives only appear as a phenomenon of old age? Or does it in fact mark every act? We all find ourselves living with the ambiguity of having a future but a limited one. Having a future enables us to create projects. The limit of our future most of the time hides its very date in uncertainty. Reaching old age, we become more and more aware of the limit on our future. Old age limits the ability to create and particularly to realize projects. No one who is young can know the experience of being old. Due to this, there is an exclusion taking place within the lived experience of being old. No one—except those who are old—can know the experience of being old. Nevertheless, even the young experience the irreversibility of time marking every lifetime-experience. Even the young experience time limiting our lives, because it, in fact, marks every act.

The irreversibility of time is a lived experience as well. Instead of focusing on the irreversibility that is at work within every act, we come up with other strategies such as habits. Habits do not only concern the past of actions. They are not only the way we have always done certain things. Habits are the way we *will* do certain things again—in the future. Habits seem to be one particular way to handle our being in time.

Beauvoir, famous for her phenomenological descriptions, analyzes the lives of elderly people as being structured by distinct habits. Habits, she argues, are sedimentations of life-long ways of acting. Due to this, habits provide protection. Habits ensure that whatever we do is done in a certain way. Structured by the moment of repetition, the habits we generate are deeply connected to our history. Habits, their steady tendency to repeat themselves throughout our acting, tell a kind of speechless story about the subject who is engaged in their realization. Hence Beauvoir realizes that habits can disclose the world; they can even have a kind of poetry and serve as an expression of love. Understood as a kind of poetry based on repetition, one may ask about the "author" of habits. Habits are not necessarily only the acts of an intentional subject who realizes them. Habits seem to develop out of themselves alongside our intentional acting. Therefore, taking habits into account enables us to rethink concepts of immanence and transcendence. This is precisely what Kruks focuses on in her essay on *The Coming of Age*.

Habits, at a first glance, do seem to belong to the concept of immanence. But Kruks argues with Beauvoir in a very distinct way. She points out that "[i]n Beauvoir's hands the practico-inert has become a more supple and ambiguous notion than it is for Sartre" (100). More precisely, Beauvoir links habits with the "practico-inert"—a term taken from Sartre's *Critique*—but she makes something out of them that is far from the "demonic" force it is in Sartre's thinking. Habits remain forms of the practico-inert but not a demonic force: they are linked to practice, which enables us to understand them as projects.

As I stressed above, habits are not only linked to the past. Habits are not only the way we have always done things, they are also the way we will do things again—in the future. I want to emphasize Kruks' view on Beauvoir's shifted thinking with respect to habits: that insofar as they are linked to practice they can be thought as projects. At the same time, in order to be relevant, the concept of immanence—the way Beauvoir and Kruks present it—is in need of more radical rethinking. Age and habit confront us with a passivity we are in touch with despite not having been its originator. Beauvoir and Kruks enhance the value of age and habit by linking both to practice and ability. Perhaps the value of immanence could also be enhanced by thinking its constitutive role in the projects of any individual.

References

Beauvoir, Simone de. 1993. *All said and done*. Trans. Patrick O'Brian, introduction by Toril Moi. New York: Paragon House.

Beauvoir, Simone de. 1996. *The coming of age.* Trans. Patrick O'Brian. New York, London: W. W. Norton & Company.

Linda Fisher

The Other Without and the Other Within

The Alterity of Aging and the Aged in Beauvoir's
The Coming of Age

Fittingly, because so much of what we think or say about old age is based on myths, false impressions, and mystification, Simone de Beauvoir begins *The Coming of Age* with a fable. This is the story she tells, part of the well-known life of Buddha. When Prince Siddhartha, who would become Buddha, was still young, he lived a somewhat sheltered life, spending much of his time confined by his father to the palace. Nevertheless, from time to time he would escape and drive around the surrounding countryside. The first time he went out he happened upon an old man, described by Beauvoir as a "tottering, wrinkled, toothless, white-haired man, bowed, mumbling and trembling as he propped himself along on his stick" (Beauvoir 1996, 1). Siddhartha was stunned by this encounter and needed his charioteer to explain to him what it meant to be old. What a pity, Siddhartha exclaimed, that "weak and ignorant beings, drunk with the vanity of youth, do not behold old age!" He wished then to return quickly to the palace. For, "what is the use of pleasures and delights, since I myself am the future dwelling-place of old age?" (1) Beauvoir goes on to say that Buddha recognized his own fate in that old man because, due to his destiny ("being born to save humanity"), he would choose to take upon himself the entirety of the human state. This sets him apart from the rest of humanity, who tend to evade the aspects of the human state that distress them; they are, after all, not Buddha. And, Beauvoir says, above all they evade old age.

But not only is old age evaded and avoided, it is in many respects suppressed. It is a taboo subject, treated by society as "a kind of shameful secret" (1), enveloped in a "conspiracy of silence" (2). It is precisely this silence that Beauvoir intends to break by writing *The Coming of Age*. As she will outline in exhaustive detail, the taboo nature of old age serves at once to repress open and realistic discussion about the social status and lived experience of the elderly, while at the same time cloaking the often desperate and degrading circumstances in which they are forced to live; a state of affairs Beauvoir considers scandalous, if not criminal. Shunned and objectified, treated as outcasts, as pariahs (*parias*), the elderly are "condemned to poverty, decrepitude, wretchedness and despair" (2), barely considered to be actual human beings.

Then again, Beauvoir says, the attitude of society towards the elderly is also deeply ambivalent. Their definition as a group or category is vague: the point at which old age is considered to begin varies according to time and place. In contrast to clearer demarcations between childhood, adolescence, and adulthood, there is little or no differentiation among adults along age lines when it comes to legal or political rights and obligations. In terms of these and other matters, the elderly are included in the general category of adults. Yet on the other hand, Beauvoir points out, when it comes to economic status, "society appears to think that they belong to an entirely different species" (3). In begrudging them anything more than a "pittance," the elderly are not considered to have the same needs as other people. As part of the "myths and clichés of bourgeois thought" (3), the elderly person is framed as someone who is different and at odds with the rest of society; someone to be ignored and forgotten. The distinction is now drawn between the "active" and the "non-active" sectors of the population, and between the workers and the unproductive. The economy, indeed the entire civilization, is based on profit, with the human working stock of interest only insofar as it is profitable; when no longer profitable, it is discarded, tossed aside (6; 543). The elderly become the cast-offs of capitalism, with little to no economic strength and limited means for ensuring their rights. This economic and institutional otherness is reflected and actualized in the abject and deplorable lived situation of so many elderly people: impoverished if not destitute, isolated and lonely, bored and without purpose, enduring the myriad physical and psychological repercussions that frequently accompany this state of affairs. Beauvoir sums it up forcefully:

> The fact that for the last fifteen or twenty years of his life a man should be no more than a reject, a piece of scrap, reveals the failure of our civilization: if we were to look upon the old as human beings, with a human life behind them, and not as so many walking corpses, this obvious truth would move us profoundly. (6)[1]

It is worth noting that Beauvoir does appear to be speaking predominantly about the situation in Western industrialized societies such as France and the United States that she often cites as examples. Thus it could be argued that such dire conditions and derogatory attitudes are not universal, that the situation for the elderly in other societies can be noticeably better, particularly in cultures where traditionally the elderly are respected, cared for and protected, even honored. And by the same token, much has changed in the social and economic sta-

1 We could add, with a human life before them as well, insofar as they are not "walking corpses," let alone actual ones. Is Beauvoir's focus on the past of the elderly, with no mention of a present or future, indicative of her own blind spot about the aged? See my discussion of blind spot and bad faith below.

tus and condition of the aged since Beauvoir wrote this in 1970, especially in countries such as France and the United States. Nowadays, in many cases, the elderly demographic wields considerable economic power, which has translated in turn into marketplace and political power, as well as the wherewithal to organize into lobbies and associations aimed at looking out for the rights and welfare of the elderly, the AARP—the American Association of Retired Persons— being a case in point. Yet even if the economic and political situation has improved for the elderly in some societies and contexts, clearly this has not been the case everywhere, when lived conditions for the elderly ranging from deprived to truly abysmal can still prevail.[2]

Beauvoir also acknowledges that not all elderly people are impoverished, and thus for those who are more privileged, the social and economic circumstances will be much more favorable, and the differences in material conditions will determine in turn a difference in status, in health, and in their overall attitude towards aging. As Beauvoir remarks, "today" a miner is finished at the age of fifty whereas many of the privileged carry their eighty years lightly (541).[3] Proceeding from an economic analysis in order to make the argument about the social otherness of the elderly clearly allows Beauvoir to meld and mirror this in a materialist analysis of the economic and political otherness of the worker. As such, the otherness of the aged person—past their prime, no longer relevant, cast aside, a species apart—easily translates into the otherness of the aged worker—no longer productive, redundant, cast off and scrapped, an alienated species apart. Thus by the time of the conclusion the plight of the aged person seems to be even more compellingly—or at least equally—the plight of the aged worker, and Beauvoir's call to arms at the end to address the state of the aged reflects to a certain extent this more materialist analysis.

Of course, the aged worker is also the aged person, and much of the materialist analysis can be re-applied more generically to the lived condition of any eld-

---

2 It can also be pointed out that in difficult economic times, the elderly (along with other vulnerable groups) are often most at risk. Such groups are frequently more vulnerable in terms of potential threats (possibly politically motivated) to needed aid and benefits, social assistance, and other entitlements, and even rights.

3 Again, it could be argued that some of Beauvoir's examples are dated or no longer relevant (though the miner example is probably still very relevant). Nevertheless, any number of other contemporary examples and cases could be cited to illustrate and ground her claims for our own times about the often deplorable situation for the elderly, thus demonstrating the continuing relevance of her overall argument and analysis.

erly person: the redundant worker becomes the irrelevant old man or woman.[4] But there is an important sense also in which the otherness of the aged is not only a function of their economic status or productivity. The myths and clichés regarding the aged involve any number of insensitive and demeaning prejudices and stereotypes, such as depicting the elderly as figures of ridicule, or even disgust when it comes to the still more taboo subject of their sexuality—a taboo which Beauvoir breaks in a lengthy discussion of the sexuality of the aged in the second part of the book. Beauvoir states that at the base of these demeaning stereotypes is the attitude that the aged are in some manner outside humanity. As such, "the world ... need feel no scruple in refusing them the minimum of support which is considered necessary for living like a human being" (4).

The preceding analysis, like many such interwoven genetic analyses, prompts a question of derivation along the following lines: Are the aged constituted as Other because of their socio-economic condition, or are they subject to that socio-economic condition because they are always already Other? Embedded in this question, of course, is the issue of the real source of the otherness of the aged. The economic/materialist analysis would point towards the former supposition, while the analysis of the myths and clichés about the aged and the social prejudices they generate supports the latter. I would suggest that in fact it is not simply one or the other of these suppositions but both, operating together in an interlacing circularity, which in turn is part of a more complex network of (pre)conceptions and attitudes about aging and the aged.

In advanced industrial societies, the aged are marginalized and framed as Other the moment they are deemed to be redundant and of no further use. They are no longer seen as part of the active (productive) community, and insofar as that community is defined and constituted as such by virtue of the productive, creative activities and projects of its members, the aged are considered to be outside of that community, outside of humanity as so constituted. The social, economic, physical, and psychological hardships and deprivations that routinely accompany this pariah status only serve to reinforce the otherness of the aged. But again there is something else, something seemingly deeper that feeds this othering of the aged, beyond simply their economic status. For even in situations where the elderly person is financially secure, and perhaps continues to be productive in some way as well, in many respects this elderly person is still often seen as different and separate; perhaps not as "outside humanity" per se, but

---

4 And this character of redundancy and irrelevance not only pertains to a felt lack of purpose and importance, but also, tellingly, to the sense of being unnecessary, superfluous, of simply not being needed anymore.

no longer as part of the community of adults as previously was the case. Thereby arise all the stereotypes and prejudices about the aged, which are not explicable solely in terms of their productivity or economic situation. So what *is* the more fundamental source of their othering, of the abjection?

In every constituting of an/some Other, there is a process which involves stipulating some perceived or supposed difference(s) which will constitute the basis and the justification for the othering. Bound up with this is a profound underlying anxiety with respect to that difference (or whatever is thought to constitute it); or indeed, more fundamentally, anxiety about difference itself. In many, if not most cases, the mere existence or even perception of difference, irrespective of what that difference might actually consist in or entail, is enough to provoke the necessary fear, mistrust, or hatred to transform that difference into alterity; and in turn the alterity into abjection in many instances. In the case of the aged, while they bear the brunt of society's reactions, it is, of course, not the aged person as such who is really at issue, but old age itself. As Beauvoir points out, while some people become reconciled to old age, and others might even settle more or less comfortably into it, for the vast majority the prospect of growing old fills them with fear and aversion. Hence the active evasion of old age mentioned above, along with the negative reactions and even anger which greeted Beauvoir's comments and claims about old age in *The Coming of Age* and elsewhere.[5] Yet while most people would not wish for a future old age of poverty, loneliness, or boredom, and may indeed worry about that eventuality, this alone does not seem sufficient to explain such a pronounced reaction to aging.

It could well be that many people fear old age because it represents the beginning of the end, as it were: the "third act" of life, and the increasing imminence of death. Death is obviously possible at any time, through illness, accident, or other mishap. But aside from the case of a life-threatening illness, death only really becomes imminent in a compelling sense in old age, simply because no matter how comfortable or healthy someone is, he or she cannot live forever. All people are mortal, after all.

Is it the fear of death, then, behind the fear of aging and old age? Beauvoir tends to discount this, claiming that old age fills people with more aversion than death itself (539). Yet while it is undeniable that many people have a strong aversion to aging, is it clearly greater than any aversion to death?[6] To be sure, our attitudes towards old age and death respectively are mediated and conditioned

---

5 Beauvoir describes the angry reactions and denouncements in *The Coming of Age* as well as in various interviews.
6 Although it does often seem that for Beauvoir herself aging was the more disturbing prospect.

by our current age and state of health: someone of twenty may well fear old age more than death, whereas for an eighty-year-old it would likely be the reverse; and Beauvoir acknowledges this. Nevertheless, whether or not old age fills people with more aversion than does death, clearly it *does* fill them with enough aversion that they seek in multiple ways to evade old age, to stave it off or to minimize its effects, to downplay or disguise it; in short, to reject it. Thus the rejection of the aged person is at bottom a rejection of old age itself. And, to come full circle, this rejection more often than not takes the form of making the aged or age itself the Other. The circle, however, now takes a turn inwards. Beauvoir states:

> Every human situation can be viewed from without—seen from the point of view of an outsider—or from within, in so far as the subject assumes and at the same time transcends it. (10)

That is, aging and the aged person can be considered from outside, from the point of view of someone not yet aged (albeit aging), or as the object of scientific, medical, sociological, psychological, etc., knowledge. At the same time, the aged person is also a subject, one who has a first-hand experience and perspective and an immanent, inner knowledge of his or her condition. Thus this situation can also be viewed from inside, from the inward point of view of the subject's lived experience of and beliefs and attitudes about aging and old age, in terms of a phenomenology of the individual's relationship to time, temporality, and mortality; to a changing, usually declining body (and possibly mind), and a modified (very often diminished) role and identity; and to the wider socio-political world and the individual's place and status therein. These two viewpoints, from outside and inside, from without and from within, correspond to the two parts of *The Coming of Age*, and Beauvoir's important contribution in this study will be to combine a literary and social anthropological examination of the lived socio-economic and political situation of the aged with a pioneering phenomenology of the lived experience of old age and aging.[7]

Human situations are enacted within the generalized context of the human condition, but they are also particularized in and for the individual subject; lived, absorbed, internalized, instantiated by the subject. As such, from an exis-

---

7 For more on Beauvoir and phenomenology, see Fisher 2002. For more on feminism and phenomenology, see Fisher 2010, Fisher 2000, Fisher 1999, and Fisher 1997. Also see the following volumes which bring together essays exploring the relationship between phenomenology and feminism and the possibility of feminist phenomenology: Stoller, Vasterling, and Fisher 2005, Fisher and Embree 2000, and Stoller and Vetter 1997.

tential-phenomenological standpoint, there is always a circling inwards, a folding or dovetailing into the subjective—if not an enveloping by the subjective—insofar as the human condition is always already individuated in the subject, and there is an existential and philosophical imperative to investigate and thematize this dimension. In this respect, I would suggest, the subjective and the "within" acquire a particular emphasis or precedence (if not thematic priority), all the while an intertwining dialectic between outside and inside operates, each mediating and shaping the other.

There is a twist, though, with respect to this circling inwards, signaled by another dimension to the quotation above. While every situation can be viewed from without and from within, in the case of some situations, the outsider and insider perspectives can co-exist within the individual subject; perhaps juxtaposed, perhaps coinciding and uniting, or perhaps—as with aging—colliding. If a significant component of the outsider viewpoint on the aged person is to constitute that person as Other, then in now considering old age from within as the subjective lived experience of old age, the alterity of the aged is inevitably reproduced inwardly. That is, as Beauvoir points out, the ostracism that we practice with regard to the aged we now turn against ourselves: "for in the old person that we must become, we refuse to recognize ourselves" (4). For the aged person is not merely "someone else" or "those others," but also ourselves. We are all potentially or actually that aged person; or better, as the old person that we must become we are always already that old person as our necessary, latent eventuality. In this manner, the aged Other is myself; the Other is within me; I am Other to myself.

The inescapable (and often dispiriting) reality is that aging is not limited or specific to any one group or unique constituency only, rather it is a fundamental element of the facticity of our shared existential situation, and as such is particularized and individuated in each of us. We are all ineluctably aging, caught up in the relentless progression of our embodied temporality. In the end, we may not for one reason or another attain old age—however that may be variously defined in a given culture—yet we are still already in some measure that aged person, as Buddha well understood, insofar as we are the anticipated future dwelling-place of old age. In other words, even before we actualize an elderly state of being, we are already that aged person; just as in our Being-towards-death, we are always already in some measure dying. As such, without yet actually being elderly, the alterity of old age already resides within us, and we are already Other to ourselves.

The process of aging is thus a process of othering, and self-othering; in a classic irony, in othering old people, we are othering ourselves. Or is it the intuition of an alterity within ourselves that causes us to project alterity outwards onto other people? One side of the movement is the internalization, the turning upon ourselves of the alterity that we have projected onto other people. In realizing that I am that dwelling-place of old age which was my basis for othering someone else—that is, I am that aged person who I have been othering—then I must recognize that Other in myself; and that I am that Other. Alternately, I discern this otherness within myself, and in an effort to deflect or exorcise it, I redirect it back onto an/Other person, as if in this manner he or she can assume this otherness for me. Once again, I would suggest that it is not one or the other, but the entwined interrelation of both movements in a characteristic dialectic.

Also characteristically, this intuition of otherness to and within myself is ambivalent and problematic. Indeed, Beauvoir does not always seem to allow for our own acknowledgement of our otherness, stating that in the old person that we must become, we refuse to recognize ourselves. As part of our overall evasive strategy, this refusal seems rooted in what I would characterize as a complex mixture of blind spot and bad faith. On the one hand, there is a kind of surprise when old age arrives, as if it has been completely unexpected and unforeseen. Beauvoir speaks of her disbelief when she looks in the mirror and realizes she is no longer a young woman, or her shock upon meeting an acquaintance after a long absence and seeing how she has aged. She quotes Proust who says, "Of all realities [old age] is perhaps that of which we retain a purely abstract notion longest in our lives" (4). There is a blind spot, an epistemological hiccup, almost a naïveté when it comes to making this abstract notion concrete, especially in regard to our own aging. As Beauvoir notes, "Nothing should be more expected than old age: nothing is more unforeseen" (4).

At the same time, while we know of course that there are old people, and that aging is an unavoidable feature of our human condition, nonetheless we do not believe that it will happen to us. An "absurd inner voice" whispers that when *that* happens it will no longer be ourselves that it happens to: "Until the moment it is upon us old age is something that only affects other people" (5). Moreover, we tend to consider ourselves a unique subject, and are thus astonished when the "common fate" becomes our own. "The fact that the passage of universal time could have brought about a private, personal metamorphosis is something that takes us completely aback" (283). Recall that, exceptionally, Buddha *was* able to think of himself as being the dwelling-place of his future old age and thus assume the human condition; however, in the existential schizophrenia in which the rest of us usually function, although we understand our situation on some level, we nevertheless often engage in willful denial of it. The fact that so many people expend a great deal of time, effort, and money in denying the realities of aging and old age indeed suggests that we know all too well that this is happening, and that it is happening to *us*, much to our chagrin; which helps explain the incensed and defensive reactions to her work on old age that Beauvoir reports. Beauvoir also recounts familiar denial tactics such as the standard mantra that as long as you feel young, you are young, and even the denial that there is such a thing as old age. But of course the operative principle in bad faith is that underlying the denial or pretense is some knowledge, an epistemic awareness, of the actual reality. Knowledge and acknowledgment can be quite distinct, particularly when there is active self-deception at work, and thus Beauvoir insists that we must stop cheating (5). We need to recognize ourselves in that old person, not only to stop acting in bad faith, but for the purpose of advancing the critical social goal of no longer acquiescing in "the misery of the last days"; given that, because we are now involved and implicated, we can no longer be indifferent (5).

There is a further scenario in the recognition of aging that I would describe as falling between bad faith and a blind spot. This is connected to Beauvoir's Hegelian formulation of the extent to which my inner self-knowledge is shaped by the apprehension others have of me. Terming this the "complex truth of old age," Beauvoir states "... for the outsider it is a dialectic relationship between my being as he defines it objectively and the awareness of myself that I acquire by means of him" (284). This constituting definition imposed from without (characteristic of encounters in the Hegelian framework of consciousness and self-consciousness) is aided and abetted in this case by aging itself. For we are often simply unable to grasp the truth of our own aging: "... our private, inward experience does not tell us the number of our years; no fresh perception comes into being to show us the decline of age" (284). If a blind spot is a failure to see it, and bad faith an unwillingness, if not refusal to accept it, at issue here is an apparent inability: the awareness of this aging process is withheld from us, all the while it is increasingly evident to those around us.

This distinguishes growing old from disease, Beauvoir claims. For while in many cases "illness warns us of its presence" (284), and therefore the existence of illness is often more evident to the individual experiencing it than to those around him or her, old age in contrast is more apparent to others, Beauvoir says, than to the individual herself. In this instance, the definition of myself from outside is not simply a matter of an imposed (and quite possibly problematic) governing characterization originating in differential power relations, as some critical analyses would argue; but in terms of the phenomenological framework that Beauvoir is also drawing on, the knowledge I might acquire from others in this respect supplements what my inner experience provides me and even redresses any gaps in that knowledge. That is, inner experience alone is not capable of furnishing the fuller account and therefore the interaction with and contribution from others is essential. *Pace* such socio-political critiques that argue that asymmetrical and hegemonic power structures invariably mediate, shape, and distort interpersonal encounters and associations, there is a compelling case for a phenomenological model of intersubjective epistemology in which the dialectic of knowledge positions—outside and inside, from within as well as without—produces an account which is less incomplete, without necessarily being skewed by power structures.[8] Subjectivity is completed intersubjectively. Beauvoir adds that although aging is obviously embodied, even our body does not always help us to a full inward realization of our condition (285); perhaps the outward signs of aging are minimal, and we remain comparatively fit and healthy, or we simply adapt to or compensate for any problems or discomforts. As Beauvoir remarks, "old age is something beyond my life, outside it—something of which I cannot have any full inward experience" (291).

Thus it is that there is this third manner in which we fail to grasp the Other that we are for ourselves, a failure due neither to disingenuous bad faith nor to a naïve blind spot, but rather to the inevitable limits of the first-person perspective. Beauvoir tells the story of a woman in a retirement home, who when interviewed stated, "I don't feel at all old; sometimes I help the grannies, and then I say to myself, 'But you're a granny too'" (*Mais toi aussi, tu es une mémé*) (294). Beauvoir observes that, when faced with the other old women, her reaction was to think of herself as ageless and not like them.

> It is significant that at this moment of awareness she spoke to herself as *tu:* it was the Other within her that she was addressing, the Other that existed for the rest but of whom she herself had no immediate knowledge. (294)

Nevertheless, as we have seen, though we may be innocent with respect to our lack of immediate knowledge of the Other within us, when confronted with this knowledge we are disbelieving and resistant all the same.

In a final circling back to this resistance and aversion to old age, I will fold in some observations about the related issues of embodied temporality, metamorphosis, and identity, issues which afford yet another clue to the source of our fear of aging. In many ways, each of these issues feeds into the next, and in probing these interrelations the deeper, possibly most troubling aspects of old age can perhaps be uncovered.

---

8 Even if we grant that any interaction is infused by power relations, and that these relations are often (or inevitably) differential or asymmetrical, it does not necessarily follow that the interaction is thereby skewed and distorted accordingly. Such an argument can be made on both a phenomenological and socio-political basis; unfortunately, space does not permit a fuller elaboration here.

Aging is embodied temporality, in the dual senses of time embodied—time "captured" or (re)presented, given a form and face, as it were, in our body, by our body; and our embodiment seen as not static but as a continuous process, unfolding and developing through time. But the issue is not merely that all embodiment and lived experience in general is temporal; presumably chronology alone or the simple fact of a certain age attained would not in itself be cause for undue concern. There is, of course, something more: that temporality leaves its unmistakable, indelible trace on our embodiment. Implicit in the notion of temporal embodiment as unfolding process—implicit in any process—are the correlated notions of development and of change. As such, the trace of temporality takes the form of a continual alteration, a perpetual metamorphosis. And as Beauvoir observes, every metamorphosis has something frightening about it (5), referring to the disruptive effect of change vis-à-vis the illusion I have of myself as stable, coherent, and continuous. Not that every bodily metamorphosis is negative; take, for example, the transformations as we progress from infancy through childhood into adulthood, or the bodily changes that occur in pregnancy. But as Beauvoir points out, there are alterations that occur up to a point, a peak as it were, after which the alterations begin to take on a very different character.

While the point of that peak is difficult to define, and the definition will vary at any rate according to time, place, and other factors, the general consensus is that what lies on the other side of the peak is a condition of decline. The metamorphoses which take place after that point are not mere neutral changes, let alone changes for the better, but in most respects are seen as metamorphoses into something lesser, something worse. As such, it is not just change per se which is at issue in old age, but a perceived change for the worse; a decline, a diminishing, a degradation.

Temporality and the metamorphosis it brings threaten, if not radically compromise, our identity, not only because my sense of self is destabilized and notions of continuity and consistency undermined, but because the ineluctable metamorphosis transforms me into something putatively worse. My "previous identity" and prior self-image have now been compromised, insofar as not only am I no longer what I was, but to my mind I am no longer as good as I was. Thus Beauvoir asks, "can I have become a different being while I still remain myself?" (283) And the answer, as we have seen, is that indeed I now think of myself as someone else, as other than myself, or as another myself: not just no longer *what*, but no longer *who* I was.

Then again this "myself" that Beauvoir invokes is not only my illusion or fantasy of a stable and unchanging subjectivity. Despite her emphasis on a continually metamorphosing embodiment and identity, and the existential imperative to stop refusing to recognize this, there is nevertheless also present through-out her analysis a notion of a default "myself." And that default "myself" seems to be my younger, more attractive, healthier, more capable self: in short, the phe-nomenological "I can" in an all-encompassing sense, contrasted now with the "I cannot" of old age. Throughout the book Beauvoir not only documents and an-alyzes, but also bemoans the typical decline of aging. Clearly this adds yet an-other dimension to the denial and otherness of old age, when Beauvoir herself appears to posit the younger self as the default self.

Stating, "what is so disconcerting about old age is that normally it is an ab-normal condition" (285), Beauvoir quotes someone who observes that "what is normal for an old man would be reckoned deficient in the same person in his middle years" (286). This is, of course, true from a strictly medical point of view, however Beauvoir's framing of old age from the perspective of health as a "normal abnormality" only seems to reinforce the notions of the default young-er self and the default healthy and fully capable body and mind; and moreover, *qua* default, as normative also. This evokes the earlier point about how death may be less disturbing a prospect than old age. Since in death we are simply nothing, whereas in old age we are diminished, lessened, in this respect, less is worse than nothing; ceasing to be is preferable to ceasing to be all that one once was. Accordingly, Beauvoir says, "it is old age rather than death that is to be contrasted with life. Old age is life's parody" (539).

If old age is not life as such, but the contrast or the parody of life, it is be-cause what "life" represents is youth, strength, beauty, good health, and capa-bility. The cruel parody is the counterpart to this younger self, which is myself in decline. (Interestingly, although aging is an ineluctable feature of the lived human situation, old age is here cast as the parody of life.) Throughout *The Com-ing of Age* Beauvoir invokes the notion of decline, and is this not indeed the com-mon principle to all of the aspects most feared in old age? Do we not fear phys-ical decline, which tends to be our most prominent association with aging, but also cognitive decline, an increasingly compelling issue as populations age, and many people live longer? Embodiment in decline, the mind in decline; the body and mind that let us down, the mind and body that now "cannot." Is the real issue in fact aging and old age as such, or rather more fundamentally the decline that goes with it; and if the real issue is the decline, then is old age the only or even the primary location for this?

If the fear of decline is indeed at the heart of our dread and aversion to old age, then perhaps what we are really rejecting is the person in decline more so than the aged person as such. Thus the feared Other within is more fundamen-tally my latent, potential self in decline rather than simply my latent, eventual aged self. Although what we are othering in ourselves and in others are the effects, symbols, and representations of old age, these constitute the branches while the roots are decline, and in this consists perhaps the true basis for alterity, more than old age itself.

To be sure, those who experience significant physical and other types of decline or disablement are not limited to the aged; and the aged are not the only, or arguably even the most disadvantaged group in this situation, given that when decline or disablement occurs in younger people it is often seen as more of an otherness within them than in the case of elderly people. Recall the comment above that "what is normal for an old man would be reckoned deficient in the same person in his middle years."

If the specter of decline and deficiency underlying this observation results in a construal of "normal abnormality" in the case of an aged person, is it simply abnormality in the case of a younger person? That is, with respect to the default and normative young, healthy, functional body and mind, the condition of an aged person is abnormal, but given their age, also normal; however, for a younger person there is nothing "normal" about this situation, therefore it is simply "abnormal." Add to this the consideration that, having reached a certain age, even if a decline then sets in, it is a decline that follows an earlier, longer life path—which, while perhaps not free of problems and limitations, was presumably more optimal than a state of decline in old age. Perhaps it is not accurate to speak of the aged as having achieved an end or a culmination, let alone completion. But if the real decline is one that takes effect only when they have attained a more elderly status, at least in most cases they have realized a certain anticipated trajectory, a life contour or arc, which for those who are subject to an earlier decline or disablement is not always the case.

With decline that is not necessarily age-related, such as the impaired, diminished, or debilitated body or mind, there can also be rejection. But unlike the rejection of the aged discussed above, tied often to a perception of irrelevance or redundancy and manifested as indifference or neglect, this rejection can take the form of an active intolerance. There is a connection to utility and relevance here also, although frequently the person in decline has to make the case that they are relevant at any time, or at all. That is, while the aged person might have to argue that they can still contribute and be relevant, the person in decline or the impaired or diminished person often has to argue that they could ever be so; since society will grant that the aged person was at least relevant at one point, but does not always acknowledge that the person in decline could ever be relevant or make a contribution. This, in addition to a frequent perception of freakishness—which the elderly generally do not have to endure—can place the person in decline or disablement in much more of a framework of intolerance. In many ways this alterity, I would argue, constitutes a deeper level of dehumanization and marginalization than that of the elderly. Obviously Beauvoir's principal concern and focus in *The Coming of Age* was the situation and plight of the aged. But probing the notion of decline is instructive both for analyzing the deeper, more fundamental source of the aversion to aging and the aged: that they (like many others) "cannot" in some respect, a grave liability in societies that place a high premium on functionality, and on conventional definitions of what constitutes such functionality; as well as for unfolding similar or related modes of otherness and marginalization, modes perhaps more pertinent for our times than issues of aging and the aged.

Nevertheless, there is no denying that old age represents a unique instance of otherness. Unlike other cases in which the constituted Other is perceived as a separate and distinct constituency set apart from the dominant group, with old age we inevitably and eventually become members of that group we are othering; we become our Other. Additionally, in most if not all cases of othering, part of the process entails framing the targeted group as deficient in some way, therefore lesser and inferior, possibly even sub-human. While the fear of the difference that the group represents may be a psychological motivator, it is usually also necessary—politically, socially, and even morally (from a self-justifying viewpoint)—for the process to be accompanied by such a twisted and manipulative logic of rationalization and justification. In the case of old age, the representation of deficiency and inferiority, especially with respect to physical infirmity, is already in place and a matter of general consensus thanks to shared beliefs and attitudes, rooted in societal and cultural prejudices regarding the elderly. The imputed lesser and othered status does not have to be projected—being already present within, in multiple ways—thus making old age arguably the quintessential alterity.

The alterity of aging and the aged is a complex, fascinating, and important instance of the process and lived experience of otherness. Simone de Beauvoir's extensive and meticulous analysis in *The Coming of Age* remains a significant and ground-breaking contribution to a phenomenology of old age and aging, while raising awareness and prodding our moral sensibilities about the lived situation of the aged by shining a spotlight on this previously neglected group, and on the grievous prejudices and social injustices to which they have been too long subjected. Fortunately, this spotlight is now also beginning to shine on the situations of other marginalized, disenfranchised, and abjected groups, from different ethnicities or belief systems, to different or challenged embodiments, who have also experienced harmful discrimination and social injustice far too long.[9]

References

Beauvoir, Simone de. 1996. *The coming of age.* Trans. Patrick O'Brian. New York and London: W. W. Norton (originally published as *La Vieillesse.* Paris: Gallimard 1970).

Fisher, Linda. 1997. Phänomenologie und Feminismus. In *Phänomenologie und Geschlechterdifferenz*, ed. Silvia Stoller and Helmuth Vetter. Wien: WUV-Universitätsverlag, 20–46.

Fisher, Linda. 1999. Sexual difference, phenomenology, and alterity. *Philosophy Today* 43: 68–75.

Fisher, Linda. 2000. Phenomenology and feminism: Perspectives on their relation. In *Feminist phenomenology*, ed. Linda Fisher and Lester Embree. Dordrecht: Kluwer Academic Publishers, 17–38.

Fisher, Linda. 2002. La phénoménologie féministe de Beauvoir. In *Cinquantenaire du deuxième sexe*, ed. Christine Delphy and Sylvie Chaperon. Paris: Éditions Syllepse, 130–38.

Fisher, Linda. 2010. Feminist phenomenological voices. *Continental Philosophy Review* 43 (1): 83–95.

Fisher, Linda, and Lester Embree, eds. 2000. *Feminist phenomenology.* Dordrecht: Kluwer Academic Publishers.

Stoller, Silvia, and Helmuth Vetter, eds. 1997. *Phänomenologie und Geschlechterdifferenz.* Wien: WUV-Universitätsverlag.

Stoller, Silvia, Veronica Vasterling, and Linda Fisher, eds. 2005. *Feministische Phänomenologie und Hermeneutik.* Würzburg: Königshausen & Neumann.

9 The research for this chapter was sponsored by Central European University Foundation, Budapest (CEUBPF).

Veronica Vasterling
Fear of Old Age

Comment on Linda Fisher

In Linda Fisher's careful and elegant analysis of Simone de Beauvoir's *The Coming of Age*, the fear of old age plays a key role. In my commentary I will discuss several issues that relate, in heterogeneous ways, to this fear of old age.

My first comment pertains to a phenomenological argument with respect to the recognition of one's aging. It is Beauvoir's argument but Fisher analyses and explicates the argument. The pervasive evasion and lack of recognition of old age is not only due to fear and, more subtly, to "othering" of the old. The argument says that there is another, more structural factor which appears to be beyond our control: we are unable to grasp the truth of our own aging due to the inevitable limits of the first person perspective. While others around us perceive clearly the process of our aging, the awareness of this process eludes us because "our private, inward experience does not tell us the number of our years; no fresh perception comes into being to show us the decline of age" (Beauvoir 1996, 284). I agree with the general gist of the argument, to wit, that we can only really know ourselves, and recognize ourselves, by acknowledging the way others perceive us. The first person perspective does, indeed, have limits. True self-knowledge and self-recognition cannot but have an inter-subjective basis. However, with respect to the specific case of recognizing one's own aging the situation seems more complicated. On the one hand, aging is accompanied by clearly perceptible signs—also for the aging person herself—of bodily change, such as wrinkles and gray hair. Even if one feels forty rather than one's real age of seventy-five, the grey hairs and wrinkles are, as it were, a daily reality check reminding one of one's true age. Hence, not recognizing one's, as it were, objective age seems more a case of intentional self-delusion than structural limits of the first person perspective. What complicates the matter, on the other hand, is the not uncommon phenomenon that our objective age does not correspond with the way we perceive and feel about ourselves. The self-perception of adults does not change that easily. The process of aging often goes faster than the pace of adapting one's self-perception. This, to me, seems to be the real problem. It is hard to keep up with the fact of aging. Once over thirty or forty, it is as if one is constantly running behind a self-perception that remains stuck at the emotional and existential level of an earlier age. Isn't that the truth about aging, that one's self-perception tends to lag behind and every now and then, with a great leap, adjusts itself to one's objective age?

At the end of the essay Fisher argues that it is not so much old age as such, but physical decline that is feared and rejected. Here again, I agree with the general point, but I want to raise two questions. First, in contemporary western countries, I wonder whether it is not Alzheimer's disease and similar conditions of dementia that are feared more than physical decline per se. And, second, if it is decline—physical, mental, social, professional—that is feared most, does not this return us to the question what is first, dread of decline or abjection of old age? Is old age abjected because we fear the decline that goes with it or does the fear of decline lead to the abjection of old age? Or are both intertwined? In any case, in modern western culture fear of decline and abjection of old age do, indeed, go in hand in hand. We should not forget, however, that this is not the universal perception of old age. In most other cultures, for instance, in many African and Asian cultures, old age is not perceived as decline but as the venerated age of wisdom.

I have a final observation on the material conditions of the aged. Discussing Beauvoir's outrage about the destitution of the aged in Europe, Fisher observes that much has changed for the better in Europe. But has it? Europe has become more affluent in general since the post-war period, including its population of aged people. But currently, as in the 1950s and 1960s, the aged are overrepresented in the low income and poverty statistics. There are other indications as well, that things have not changed much for the better. Most European countries are sitting on a demographic time bomb which will double or triple the proportion of the aged of the total population in the near future. As far as I can see, most European countries deal with this demographic emergency in the same way. They plan to cut state supported pension plans, medical care and general elderly care provisions, even as they raise the contributions citizens have to pay for these services. These measures are especially painful in times of increasing numbers of old people dependent on these provisions. Lack of nursing homes for people with Alzheimer's, lack of help at home, and similar consequences are the result. An important political consequence of the tendency to neglect and abject the old is that governments can take draconian measures, resulting in declining provisions for the old, without anybody paying much attention and without any public discussion or outcry. If we don't start paying attention soon, the material conditions of many old people—and of ourselves when we are old—may deteriorate even beyond the bad conditions that filled Beauvoir with indignation.

References

Beauvoir, Simone de. 1996. *The coming of age.* Trans. Patrick O'Brian. New York, London: W. W. Norton & Company.

Debra Bergoffen
The Dignity of Finitude

Simone de Beauvoir opens *The Coming of Age* with two declarations: one that she will break the silence surrounding the indignities of old age; two that she will expose the bourgeois myths glorifying old age. Breaking the silence, she listens to the aged as they voice their experiences of aging and being classified as old. Detailing this lived experience, she discovers a common condition of old age —a unique relationship to time characterized by experiences of a closed future, an overwhelming past, a diminished if not extinct passion, and a curtailed if not broken relationship with others and the world as epitomized in the moods of boredom and melancholia. Taking a Marxist lens to bourgeois myths she details the economic and social structures that alienate not only the old, but all of us, from our humanity. In a world where our dignity is tied to our commodification as hours of productivity, the unproductive person is despised as worthless and considered dispensable (Beauvoir 1996, 6).

As set up in the introduction and pulled together in the conclusion, Beauvoir would have us believe that the Marxist and existentialist meanings of old age intersect, that were the structural changes necessitated by the Marxist critique enacted, the existential miseries of old age would wither away. Without suggesting that there is no relationship between social institutions and lived experience, I do not see things coming together as neatly as Beauvoir's Marxist analysis seems to suggest; for if we read Beauvoir's description of the lived time of the aged in the *Coming of Age* within the context of her *Ethics of Ambiguity* and *All Men Are Mortal* we see that our changed relationship to time, so critical to the altered relationship of the aged to the world and others, will not be ameliorated by altered political structures. Changing the situation of the aged requires changing our understanding of the body, finitude and time.

In *The Coming of Age*, the old person's changed relationship to time is linked to their unique experience of finitude. This experience—the discovery that the future as inherently contingent is neither amenable to the idea of progress nor to the closure our projects would impose on it—provokes the sense of being without a future insofar as we see ourselves as superfluous to it. It is responsible for the mood of despair. In *All Men Are Mortal*, however, this discovery with its accompanying despair comes to an immortal man, not to a person facing imminent death. In both cases, that of the aged and that of the immortal man, the meaning of the future, concealed from finite humans in their prime of life, is revealed and in both cases the implications of this revelation provide criteria for what Beauvoir calls authentic projects in *The Coming of Age* and a politics of the appeal in *The Ethics of Ambiguity*.

Finitude as an Ethical Issue

The Ethics of Ambiguity identifies the ethical problem of freedom as a particular instance of the problem of the particular and the universal. It asks how a "plurality of concrete, particular men projecting themselves toward their ends on the basis of situations whose particularity is as radical and irreducible as subjectivity itself ... [can] at the same time be bound to each other ... [and] forge laws valid for all" (Beauvoir 1948, 17–18). In the course of *The Ethics of Ambiguity* Beauvoir answers this question by appealing to the irreducible truth that "The me-others relationship is as indissoluble as the subject-object relationship" (72). From this irreducible truth, Beauvoir discerns an ethics of ambiguity and advocates a politics of the appeal. She writes, "thus we see that no existence can be validly fulfilled if it is limited to itself. It appeals to the existence of others" (67). She continues, "Thus every man has to do with other men ... this means that ... [h]e must disclose the world with the purpose of further disclosure and by the same movement to try to free men by means of whom the world takes on meaning" (74).

Considered as an ethical issue, finitude has two dimensions. One, the dimension of singularity—we exist as particular individuals in discrete situations; two, the dimension of time. The particulars of our situation are in flux. They are bordered by birth and death. The ethical project of disclosing the possibilities of freedom is directed toward the future. Its purpose is "further disclosure" that "appeals to the existence of others." These others are both my contemporaries and those yet to come. As directed toward the future, ethical action is also grounded in the past. Our temporal finitude is ethical in that, "One can reveal the world only on a basis revealed by other men ... freedom cannot will itself without aiming at an open future ... only the freedom of other men can extend [my goals] beyond our life" (71).

In *The Coming of Age*, these ideas of temporal and singular finitude, and the me-other relationship become more specific. Drawing out the ethical truth of the temporal flow, Beauvoir reveals the ways that the realities of contingency bind us to each other across the generations. Bringing the ethical truths of *The Ethics of Ambiguity* to the realities of aging described in *The Coming of Age* I find Beauvoir arguing that our current treatment of the old constitutes a form of oppression. She asks us to examine the ideologies that "legitimate" this oppression.

There may have been a time when the question of aging and the aged were issues of limited public importance. Though the Marxist argument of Beauvoir's

Coming of Age insists that the matter of the aged and aging are matters of state insofar as they are tied to the politics of economic and social structures, this argument carries little weight in a world where Marxism is said to be dead. The world of capitalist politics, like the worlds before it, considers the matter of the aged a family affair. Demographic realities conspire to make this privatization of aging untenable. The recent UN report titled, "World Populations Ageing 1950 – 2050" called global aging an unparalleled historical process and predicted that people over 60 would outnumber those under 15 for the first time in 2047. In some nations that future is already visible. More than one quarter of the population is over 60 in Japan, Italy, Germany, Poland and Russia. Noting that in most countries older women outnumber older men so greatly that the issue of aging should be considered a woman's issue, aware of the inter-generational conflicts emerging as a result of this demographic change, the report found that the "rights of older persons should not be incompatible with those of other age groups." It also urged that "the reciprocal relationships between generations must be nurtured and encouraged" (United Nations 2006, 34).

Given Beauvoir's descriptions of the realities of aging these figures should give us pause. If we listen to the frequent charge leveled against the Enlightenment—that by equating reason with human dignity it deprived much of humanity of their human status and legitimated their exploitation and abuse—and if we note the ways that the old are marginalized today, the fact that this marginalization will soon become the fate of more than half the world's population, should prompt us to interrogate the exclusionary effects of current descriptions of the human as vigorously as we have interrogated the exclusionary effects of Enlightenment definitions of "man." We pride ourselves in having exposed the ways that the link between reason and the human produced imperialist discourses of the white man's burden and self-righteous justifications of slavery. We say that we have learned from this mistake; that we now define the human in ways that are open to the full diversity of human life. The old, however, do not seem to have benefitted from this celebration of difference. Jane Gross reports in the *New York Times* that the elderly suffer from physical neglect and abuse at alarming rates. The veracity of these reports may be confirmed by the fact that of those cases prosecuted ninety percent result in convictions (Gross 2006). Our notions of the human are not, it seems, as inclusive as we claim.

Beyond the Dignity of the "I-can" Body

Beauvoir traces the humiliations suffered by the aged to a capitalist, utilitarian attitude toward human beings. Within the capitalist frame, to be treated with dignity requires that one be useful. While Beauvoir objects to this way of conceiving human worth and provides structural antidotes to the ill treatment of the aged, her own examples of traditional societies, where criteria of utility are also often used to discard the old, indicate that something more than the flaws of capitalism are at work in this denigration of the aged. In Beauvoir's examples of places and times where the aged were treated well, this treatment was the effect of one of two sources: either the elderly were valued for their knowledge and experience (Beauvoir 1996, 90), a utilitarian value that cannot be appealed to in a rapidly changing information age where yesterday's knowledge is an obstacle to operating today's computers (210); or they were cared for out of the affection their children bore them (58, 72, 80), not something to be counted on and certainly not the ground of a dignity claim.

In her critique of the situation of the aged, Beauvoir draws a sharp distinction between the situation of the aged in modern and traditional societies. She also presents capitalism and Marxism as staking out incompatible economic principles. This accepted truth hides the shared capitalist and Marxist attitude toward the relationship between work and human worth. The depth of this modern commitment to the worth of work is reflected in the existential notion of the project and the phenomenological focus on the "I can" body.

Though Marxism rejects Adam Smith's economic man, like capitalism, it identifies work as the process through which human beings create and liberate themselves. This is the legacy of Hegel's Master-Slave relationship. It is the work of the slave that moves the Spirit to the next level of consciousness. Through its labor the slave undergoes the self-transformation that recognizes the relationship between one's freedom and the freedom of the other. As Hegel looked at the labor of the slave as liberatory, Marx identified the worker as the beacon of freedom. We might not be surprised to find the prints of this Hegelian legacy in Beauvoir's writings given her sympathies for Marxism and the influence of Hegel in her intellectual development. The depth of this attitude toward work is revealed when we find that it is critical to both Merleau-Ponty's and Beauvoir's phenomenology of the body. Beauvoir's focus on the "I can" body is revealed in her understanding of the body as the instrument through which we engage the world. She challenges the Hegelian-Marxist liberatory view of this engagement, however, when she critiques the ways that women have been alienated from their bodily "I cans" (a theme central to Iris Marion Young's "Throwing Like a Girl" [1990]), and exposes the ways that women's unique bodily "I can," the birthing body, has been used against them. Challenging the exclusive focus on the "I can" body, Beauvoir introduces us to another body—the erotic body. She marks this body as the site of a possible radical transformation of subjectivity. In the section of The Second Sex titled "The Independent Woman" the tensions between the erotic body and the "I can" body are noted. They are not, however, fully explored. *The Coming of Age*, however, makes it clear that ignoring these tensions by allowing the "I can" body of work and the project to dominate the account of our embodiment is both inadequate and immoral. Refusing to let the "I can" body monopolize our account of the body she directs us to the erotic body in *The Second Sex*, the finite body in *The Coming of Age* and *All Men Are Mortal*, and the pleasurable body in *The Ethics of Ambiguity*. Given Beauvoir's accounts of the ways that the old are alienated from their pleasures in *The Coming of Age*, her description of the relationship between the working and the pleasure body in *The Ethics of Ambiguity* is especially significant. Beauvoir writes, "If the satisfaction of an old man drinking a glass of wine counts for nothing then production and wealth are only hollow myths; they have meaning only if they are capable of being retrieved in individual and living joy" (Beauvoir 1948, 135).

There is in short, more than one body in play in our relationship to the world and each other. Often these bodies complement each other. Often they do not. When one mode of embodiment becomes definitive, however, we can be sure that some part of our humanity is being sacrificed, and that some people will suffer. Bringing the prejudice for the "I can" body to Beauvoir's *The Coming of Age*, where the issue concerns the ways that the aged, those whose I can bodies are in question, are stripped of their dignity, alerts me to the need to challenge this contemporary prejudice. Taking up this prejudice within the context of *The Coming of Age* where finitude plays a crucial role, I am led to explore the matter of dignity through the question of the body and time.

The Flight from Finitude, Vulnerability, and Contingency

As I consider Beauvoir's analyses of aging, I am struck by the ways that the melancholia of the aged is tied to their exaggerated sense of finitude, triggered by their experience of being at the end of "their" time, and by the ways that those who are not yet old are repulsed by the unmistakable ways that time has marked the bodies of the aged as unfit for work—frail, fragile, and vulnerable.

The irony is this: finitude and vulnerability are essential markers of the human condition. Both the old in their melancholia and those repulsed by them seem to be fleeing their own humanity. Examining the meaning of this flight may provide the ground of a genuinely inclusive human ontology. It may help us find ontological grounds for the universal claims of human dignity, which because they are genuinely ontological, do not commit the universalist errors that have haunted the humanist project.

As human we are the finitude of the between. We live in the flow of a present, moving from an accomplished past toward an anticipated future. This future, though fundamentally unlike the past in its unpredictability, possesses one certainty—death. It is tempting to say that it is our flight from death and the ways that death confronts us in the person of the old man and woman that accounts for the indignities suffered by the old, but this is too quick. It gives us no way of understanding the dignity we accord the reality of death in funeral and burial rituals. If Beauvoir is correct in her observation that burial rites reflect the collectivity's homage to the individual (Beauvoir 1948, 106), then we must ask how and why the old are stripped of their individuality. What is it about the embodiment of approaching death that humiliates and offends us?

Beauvoir characterizes the unique relationship of the aged to time in two ways. One deploys the categories of immanence and transcendence and is marked by the existential concept of the project. The other depicts the old person experience of time's flow toward the future as clogged by the weight of the past. Here too the concept of the project is at work; for as consumed by the past (memories) the elderly are said to be unfit for the creative engagements with the future so critical to the task of freedom, the essence of the project. Beauvoir's distinction between immanence and transcendence, both in *The Coming of Age* and in *The Second Sex*, is materialized in the lived difference between the static and repetitive activities of maintaining life and the creative and transformative activities that revitalize it. Though Beauvoir notes that both are necessary for living, in *The Second Sex* she argues that women confined to the home as mothers and homemakers and restricted to the task of maintaining life are dehumanized. This feminist rejection of housework is anticipated in Beauvoir's earlier work, *The Ethics of Ambiguity*. There she equates repetitive work without purpose with oppression and condemns it as the worst form of punishment. Unlike Camus, Beauvoir could not imagine Sisyphus happy.

Like the unemancipated women of *The Second Sex*, the aged are consumed with tasks necessary for the maintenance of life. Unlike the women, however, who are candidates for liberation once arguments that naturalize their socially constructed positions are debunked, there is nothing socially constructed about the maintenance necessary for the aged and aging body. Here Beauvoir notes, the situation is more analogous to the ill than to women.

In growing old and falling ill, the "absent body" (Leder 1990), in Drew Leder's apt phrase, becomes irreparably present. My taken for granted "I cans": I can walk, I can grasp the coffee cup, I can enjoy my dinner, I can breathe freely, are disrupted. My body, once a source of pleasure and competence is now a site of betrayal, of aches, pains and disgust (Beauvoir 1996, 320). Instead of being the instrument through which I engage the world the body becomes a hindrance (317). The ailments of old age, the arthritis of Beauvoir's mother, the rheumatism of Sartre's mother are illnesses, which like the illnesses of the young, come between the body and the world. Instead of beckoning me, the world now "bristles with threats" (304–305). The work of disability theorists and activists alerts us to the ways that these threats are constructed as well as given. They also challenge the assumption that the loss of bodily "I cans" necessarily entails the loss of sensuality.

The analogy between old age and illness breaks down rather quickly, however. I expect to recover from the flu. There is no antidote to old age. Hence the different discourses associated with illness and aging. We expect the sick person to fight the disease. We ask the old person to accept the inevitable—age gracefully is the euphemism. Here, resignation prevails. Nothing can be done. The slide from this resignation to "who cares" is not very far. Once we are here, at who cares, the realities of abuse that accompany the loss of respect appear.

Bleak, as this sounds, there is nothing inevitable about this attitude toward the old. It depends on establishing a hierarchal bifurcation between transcendence and immanence rather than validating the ways that both mark us as human. It also depends on describing the privilege accorded to transcendence in terms that are generally associated with youth: risk taking, passion, aggression, and power. It is not only the case that privileging transcendence privileges the future, it is also the case that privileging the future in terms that are associated with youth supports the idea that it is the young who have a monopoly on transcendent activities and claims to the future. Further if we mark these transcendent activities as distinctively human and tie them to human dignity claims, the young will insist on exclusive rights to these claims. Since those who are old were once young and made these claims for themselves, they will be reluctant to see themselves as old. Clinging to their dignity as guaranteed by their youth (plastic surgery cannot be reduced to a narcissistic impulse), they will refuse to render themselves superfluous by recognizing the claims of the next generation (Beauvoir 1996, 4–5, 284–301).

These descriptions of transcendence, by associating it with the vigorous activities of the young, carry a subtext that suggests that the future, if approached with sufficient power, can be commanded by our will. But here is the rub. The essential feature of the future is that it does not belong to anyone. It can neither be possessed nor controlled. It is not the time of the not yet as that which is ready to be conquered and molded according to our desires. It is the time of the not yet of radical contingency. Insofar as human life and the dignity accorded it must be considered, at least in part, in terms of its temporality, these too must be grounded in an ontology that recognizes this radical contingency of the future. If we intend to support the value of transcendence and the activities associated with it, we must reject the idea that our projects will set the course of the future. We must combat the idea that those at the end of their lives are worth less than others because they have little at stake in a future that will not be theirs.

Whether Beauvoir in particular or existentialism in general can provide us with this ontology is the question. In linking our attitude toward the aged with a primitive revulsion toward the aged present in all cultures and thereby seeming to naturalize it (18, 40); in often describing the project in ways that idealize work and the young; and in indicating that it is through our projects that we assume responsibility for the future; Beauvoir unreflectively reproduces the assumptions about work and the illusions of youth so detrimental to the aged. The thought of radical contingency and finitude, central to her politics of the appeal, however, render her concepts of transcendence, immanence, and the project unstable and ambiguous. They do not always support the ideologies of youth, power and will. Further if we turn to *All Men Are Mortal* we find Beauvoir suggesting that the ideologies of youth, power, and will are dangerous and immoral illusions. We discover the necessary resources for combating the injustices suffered by the old.

Combating Immoral Illusions

Beauvoir guides us through her investigation of the aged and aging by reminding us that we can neither reduce the phenomenon of old age to a biological fact, nor equate it with a social construction. Biologically the process of aging is an irreversible decline. We view this decline unfavorably and this too seems natural; but for Beauvoir this taken for granted idea needs to be scrutinized. It is a judgment, the result of accepting certain arguments concerning the goal of life and the meaning of the future. It is in this sense that old age is a cultural as well as a biological fact (11–13). Taking aging as a biological and a natural fact and viewing this fact from a temporal perspective, the question may be put as follows: If from the perspective of time the decline of old age marks the fact that the chances of continuing to live are exponentially reduced, (17), what is it about the frail body with a shortened life span that devalues the old? What concepts of the human induce us to ascribe dignity to virile bodies with a long future and withhold it from vulnerable bodies with a short one? Beauvoir gives us a clue to this puzzle when she notes that the decline of aging is the other side of the optimism of progress (302). We can pursue this clue by turning to *All Men Are Mortal.*

All Men Are Mortal is the story of a man, Fosca, who chooses immortality in order to have enough time to complete his project of creating a perfect world. It is also the story of a man who in becoming immortal suffers the indignity of losing his humanity. This is Beauvoir's way of telling us that finitude is not, as the myth of the Garden of Eden would have us believe, a curse, but an ontological necessity. It is the ground of our desire, the anchor of our humanity, the condition of the possibility of justice.

There are striking parallels between Beauvoir's descriptions of Fosca, a man who cannot die, and the old, those about to die. Both have lost their passion for life. Both see the future as closed. Both feel superfluous. Seeing how Fosca, a man who cannot die comes to experience time as if he were about to die, shows us that it is not the aging body, as immortal Fosca is eternally young, but a misunderstood attitude toward youth and the future that contaminates the old person's experience of life.

Fosca is haunted by death—not because he fears dying per se, but because if he dies, his project will die with him. When offered the chance to become immortal, a chance that to him means the power to ensure the success of his project, he takes it. Beauvoir keeps it complicated. Fosca does not want the power that comes with immortality for himself. He pursues eternal peace and the happiness of humanity. Fosca is a humanist who in pursuit of his humanist goals exposes the perils of the illusions of youth. The illusions of youth are so common we take them for granted. We expect young people to act as if they were invulnerable and immortal. They say they are not afraid of death. They mean they do not believe that it is one of their possibilities. For the young, this is an illusion; for Fosca, however, it is not. His perennial future is guaranteed. As the one who has a guaranteed future, Fosca, like the young who think their future is guaranteed, comes to denigrate those whose time is limited. For the young this attitude is directed toward the old. For Fosca it is directed to all mortals. Determining that by virtue of their finitude mortal human beings have no right to the future, Fosca strips them of their rights to the present. They become the means to the realization of Fosca's future.

The illusions of youth and humanism are joined to another illusion in Fosca's decision to become immortal—the illusion of the idea of progress. Fosca does not believe that time as the power of change and transformation is necessarily progressive. Rather he believes that time, guided by reason and powered by his will can be used to realize humanity's goals (Beauvoir 1955, 147, 151, 157).

It takes Fosca several hundred years to outlive these illusions. Without them, however, he loses his passion for life. No longer a tyrant or a danger to others, he turns on himself. Condemned to eternal youth, Fosca is an old man. This has nothing to do with a failing body. As forever young, Fosca's body remains the site of unimagined powerful "I cans." It has everything to do with his relationship to time. His past, like the past of the old weighs too heavily on him. He no longer believes in freedom or the future. Bereft of these beliefs his sensual body dies.

If we stay focused on Fosca, the lesson taught by the immortal man is twofold: One that youth is not so much a time of life as an illusion regarding life; and two, that once this illusion is destroyed the passion for life and all that makes it desirable is also destroyed. These lessons seem to be captured in the closing line of the book: Regina's scream. If this horrific sound is the last note of the book, it is not, I think, Beauvoir's last word; for as I read *All Men Are Mortal* I find it asking a question in the figure of Fosca and answering it in the person of his great grandson Armand.

Reading Fosca as a question: Can life be lived without illusions? Rather than as a statement: Life without illusions is unlivable; I find Beauvoir posing the question of our relationship to time and answering it in terms of the meaning we give to the relationship between the past, present and future. Armand looks just like his great grandfather. In addition to having Fosca's looks, he seems to have inherited his experience; for he neither believes that he has the right to control people (even for their own good), nor lives under the illusions of youth, humanism, or progress. Instead, he embodies the value of freedom, understood as the unpredictability and instability of desire. He aligns himself with other revolutionaries who share his commitments and in this allegiance engages in liberatory action. Here liberatory action is not grounded in notions of work or power. It is grounded in the realities of finitude, failure, and contingency. Thus, after the defeat of the 13th of April uprising, Granier tells Fosca: "We don't have to count on the future to give meaning to our acts. If that were the case all action would be impossible. We have to carry on our fight the way we decided to carry it on. That's all" (Beauvoir 1955, 312). Projects in other words must respect the radical contingency of the future. The only legitimate goal of the project is freedom; for this is the only goal that respects the radical impossibility of foretelling the desire of those yet to come.

Fosca is suspicious of Armand. "What", he asks, "will man do with this freedom?" Armand replies, "What's the difference, he'll do whatever he likes" (319). Fosca presses Armand insisting that the future he dreams of will never be realized. Armand replies, "Of course not. ... Paradise for us is simply the moment when the dreams we dream today are finally realized. We're well aware that after that other men will have new needs, new desires, will make new demands" (327). Here Armand turns the tables to criticize Fosca for treating the present as if it were the past instead of seeing the past as other men's present. Fosca's mistake of seeing "all past enterprises [as] decisive ... dead, embalmed, buried" (328), however, is a common one. Its power is reflected in our denigration of the old.

The analyses of *The Ethics of Ambiguity* provide the context for Armand's critique of Fosca's politics. *The Ethics of Ambiguity* establishes freedom not happiness as the criteria by which our projects must be measured. Arguing that freedom must aim at an open future; that the purpose of disclosing the world is that of further disclosure; and that we can reveal the world only on a basis revealed by others; Beauvoir establishes the intersubjective realities of freedom. It is on the basis of this intersubjectivity that Armand challenges Fosca.

On meeting Armand, Fosca already knows that the future cannot be controlled. Armand teaches him that it is immoral to try to control it—that a temporal reality, the open future—is also an ethical mandate—pursue the other's freedom by ensuring that the future will remain open to their desire. The undecidability of my project grounds the possibility of the next generation's passion and action. If it is the case that as human I am drawn toward a future, it is also the case that to be drawn toward a future without illusions is to be drawn toward its contingencies and unpredictabilities. From this perspective whether I am young or old, whether I believe that I have a long or short future before me does not matter; for if the goal of the living ought to be that of preserving the other's freedom to engage the future, whether I have one day or hundreds to live is a matter of indifference.

The Intergenerational Bond

The indignities of old age come from the ways that I experience myself and the ways that I am treated by others. If it is the case that I must experience my youth without illusions in order to value myself in my old age, and if it is the case that living youth without illusions requires revaluing the relationship between the present and the future, it is also the case that for the old to be treated with dignity by others a reassessment of the past is necessary. So long as the past is understood as "dead, embalmed, buried" (Beauvoir 1955, 328) such that those with a long past are said to be burdened by it, immobilized, good as dead, it is difficult to see how the old can be viewed as relevant to either the present or the future. Beauvoir, however, rejects this view of the past. She writes:

> [t]he fact of having a past is part of the human condition; if the world behind us were bare we would hardly be able to see anything but a gloomy desert. We must try, through our liv-

ing projects to turn to our own account that freedom which was undertaken in the past and integrate it into the present world. (Beauvoir 1948, 93)

As a time that was not ours, the past is the time of the passion of the other. In this it is like the future. If it is the responsibility of the present generation to preserve the present of the future for the next generation, it is also the responsibility of the generation in the prime of their life to see that the elderly, as carriers of the past, are a unique opening toward the future. Their extensive experience with contingency and failure, and their marked vulnerability remind us that it is our finitude that makes us human and that it is as finite that we deserve to be treated with dignity and respect.

There is another consequence of having a long past, however, which requires our attention. With a "long habit of the same perceptions," Beauvoir writes, the present loses its freshness. No new impressions come (Beauvoir 1996, 449–50). The past as the solidification of habit destroys the present as the time in which consciousness reveals the possibilities of the world—a revelatory power described by Beauvoir in *The Ethics of Ambiguity* as a source of joyful world engagement. Like Fosca, the old lose their capacity for taking up projects and pleasure (451).

Not long after this denigrating description of the old as living in dead time, alienated from life, others, and the world, Beauvoir seems to remember Armand. Suddenly she commends this changed relationship of the aged to time as revealing the illusions of youth and progress. The aged, Beauvoir writes, realize that "the idea of advancing toward a goal was a delusion" (491). She continues, "This sweeping away of fetishes and illusions is their truest, most worthwhile of all the contributions brought by age" (492). One might think that the idea of the project, caught up as it seems to be with the idea of advancing toward a future goal would now also be exposed as a fetish and an illusion. Beauvoir will not go this far. Instead she allows us to see that the old, by sweeping away fetishes and illusions provide us with the criteria for distinguishing moral from immoral ways of engaging the future. They teach us the difference between despotic projects and authentic ones. For what Beauvoir asks us to learn from the old is to act "while at the same time placing one's activity into a parentheses" (492). This is the language of phenomenology. We need to listen for echoes of the *epoché*, where it is by not assuming we already know the world that we begin to experience it. Here, what needs to be put into parentheses, are our assumptions about our relationship to our projects. They are not ours. They belong to those we engage. The older dancer's project now belongs to her students (386).

It is commonly assumed that the old need the young. Beauvoir supports this assumption when she writes:

> I want this adventure that is the context of my life to go on without end. I love young people: I want our species to go on in them and I want them to have a better life. Without this hope I should find the old age towards which I am moving utterly unbearable. (Beauvoir 1996, 412)

This touching personal note is also disturbing. The illusions of youth and progress sustain her hope and her capacity to bear the burdens of aging. There is nothing here to suggest that the young should love or care about her. Nothing to indicate, that, as an old woman, she should be treated with dignity and respect. We can, however, use her texts to plead her (and our) case. To do this we need to move to phenomenological territory.

So long as we use the criteria of usefulness and work to assess the value of a human being and so long as we measure the humanity of the body in terms of the range of its "I cans," the old will live at the mercy of the young. If they are treated well it will be a matter of generosity not of dignity. As a matter of generosity the situation of the old will call for an ethical response but not necessarily a political one. As a matter of dignity, however, the respect due the old can become the stuff of human rights and other political demands.

Once we put the category of finitude in play, things change. Now the respect due to us as human has no relationship to my usefulness or embodied "I cans" but to my changing relationship to time and to the ways that my body is marked by time. So long as we value ourselves and others in terms of their "I cans" this changing relationship to time called aging will be seen negatively. Seen in terms of finitude, however, the meaning and lived experience of finitude of the young, the mature, and old embody different finite realities. No single age captures the full meaning of our humanity. The vocabulary of phenomenology is particularly helpful here. It invites us to see the aged as the bulwark of the *epoché*. Their frail bodies confront the illusionary assumptions of the young. Their marked vulnerability, instead of becoming an invitation to abuse becomes a check on the despotic tendencies of the younger generation as characterized by Fosca. As the *epoché* is not the whole story of phenomenology, however, the need of the young for the old is not the whole story of finitude. If the aged save the young from the tyranny of their illusions, the young save the old from the power of their habits. Listening to the young, the old recover the freshness of the world and rediscover the joys of revealing the possibilities of existence. Their phenomenological sensual capacities are reawakened.

Materializing the phenomenology of Beauvoir's two moments of intentionality in the embodied relationship between the generations reveals a mutual dependency mandated by the ontology of finitude and time. The dignity of the young and old is neither tied to their commodity value nor to the liberatory power of work. Neither does it appeal to myths about the wisdom of the old or the vision of the young, at least not in the ways these myths are usually presented. If there is a wisdom of old age it is not about the good old days or about maintaining the status quo, but about recognizing the impossibility of imposing one's will on the world and of seeing this failure as a virtue rather than as a defeat—as essential to the regeneration required by finitude. If there is a vision of the young, it is not about changing the world so that it will reflect their desire but about revealing the world in all of its possibilities so that it may refresh our desire and keep it open to the possibilities of freedom. Between the young and the old we learn that visions of the possibilities of the present for the future are the stuff of our desire. We also learn the difference between re-visioning the world and imposing our visions on the world. The first welcomes the revelatory power of others. The second violates the demands of finitude.

As described in *The Ethics of Ambiguity*, the two moments of intentionality, a first joyful mode of disclosure followed by the attempt to instantiate the newly disclosed meaning of the world on the world, are contentiously and necessarily bound to each other (Bergoffen 1996, ch. 3). This is also true for the generational bonds of finitude. If we segregate the generations from each other; if we marginalize the old and set them aside; the illusions of youth will remain uncontested and the melancholia of the aged will persist. Recognizing that the generations need each other to adequately understand and ethically live the fullness of their finitude ought not lead to romantic visions of inter-generational life. The conflict between the generations, like the conflict between the two moments of intentionality, is real. Viewed phenomenologically, however, this conflict is not essentially about money or power, it is a conflict about assumptions and illusions which are turned into a conflict about rights—specifically about who has a right to the present and the future. To get to the ethical answer to this question: We all have a right to the present. None of us has a right to the future; and to institute a politics of finitude reflective of this answer, we need to take up the difficult work of inter-generational dialogue—the work Merleau-Ponty called the violence of dialogue which forces us to engage the other whose otherness requires that we interrogate ourselves (Merleau-Ponty 1973).

References

Beauvoir, Simone de. 1948. *The ethics of ambiguity.* Trans. Bernard Frechtman. New York: Philosophical Library.
Beauvoir, Simone de. 1955. *All men are mortal.* Trans. Leonard M. Friedman. New York: W. W. Norton.
Beauvoir, Simone de. 1996. *The coming of age.* Trans. Patrick O'Brian. New York and London: W. W. Norton & Company.
Bergoffen, Debra. 1996. *The philosophy of Simone de Beauvoir: Gendered phenomenologies, erotic generosities.* Albany: State University of New York Press.
United Nations, Department of Economic and Social Affairs, Population Division. 2006. *World Population Ageing: 1950–2050.* http://www.un.org/esa/population/publications/worldageing19502050/ (accessed December 30, 2008).
Gross, Jane. 2006. Forensic skills seek to uncover elder abuse. *New York Times,* September 27, 2006. http://www.nytimes.com/2006/09/27/us/27abuse.html (accessed December 30, 2008).
Leder, Drew. 1990. *The absent body.* Chicago: University of Chicago Press.
Merleau-Ponty, Maurice. 1973. Dialogue and the perception of the other. In *The prose of the world.* Evanston: Northwestern University Press, 131–46.
Young, Iris Marion. 1990. Throwing like a girl. In *Throwing like a girl and other essays in feminist philosophy and social theory.* Bloomington: Indiana University Press, 141–59.

Gertrude Postl
Different Finite Bodies

Comment on Debra Bergoffen

Agreeing with Beauvoir's critique of a utilitarian attitude towards the aged, Debra Bergoffen suggests that we should focus on humans' relationship to temporality and finitude rather than on old people's contributions to society and the failing usefulness of their "I can" bodies. Relating to the story of Fosca, the main protagonist of Beauvoir's *All Men Are Mortal*, Bergoffen shows that immortality is no guarantee for humanity. Forever frozen in the illusion of controlling the future through his project, Fosca loses his humanity. In that, he is comparable to the illusion of the young who also assume a monopoly over the future, which in turn, results in treating the old with indignity. Thus, "it is not the aging body ... but a misunderstood attitude toward youth and the future" (135) that is responsible for the misery of the old.

The realization of finitude—"an ontological necessity," (135) which we all have to face—changes this picture. Rather than being caught in the illusion of controlling the future, finitude makes us aware that the future "can neither be possessed nor controlled" (133) and that it consists of contingencies and unpredictabilities. If nobody can lay claim to the future then there is no reason for treating the old with indignity. And since all of us, young or old, have to face our finitude, the differences between age groups dwindle. "From this perspective whether I am young or old, whether I believe that I have a long or short future before me does not matter" (137). As a result, having projects is not the privilege of the young, and being burdened by the weight of the past, materialized in habits, is not the predicament of the old. The actual physical differences between the young and the old seem to lose their significance—the frail, aging body might be a hindrance for the realization of certain projects, but it does not any longer prevent a dignified treatment.

While both the young and the old have to face their finitude and are thus alike with respect to the contingencies of the future, they also differ: "the meaning and lived experience of finitude of the young, the mature, and old embody different finite realities. No single age captures the full meaning of our humanity" (139). These differences in the lived experience of the different age groups allows for an exchange of perspective or "mutual dependency": "the aged save the young from the tyranny of their illusions, the young save the old from the power of their habits" (139).

In order to explain the differences between age groups, Bergoffen evokes the language of phenomenology, in particular the notion of the *epoché*. Unquestioned assumptions (in this case the future of one's projects) have to be put on hold. Translated into the situation of the old, this means that they need to put the relationship to their projects in parentheses. "The older dancer's project now belongs to her students" (138; cf. Beauvoir 1996, 386). The balanced interaction between the generations, with each group making available the insights of their own situation to the other, is achieved only at a price. Although Bergoffen admits differences in the lived experience of the different age groups, she basically—with Beauvoir—expects the older dancer to put her aging body and all the now impossible projects that once were tied to it into parentheses. I agree, "[n]o single age captures the full meaning of our humanity" (139), but the olds' finite reality entails a loss which is not part of the experience of the young, a loss that has to be accounted for somewhere—if it cannot be accounted for, what then, would be the meaning of a lived bodily experience or, in this case, the "lived experience of finitude"?

In my view, the lived bodily experience of the young differs significantly from those of the old. The older dancer's body is no longer an "I can" body. At the point where able "I can" bodies confront the bodily decay of the old it becomes obvious that the mutual encounter of each other's experience places a higher burden on the one group than on the other. Even if the future is contingent and cannot be controlled by either group, the realization of one's finitude is yet a different one if accompanied by frailty, pain, or loss over one's senses. Putting into parentheses unquestioned assumptions is one thing, losing control over one's body yet another—the first is an intentional act, the second is not.

Granted, having a feeble and perhaps pained body captures the meaning of humanity as much as engaging in a multitude of projects without bodily hindrance. But it seems that in Bergoffen's account more is required from the old than the young for this diverse manifestation of humanity to unfold. Can the finite reality of the aging body be ignored just because the project continues through somebody young? Can the continuation of the older dancer's project through the student make up for the physical frailty and the loss of bodily integrity she most likely is to experience? Does this passing on of one's project to the younger generation eliminate the importance of embodiment and the lived bodily experience? If the "I can" body should not monopolize the entire spectrum of the human bodily experience (131), then the loss of the "I can" body has to be more prominently addressed. Otherwise we end up with a scenario where displacement rules, and older people are able to transcend only through passing on their projects to the younger generation.

While Bergoffen's attempt to do justice to the diversity of human life and to include the old in the current "celebration of difference" (129) requires an attention to differences (the embodiment of different finite realities), the demand for a dignified treatment of the old relies on a notion of equality (we all are finite beings). No, the shortcomings of the aging body should not be the reason for treating the old with indignity, but those shortcomings should not be argued away either. If our finitude forces us to rethink our projects with respect to an unpredictable future then the differences in the bodily enactment of these projects have to be taken into consideration—something, I think, Bergoffen fails to clearly address. Only if these differences are accounted for can we all fully claim our "right to the present" (145)—a prerequisite for the inter-generational dialogue to work.

References

Beauvoir, Simone de. 1996. *The coming of age*. Trans. Patrick O'Brian. New York and London: W. W. Norton & Company.

Dorothea Olkowski
Letting Go the Weight of the Past
Beauvoir and the Joy of Existence

Aging and the Relation to Time

In *The Coming of Age*, Simone de Beauvoir focuses one chapter on the question of how age changes the human relationship to time (Beauvoir 1972, 361). At first, the passing of time appears to be entirely a loss. For some aging people, their experience is centered on the refusal of future time as they embed themselves in their past. So the "I" of their past, their middle years, youth or childhood, is the "I" in which they remain unaltered, a fixed, unchanging essence (363). This is reflected in the stories they tell about themselves: hero, glamorous woman, good mother, soldier, blooming adolescent. But as Beauvoir rightly points out, such story telling requires physiological data, images, knowledge, and logic to produce a still functioning social memory that reconstructs and localizes facts from the past. Some things must be forgotten so that others can be remembered. Nerve-circuits for the renewal of images must function undiseased and even under optimal conditions, the images left to us are impoverished, so that most of the time we are just guessing about the past (362–64). As such, very old people generally do not have a long past, as we move forward with our lives, the past crumbles and even its meaning escapes us (365).

But into this gloomy picture of the passing of time and memory, Beauvoir begins to admit something else. Is it not possible, she asks, that the past, our own past and the past we shared with others, can it not be an object of enjoyment? This possibility is available to us but it requires a certain point of view. It requires an ability and desire to admit that one does not *have* a life, neither a fine life nor a poor one, and that it is only our determination to contrast the past with the present that turns the past into a gloomy and pitiful saga or a saga of former glory, pleasure and success, now faded. For Beauvoir, life is based on self-transcendence. It is one's future oriented projects, not yet accomplished, that give life meaning. As such, we never really have an identity, and in-itself but we are always transcending, always a for-itself (Beauvoir 1972, 368). The question that she presents is this: how can an aging person find joy in self-transcendence while remaining fully aware of the limitations of time? This is not a simple matter and often the aging are paralyzed by the future which they fear and the past which they recall only poorly. Yet, it seems that Beauvoir remains positive and cheerful about the future of an aging person and that throughout her work she contrasts those persons who have failed at the project of aging with those who have succeeded. Let us therefore begin by looking as some examples of each of these in Beauvoir's work in order to make sense of how even the aging can experience the joy of existence.

Two Women, Two Futures

A woman of 60, possibly a philosopher, married, it seems, to André, a scientist, reflects on their life, past, present and future. "How many times had we sat there opposite one another at that little table with piping hot, very strong cups of tea in front of us? ... The moment possessed the sweet gentleness of a memory and the gaiety of a promise. Were we thirty, or were we sixty?" (Beauvoir 1969, 12). How many times *had* the couple sat in the sun filled library in an ordinary, easy-flowing way? How sweet *is* the gentle present moment of this thought? How gay, the promise of future days, the very strong and very hot cups of tea to come? The woman recognizes that together, she and André have had a long life filled, as she says, with laughter, tears, quarrels, embraces, confessions, silences and sudden impulses of the heart, yet "sometimes it seems that time has not moved by at all. The future still stretches out to infinity" (12). And so it does, for the implication of these realizations will be that no existence founds itself only from moment to moment, that moral freedom requires a past and a future, a past and a future that belong to the temporal unity of one's current projects, projects that, in turn, may become the starting point for other projects to be carried out by other people, on and on into the infinite future, well beyond the strong cups of tea, the sun-filled library and day's post (Beauvoir 1976, 27).

Soon, André will go off to the laboratory where he conducts scientific research and the woman will attend to the card indexes and blank paper that, sitting on her desk, urge her to work. For the woman and her husband, what matters is not falling into the paralysis of what Simone de Beauvoir has elsewhere described as a limited future and a frozen past, a situation that the aging and elderly often face (Beauvoir 1972, 378). The question Beauvoir fearlessly raises is precisely that of the weight of this past. Will the shortness of their future and the weight of the past necessarily close off all outlets to the woman and her husband? Will the process of aging lead them to cling to routine, to the advantages of their experience, to the point where they do not merely fall behind the times but stubbornly come into conflict with the present age because it endangers their economic or ideological interests? (382–83).[1] But such circumstances, whereby one clings to the weight of the past do not happen for an individual in isolation. The life of the individual takes place only in the context of the society, the life with others. Perpetually out of date, the aging woman or man must find a way to tear themselves free from a past that holds them in its grip, but even as they *become*, they seem to loose ground. The sciences grow more and more complex, the number of things one neither knows nor understands increases. Given this situation, some individuals, unable to face the expanding and infinite future, begin to loathe novelty, to despise change, and even to deny what Beauvoir takes to be human nature itself, that is, the very fact of our transcendence (382–83).[2]

The question she raises is obviously one of great importance. How are we to will ourselves free? All humans are mortal, all feel the tragic ambiguity of existing the past and the future in a moment that seems to be nothing, but if it is truly the case, as Beauvoir claims, that no existence founds itself moment by moment, on the model of the natural sciences for which each moment is exactly the same as any other, and no moment has special significance, then we must ask ourselves what structure and what ethical stand makes the gentleness of memory and the gaiety of future promises possible for mortals (Beauvoir 1976, 25, 27)? How can we realize the joy of existence even in our aging years? How are we to continue to effect the transition from nature to ethics in the process of aging (25)?

Classical Science and Natural Law

Let us begin with the question of nature. If, for Beauvoir, we must effect the transition from nature to ethics, this is because human life is circumscribed by nature and natural laws. What are those natural laws? The laws of nature that are relevant for the organization and evolution of life are the laws that give an account of nature as it evolves from moment to moment in an open system through which matter and energy flow (Margulis and Sagan 1997, 32).[3] Since

---

1 Beauvoir notes that some very old people delight in innovation even though they feel themselves unable to participate in it.
2 Beauvoir cites many old persons amazed and delighted by the modern world as well as those who refuse it by shutting themselves up in the past.
3 These are the structures described by non-linear thermodynamics. Margulis is an evolutionary biologist whose work focuses on the relation between the evolution of life and thermodynamics. Sagan is a science writer.

the time of Isaac Newton, the efforts of classical science were directed toward explaining these processes. In her novel, *She Came to Stay*, each of Beauvoir's principle characters, Xavière, Françoise and Pierre exist as the embodiment of these laws. According to these natural scientific principles, existence, as determined by nature's laws, seeks to found itself moment to moment through the limit or negation of what has come before so as to remain absolutely free of the past. But Beauvoir refers to this as "the absurdity of the clinamen," the absurdity of homogeneous moments in which the direction of an atom is absolutely determined through the negation of what took place the previous moment (Beauvoir 1976, 26). The clinamen is a concept attributed to Lucretius who defines it as a type of atomic motion, a moment to moment motion that is a spontaneous and infinitely small change of direction in the course of an atom's downward fall resulting from the chance collision of one atom with another, without which nothing could be created in nature (Serres 2000, 21).

Although the clinamen is a physical concept and appears to epitomize nature's deterministic pathways, at least as classical science theorizes them, philosopher of science, Michel Serres, has put forward the thesis that Lucretius conceives of the clinamen in relation to free will or change. Rather than following a determinate path prescribed by a causal sequence of events, as Beauvoir's criticism of the term implies, Serres's maintains that atoms swerve, thereby originating a new movement that appears to "snap the bonds of fate, the everlasting sequence of cause and effect."[4] This, he claims, is the clinamen. In this sense, to exist, to be a being, is to escape the causal determination of the past; it is to deviate moment by moment, from nothingness to nothingness, where each new moment is an effect of the past but breaks completely with that past and so can be defined as nothingness. In this sense to exist is to deviate from a state of equilibrium that is mute, motionless and passive, governed wholly by natural forces outside of oneself. This means that existence or being, what Beauvoir calls transcendence, denotes deviation from the position in which one has been fixed by other forces that are necessarily external forces. As Serres writes, "we do not exist ... except through and by this deviation from equilibrium. Everything is deviation from equilibrium, except Nothing. That is to say, Identity" (21).

According to the theory of the clinamen, nature runs its course toward an equilibrium, but deviations appear stochastically. Unable to be predicted precisely, they swerve forth as minute, infinitesimal deviations from equilibrium, thereby producing something new rather than nothing new, which would be some-

---

4 Cited in Susan Mapstone (2008, 8). Mapstone cites Lucretius' *On the Nature of the Universe* (1994, 44).

thing that is identical with the past (22). As such, this description appears to conform to the very idea of transcendence, to the idea that we are beings who make ourselves a lack of being, a nothing*ness*, in order that there might be being, in order that there might be something new (Beauvoir 1976, 11). And yet, Beauvoir objects to this. What is it, for Beauvoir that makes this conception of nature absurd for existence? Crucially, it is that ethics is not physics and that we must find a way to transition from nature to ethics (25).[5]

We have said that the characters Xavière, Françoise and Pierre embrace and embody the clinamen. Xavière, in particular, characterizes the world and other people as physical entities that attempt to resist her deviation, thereby limiting her power to exist, that is, to change course in infinitesimally small increments through chance collisions with other atomistic entities. It is the resistance of other entities, be they persons or events, to her changes of direction, which are the negation of being, that she wishes to overcome. "'I'd like to live alone in the world and keep my freedom'" declares Xavière. To which Françoise counters, "'You don't understand; to follow a more or less consistent line of conduct does not constitute slavery' ... 'You give them rights over you,' Xavière said scornfully" (Beauvoir 1990, 103). Xavière disapproves of and is disgusted by the idea of other people to the extent that she takes any interaction with others to be equivalent to being bound by shackles that inhibit her spontaneous changes in direction, her deviations from consistency. As such, other people are nothing but what fix you. Like atoms in the void, they force you into equilibrium, the zero degree that is deterioration, ruin and death (Serres 2000, 22). In this sense, it is not surprising that Xavière resents any others who take an interest in her well being, including Françoise and Pierre, for she can only imagine that this is an attempt like her own, at objectification, fixing her existence in a set trajectory, as certain as it is final. Nevertheless, her fear of being fixed does not keep Xavière from extending invitations to Françoise, but such invitations seem much more like "imperious orders" giving Françoise the feeling that one could never live with Xavière, but only beside her (Beauvoir 1990, 136). To live with Xavière, it would be necessary that she ceases objectifying others, that she recognizes them as existing independently, as free beings, in relation to herself.

Alternating, as she says, between "brainstorms and lethargy," Xavière's determination to evade all consistency also keeps her from taking up a profession; she both denigrates any possible course of study offered to her and despairs of

---

5 Contrast this with Serres's view: "Morality is physics. An exact knowledge of natural things. ... Its reduction to the objective is a part of the system. ... The theory of knowledge is isomorphic with that of being." So says Michel Serres of Lucretius' atomism in *The Birth of Physics* (Serres 2000, 38).

her own abilities (108, 127). Given the opportunity to study acting with the great professionals of Pierre's theater, Xavière ends by declaring the profession of acting and those who engage in it not worthy of her time or effort. In this manner, Xavière is even more insolent and full of pride than Pierre, who also rejects the idea of consistency, and "with the fury of a renegade offered up his past in sacrifice to his present" (127).[6] But each time Pierre moves on, he deliberately places in Françoise's hands the dark responsibility for his former self which he now rejects and condemns, leaving Françoise in the cold and wondering, once Xavière and Pierre join forces, to what extent if any she is protected from the two of them.

Although it is Beauvoir who first realized and gave voice to the idea of the clinamen as the nothingness of identity, it was an idea extensively adopted by Jean-Paul Sartre two years later in *Being and Nothingness*. Beauvoir came to reject the *naturalism* of this position, this *transcendental* position, in favor of an ontology and ethics of ambiguity that does not demand consistency, insofar as the latter might well condemn the aging to the frozen past, but that also is not caught up in the arbitrary moment by moment destruction of the past and of other human beings. Let us try to see how she works this out.

The Weight of the Past

In *The Coming of Age* Beauvoir reaffirms the idea that life is based on self-transcendence, but it seems as though this has taken on a new meaning. The nihilistic self-transcendence of Xavière means that she avoids any commitments to persons or projects. The French title, *L'inviteé*, indicates clearly that Xavière is in Paris at all at the *invitation* of Pierre and Françoise. However, although Françoise and Pierre support her financially and mentor her professionally, she remains indifferent and without gratitude toward them. With Pierre, whose creative intelligence and life she admires and envies, Xavière seeks to make herself into a fascinating object, an "I" who puts herself beneath the look of the Other to make him look at her as a privileged and meaningful object, infinitely and unsurpassably deep. This is not, of course, love; it is the project of trying to make herself be loved to the exclusion of Françoise. Once she has succeeded in being recognized by Pierre as a free subjectivity, Xavière refuses to recognize his own free, subjective existence, objectifying him as her admirer alone and driving to an end the intellectual and intimate relationship between Pierre and

---

6 This negation of the past is the effect of the clinamen. It is a limit or a change of direction in the smallest possible time.

Françoise.[7] Offered friendship by Françoise, Xavière instead objectifies her, remains cold to friendship and oblique to Françoise's own subjectivity, until, beaten down by Xavière's superiority and open contempt of her, Françoise becomes so ill that she must be hospitalized.

Although she is only 30, Françoise begins to see herself as a mature, meaning old woman. Her illness reduces her to an inert mass such that "she was not even an organic body" (179). Xavière makes it clear that becoming ill is a serious fault, that the struggle for life is a humiliation and weakness that cannot be accepted. Like the adventurer, Xavière asserts her existence without taking into account that of others. Françoise, attuned to and infuriated by Xavière's objectification of her, can find no solution here but that of nature's clinamen. In order to go on with her own life, to open a new direction, Françoise negates and eliminates Xavière wholly; she turns on the gas in her room: Xavière dies. But this action simply follows nature, or more accurately, one aspect of nature. Françoise does not plan to destroy Xavière, it simply happens. It is the turbulent and unexpected negation of an otherwise objectified state of affairs that has the effect of freeing Françoise. It negates the objectification of Françoise by Xavière, but only by negating Xavière absolutely, an act in accordance with nature's contingent possibilities. But insofar as this act follows from the absurd law of the clinamen, it is not ethical, and so it seems that, for Beauvoir, in *The Ethics of Ambiguity* and *The Coming of Age*, as well as in other literary works, self-transcendence must take on a new meaning.

In the latter text in particular, it is one's own life and not other people that set one up as "Another," as objectified, it is "the books I have written, which now *outside me* constitute my works, and define me as their author" (Beauvoir 1972, 373, emphasis added). And with age, our own past weighs us down more and more. The future we had freely chosen for ourselves has turned into a fact, a necessity; our own past is an otherness and our projects are frozen in that past. Yet, for Beauvoir, this view fails to be an ethical view insofar as it corresponds only to the physical view of deterministic, that is, rule-following, classical nature. Freedom is not a thing or a physical quality of things, and unlike physical nature, freedom has a specific direction as well as a unique founding moment, which is the moment of choice (Beauvoir 1976, 24–25). For human beings, the world, objects, bodies, are finite physically, physically destined to wear down and wear out, to fall apart and die in what Serres describes as the "shifting aggregations of atoms," so that, following Lucretius, it appears that "the world, objects,

---

7 Sartre's view of love seems to be a perfect reflection of the conflicts characterized by objectification in Beauvoir's novel (Sartre 1984, 488–90).

bodies, my very soul are, at the moment of their birth, in *decline*. ... Nature declines and this is its act of birth. ... The past, the present, the future, the dawn of appearance and death, tenacious illusions, are only the declinations of matter" (Serres 2000, 34).[8]

This purely physical decline is also purely external, purely outside oneself, an effect of external forces, nature's laws, driving atomistic entities to collide with one another. But Beauvoir has already, in her ethics, discovered something more than the purely external, physical view. She accepts that one's own mortality is something only the outsider can see; it is something general, abstract and assumed from without. In other words, mortality is not the object of an inward experience so "I do not *feel* it" (Beauvoir 1972, 441). However, Beauvoir asks, is there not, in addition to this view, the ontological structure of being-for-itself, so that even if we were to live an additional hundred years, or forever, finitude would not be taken from us? Unlike the immortal Fosca, in Beauvoir's novel, *All Men Are Mortal*, who ceases to be human when he ceases taking up projects and turns away from all activities, when we make ourselves, when we take up a project in the world, that is how and when we make ourselves finite, and that is when we have only ourselves, our own past, our own skin to outstrip.[9]

In other words, ontologically, our own finished projects fall back into the realm of our own Other, and we are left, finite, always seeking the new, in order to be at all. Such a "passionate heroism," is precisely what the aging must embrace, "delighting in a progress that must soon be cut short by death, [the] carrying on, the attempt to outdo oneself in full knowledge and acceptance of one's finitude" (410). This ontological view, we maintain, is not the abstract and universal view of classical physics, which is an external view of objects in motion, nor is it pure inwardness, matter reduced to mind. In what does it consist? How is such a view possible? It is discoverable, we will argue, in a philosophy of ambiguity, a philosophy for which human beings are neither purely the effects of external relations nor pure mind and inwardness, nor a synthesis of the two.

---

8 "Physics is concerned with weight, heat and fluids. Hence with falling, with the irreversible and with flow. All this needs a slope. The *clinamen* produces just this inclined path. It quantifies a minimal sense, by which all things have existence and meaning [sens]" (35).
9 See Beauvoir 1992 and 1972, 377–78.

The Logic of Ambiguity

Beauvoir states that humans *feel* their tragic ambiguity; they *exist* the past and the future in a moment that is itself nothing (Beauvoir 1976, 7). This is the meaning of the claim that they are the beings that make themselves lack in order that there might be being. In denying this, philosophers deny ambiguity, they deny that subjectivity realizes itself only as a presence in the world, a surging for-one-self but one that is always and immediately given for others. If this were a purely natural process, there would be no ethics. When Françoise unexpectedly opens the gas valve in Xavière's room, she does so impulsively, driven by Xavière's brutal collision with and intrusion into Françoise's attempts to be free, to free herself from Xavière's objectification of her. But ethics implies intentionality, it implies that we *make* ourselves lack, not to destroy but in order to *disclose* the being of the world and the being of others (7–12). "I should like this sky, this quiet water to think themselves within me, that it might be I whom *they* express in flesh and bone," says Beauvoir, while "I" joyfully remain at a distance so that sky and water may exist before me (13, emphasis added).[10]

In *Being and Nothingness*, Sartre argues that we humans are encompassed by nothingness, the permanent possibility of non-being such that what being will be arises on the basis of what it is not. Logically, we may formulate this by saying that being is x and outside of x, it is nothing, although, for Sartre, non-being is real (Sartre 1984, 33–36). Of course, given the law of conservation of mass in a closed system, it might be argued that being-in-itself is fully positive and according to nature's laws, can contain no negation, that negation and nothingness only imply failed expectations, thereby making the proposition "X is not," only a judgment, nothing real. So it seems that it is only for humans that a storm or earthquake destroys and not for the earth. But, for Sartre, we must come to understand that the proposition "X is not" presupposes a comprehension of nothingness as such, and conduct in the face of nothingness which is a human fact. The ground of *human* perception is for this reason an original nihilation necessary for a figure to appear but into which it melts like unwanted faces in a café when one is searching for one who is not there and who thereby appears but only as a nothingness on a ground of nihilation that is the cafe, a nothingness that is real for the searcher and not merely a thought. Such negation, Sartre claimed, is an abrupt break in continuity; an original, irreducible event, but also a perpetual presence in and outside us (36–44). It is, in short, the clinamen, that unexpected change of direction, that swerve in nature that

---

10 The "I" must remain at a distance for there to be an ethical stance.

originates new movement, and that appears, as was said above, to snap the bonds of fate, the everlasting sequence of cause and effect.

Being and nothingness rests on the law of non-contradiction, which claims that for any proposition, that proposition and its negation are never both true, however both may be false. It also seems to require the law of excluded middle, namely, that for a given proposition and its negation, at least one must be true *and* they cannot both be true. This means, of course, that for Sartre, Being cannot be both some x and its negation, only one can be true and at least some position x is true until superseded by its negation. By negating the being that we have been, we declare the past to be false and the present to be true.

It seems, however, that Beauvoir denies this. Transcendence cannot be just a formal mathematical or Stoic freedom. She proposes that it is a sort of a double negation in which we first make ourselves lack, but then we go on to negate the lack so that it can be filled by the Other expressing itself *in me*, even as I remain distant from my "I." As my lack is filled by *the other in me*, I may affirm both of our positive existences. But logically, this double negation is somewhat problematic, for it presupposes that the future is already actual, that we have a God's eye view of it insofar as we know it will be true, when in fact, the future is open.

Among logical axioms, the Principle of Excluded Middle has been called the most flawed and obvious misstatement of fact. The Principle of Excluded Middle, we recall, states that for a given proposition "P," either "P" or "not-P" *must be true*, thus it affirms the fundamental principle of binary thinking and the logic of identity (Tasić 2001, 40–41). However, for the branch of mathematics and logic, called "Intuitionism," (which has been associated with Henri Bergson and Edmund Husserl) mathematical or logical statements, whether affirmative or negative, express completion in a temporality that "flows with the flux" of the thinker's own inner time, with an open future and unpredictable free choices, there is no a priori fixed determination of the elements of a proof (40). Given the temporal nature of existence, a negative statement that expresses the incompatibility of two mathematical constructions that are represented by the subject and predicate of a sentence is, as Beauvoir has stated, absurd. Time is nonatomic, it does not consist of infinitesimally divisible points each of which negates the previous, but is more like a "fluid paste from which points cannot be picked out with atomist accuracy" (Van Stigt 1998, 40). The mathematician or logician is always able to choose how to construct any given sequence, thus every element in a construction has an *indeterminate future*. And the same structure could account for choice in all human endeavors.

In this logic as in Beauvoir's ethics, failure or lack is not overcome or negated, but is assumed as ambiguity, the ambiguity of existence that each human must accept and realize as the passage from a deterministic view of nature to ethics. We rejoin ourselves only to the extent we agree to this distance from ourselves. With age, this distance becomes all the more crucial, for what we must negate is our own past, the weight of our own past projects as they define us. And what, we ask, what will take up the place of the other within?

Beauvoir argues that a mathematician or a scientist, like André in "The Age of Discretion," has already done away with his subjectivity in order to think along the lines of a universally valid rational system. In this sense, he or she has been fortunate to have never worked alone but to have always taken part in a collaborative effort. But the evolution of science relentlessly demands the new, and that does involve an intellectual break with what has come before, with habits of mind, out-of-date methods and seemingly self-evident ideas. To accomplish this, the aging scientist may find it necessary to follow the lecture courses offered to students, doubly negating one's own expertise to make room for something new. Or the scientist may have to follow out the implications of contraries, ideas that conflict with his or her own earlier work (Beauvoir 1972, 388–91). Euler, Galileo and Laplace carried out important mathematical work in their seventies. Michelson published his experiments on the speed of light in his eighties, yet there is no denying that these accomplishments were quite unusual (387).

Beauvoir's character André takes the route that is most likely. He carries out his research in a group with other younger scientists. His project will continue into the future with or without him as long as he keeps adequate distance from himself in the present. He has a "fine team," source of all the "fresh ideas," but as the chief investigator, he must allow these fresh ideas to be asserted even if they are ambiguous, that is, even if they are contraries, for contraries in the work may be asserted without collapsing the system. They make the future possible since at some stage one or another of them may be shown to be true in a manner that leads to other new ideas. Unlike the scientist, who describes the world from outside, the philosopher, "wishes to understand the relationship between the world and man posited as a subject" (395).

And, given that it may take a lifetime to grasp all the implications of her original philosophical intuition, the philosopher's task proceeds well according to a logic of ambiguity. Having arrived at a philosophical intuition, the philosopher must lay out a system but then, *stand back*, distance herself from it, criticize it and allow it to be the site of fresh problems. The philosophical system must remain open, open to its own ambiguities (396). So when the scientist, André, decides to go back to being a student and the philosopher-writer reluctantly discovers her own resistances to altering her habits of mind, they are both, in their own way, plunging back into ambiguity.

The Ethics of Ambiguity

Therefore, unlike Françoise in *She Came to Stay*, the woman does not resolve her conflicts with others naturalistically, which is to say, nihilistically, but resolves them ethically. Extremely disappointed and suffering from her son's decision not to pursue the intellectual life but instead, and with his father-in-law's assistance, to go into government service, the woman cuts off all contact with him. She objectifies her son, Philippe, and his wife, Irène, calling them "half-wits" mired in bad faith, seeking only success and dishonoring themselves by this choice (Beauvoir 1969, 40 – 41). In her fury, she objectifies André, accusing him of being a plotter, plotting against her, behind her back, with their son, until she is carried away "thousands of miles from him and from ... [herself], into a desert that is both scorching and freezing cold" (42). And she wonders if she and André will simply end their days together, but this time, living only side by side, two atoms in chain.

Even worse, it is just at this moment that the first harsh criticisms of the woman's book appear. Shocked, she characterizes her critic as an old fool and bitterly decides that she herself is no longer capable of writing. In her fury, she sends André off to visit his mother in the countryside without her. Yet by existing under conditions that can only be characterized as contraries that violate the Law of Excluded Middle, *both* scorching *and* freezing in the desert, the woman finally begins to act ethically. She follows André and walks with him under the moon. "Little star that I see, Drawn by the moon. The old words, just as they were first written, were there on my lips. They were the link joining me to the past centuries, when the stars shone exactly as they do today" (82). And listening to André's familiar voice, finally, her anger dissipates as she admits the other within.

For her sake, he will quit playing at being old, pitying himself and viewing himself as finished as a scientist. Thus he decides to stop his current research in order to bring his knowledge up to date in his field. But André also tells her that her book failed because she wrote it following the rule of the clinamen. "You set off with a sterile ambition—an ambition of doing something quite new and of excelling yourself" (Beauvoir 1969, 84). In other words, the book was an absolute negation of her previous literary work. For her husband's sake as much as for her own, the woman admits that she will write again and that she will find a new way to exist with her son and his wife, to recognize their subjectivity, their independence from her objectification of them. In short, she will learn to love her son and his wife independently of herself.

Still, Beauvoir cautions, this is not enough. The dilemmas of old age expose the failure of our entire civilization. André suggests to the woman philosopher, his companion and partner, that "from a self-regarding point of view," she may not be able to fulfill her ambition for something quite new, a swerve or unexpectedly new direction that echoes the motion of the clinamen, but that she can still interest readers, she can make them think and enrich them (84–85). But even when our projects aim at goals that lie beyond the limits of our own self-regarding point of view, what hope do we have that our efforts will not be lost? For men and women who are the least exploited, who can make a place for the other within, it is a matter of breaking the silence between them, of finding one another again, and of not looking too far ahead. When the couple sits under the stars, their hands touching, time stops and the fears of old age are allayed by the good fortune of their being together (85). Apart from this, they decide to live for the short-term. There is no question, for them of achieving eternal fame, so that the increased pace of civilization, whereby the present is outdated and lost even before it becomes the past does not overwhelm them (Beauvoir 1972, 379–80).

But beyond this fortunate pair, fortunate in having interesting work and one another, old age is a matter of the exploitation of some groups of human beings by others. Among those who have been most exploited, aging harshly reveals that "the meaning of … [their] existence has been stolen from … [them] from the very beginning," and that although women and men are allowed to reproduce life, they are not given the opportunity to commit themselves to projects that "peopled the world with goals, values and reasons for existence" (542). Life without culture, interests and responsibilities denies transcendence; it denies ambiguity. In order to embrace ambiguity, each and every human being should not look forward to the coming of age alone and empty handed. Ambiguity demands that society look upon women and men as useful at every age, not as atoms able to be negated by other atoms, but as part of a collective in which even the old can fulfill and renew their lives as they prepare to distance themselves one last time from the weight of the past (542–43).[11]

References

Beauvoir, Simone de. 1969. The age of discretion. In *The woman destroyed*. Trans. Patrick O'Brian. New York: Pantheon Books.
Beauvoir, Simone de. 1972. *The coming of age*. Trans. Patrick O'Brian. New York: G. P. Putnam.

---

11 A longer version of this paper appeared in my book, *Postmodern Philosophy and the Scientific Turn*, published by Indiana University Press (2012).

Beauvoir, Simone de. 1976. *The ethics of ambiguity*. Trans. Bernard Frechtman. New York: Citadel Press.

Beauvoir, Simone de. 1990. *She came to stay*. New York: W. W. Norton.

Beauvoir, Simone de. 1992. *All men are mortal*. Trans. Leonard M. Friedman. New York: W. W. Norton.

Hass, Marjorie. 2002. Fluid thinking: Irigaray's critique of formal logic. In *Representing reason: Feminist theory and formal logic*, ed. Rachel Joffe Falmagne and Marjorie Hass. New York: Rowman & Littlefield, 71–88.

Lucretius. 1994. *On the nature of the universe*. Trans. R. E. Latham, revised by John Godwin. Harmondsworth: Penguin Group.

Mapstone, Susan. Non-linear dynamics: The swerve of the atom in Lucretius' *de rerum natura*. http://www.londonconsortium.com/wp-content/uploads/2007/02/map stonestoicsessay.pdf (accessed July 31, 2013).

Margulis, Lynn, and Dorian Sagan. 1997. A universe in heat. In *What is sex?* New York: Simon & Schuster.

Olkowski, Dorothea E. 2012. *Postmodern philosophy and the scientific turn*. Bloomington: Indiana University Press.

Sartre, Jean-Paul. 1984. *Being and nothingness*. Trans. Hazel Barnes. New York: Washington Square Press.

Serres, Michel. 2000. *The birth of physics*. Trans. Jack Hawkes. Manchester: Clinamen Press.

Tasić, Vladimir. 2001. *Mathematics and the roots of postmodern thought*. Oxford: Oxford University Press.

Van Stigt, Walter P. 1998. Brouwer's intuitionist programme. In *From Brouwer to Hilbert: The debate on the foundations of mathematics in the 1920 s*, ed. Paolo Mancosu. Oxford: Oxford University Press, 1–22.

Annemie Halsema
Ethics and Nature

Comment on Dorothea Olkowski

In her essay, Dorothea Olkowski, on the basis of Beauvoir's novels and philosophical works, reflects upon the dilemmas of aging. She asks how we are to prevent falling into the paralysis of a limited future and a frozen past. Olkowski shows that for Beauvoir aging includes the specific problem of upholding the general anthropological feature that characterizes humanity, namely transcendence. The weight of the past for the elderly endangers closing off all outlets, tempting them to cling to routine, instead of embracing novelty and change. The ethical problem for the elderly is how not to surrender to the weight of the past but to keep on living with an eye to the future.

Intermingling Beauvoir's novels and philosophical works, Olkowski not only demonstrates that both genres benefit from each other in Beauvoir's œuvre but also mimes her literary philosophy. Olkowski's narrative style allows her text to vividly illustrate Beauvoir's ideas on ethics and aging. However, in her interpretation Olkowski at some points follows her own path, which is radically different from Beauvoir's.

In the first half of the essay, she relates the problem of aging to "the transition from nature to ethics" (149) that Beauvoir raises in *The Ethics of Ambiguity*. She argues that for Beauvoir transcendence is central to human nature and relates it to the notion "willing oneself free" (cf. 149) that Beauvoir develops in the same essay. Olkowski understands "willing oneself free" as an ethical task that differentiates humans from their nature. And indeed Beauvoir claims that willing oneself free means effectuating the transition from nature to ethics in founding an authentic freedom upon the original freedom of our existence (Beauvoir 1962, 35). In what follows, Olkowski concentrates upon the question of nature, claiming that for Beauvoir "human life is circumscribed by nature and natural laws" (149). For Beauvoir, however, "nature" does not so much imply the naturalness of humankind that we have to overcome; rather, she differentiates herself from philosophical notions of man's naturalness, precisely because ethics *excludes* nature. She refers to Hegel's radical differentiation between nature and ethics and to his claim—in opposition to Kant—that in understanding humankind as being natural we cannot propose an ethics for it (Beauvoir 1962, 14). For Hegel, ethical consciousness can only subsist if there is a sharp distinction between nature and ethics. The ethical law is not a natural one, and humans can only be ethical as social beings—living in a society—and not as natural ones. Hegel's argument is used by Beauvoir in order to show that an ethics cannot be based upon human nature, any more than it can be based upon God; thus, it cannot be proclaimed that human life follows natural laws.

When we follow Olkowski's route, it should be noted that she brings forward an interesting thermo-dynamic conception of nature in which the laws of physics "give an account of nature as it evolves from moment to moment in an open system through which matter and energy flow" (149). Nature in this account already in itself implicates change and contingency. Such a concept of nature contradicts one that takes nature as being fixed and determined and thus allows for thinking transcendence and freedom. The notion of transcendence that results from this conception of nature, however, is, as Olkowski shows, not the one that Beauvoir embraces. Beauvoir rejects it because natural freedom and transcendence are not willed, and not directed, but erupt spontaneously. This raises interesting questions with respect to Beauvoir's supposition of free human will as being opposed to will-less nature. It is a pity that Olkowski does not further elaborate this argument but instead follows Beauvoir in the transition from nature to ethics.

The thermo-dynamic notion of nature also leads Olkowski to considering nature a very broad concept that applies to human relationships and to the way we relate to our creations and projects. Therewith she undoubtedly takes another route than does Beauvoir, which is perhaps legitimate in the light of Serres' work on physics that she refers to but leads to problems in interpreting Beauvoir. Olkowski refers to the Lucretian notion of "the clinamen" in order to describe a manner of existing in the context of which we treat others as objects or instruments, which is exemplified by the character of Xavière in *She Came to Stay*. The notion of the clinamen makes change understandable without determining a cause, yet also without understanding the atom as being absolutely free. Michel Serres explains that the theory of the clinamen has found a haven in subjectivity, "moving from the world to the soul, from physics to metaphysics" (Serres 2000, 3). Following Serres, the clinamen theory could be applied to the problem of human free will, as opposed to destiny and causation. But for Beauvoir in her novel, reducing others to objects (or holding on to one's past projects) is an ethical problem and not a natural one. For Beauvoir it is not a consequence of human nature but rather of not realising one's ontological freedom. It is a problem of not *willing* oneself free although *having* ontological freedom. Beauvoir compares ontological freedom without willing oneself free, that is, without choosing a direction towards something, with the random indirection of the movement of the atom (Beauvoir 1962, 35). She distinguishes undirected or willed human spontaneity from the positive assumption of projects. Subjects who are lazy, cowardly, impatient, and deny their projects while committing them, do not will their freedom and resemble the useless pulsation of life. In order to will their freedom, they need to identify positively with their projects and with others. For, willing oneself free for Beauvoir includes willing others free (Beauvoir 1962, 104), and precisely not treating them as objects. Thus, for Beauvoir ethics starts with realizing one's ontological freedom, with using one's freedom in order to liberate and engage with others. Not realizing one's freedom is not a natural problem which leaves one into the realm of nature but rather is unethical.

Olkowski recognizes relationships of the clinamen-kind between individuals in Beauvoir's novel *She Came to Stay*, and relates the fixation of the aging individual to its past to the physical view of nature. Therewith she not only gives another interpretation of nature and of the transition between nature and ethics in Beauvoir's works, but she also enlarges the conception of nature to the domain of ethics.

References

Beauvoir, Simone de. 1962. *Pour une morale de l'ambiguïté suivi de Pyrrhus et Cinéas*. Paris: Gallimard.
Serres, Michel. 2000. *The birth of physics*. Trans. Jack Hawkes. Manchester: Clinamen Press.

Part Three: **Age and Time**

Sara Heinämaa
Transformations of Old Age
Selfhood, Normativity, and Time

> *Also I myself will die—like I was once born, developed into adulthood and got old. But the question is, what this means.*

This statement could well be from Simone de Beauvoir's late work, *The Coming of Age*, but it could equally well belong to Sartre's or Merleau-Ponty's reflections on the temporality of the human condition. It comes, however, from a more distant source which is less familiar to contemporary feminist theorists and philosophers of life: the quote is from Husserl's reflections on the finiteness of human existence.[1] The cited paragraph illustrates well Husserl's mature insight that death and birth, together with historicity, unconsciousness, and sexual difference, belong among the transcendental problems to be studied by genetic phenomenology (Husserl 1970, 187–88).[2] The philosophical task is not to explain these phenomena but to explicate their meanings and their roles in the constitution of intersubjectivity and objectivity (Husserl 1970, 187–88).[3]

This chapter discusses Simone de Beauvoir's approach to old age within the methodological framework of classical Husserlian phenomenology. My aim is not to offer a historical reconstruction of Beauvoir's *The Coming of Age* nor a comprehensive reading or a detailed interpretation of her text. Rather, I will focus on three insights that I find philosophically most important and tenable in Beauvoir's work, and I will develop these insights into a systematic account of the phenomenon of aging. I will argue that aging is fundamentally a personal transformation, a change in one's relation to oneself, to others and to the world which is not accountable by mere biological or social factors. My critical-con-

---

1 Husserl 1992, 332; cf. Husserl 1989, 89.
2 Genetic phenomenology studies the *temporal* order of meaning constitution. It does not confine itself to the investigation of particular histories but, by the methods of eidetic variation, aims at illuminating the essential steps and phases in all temporal institution or establishment of meaning and sense. The mature Husserl argues that static analyses are a necessary part of phenomenology but not sufficient in themselves because phenomenology aims at accounting for the structures of meaning as well as for their geneses and origins (Husserl 1960, 66–81; 1968, 208–17; 1978, 316–20). For an introduction to genetic phenomenology, see Steinbock 1995; cf. Bachelard 1968; Sokolowski 1964.
3 For an account of birth and death as transcendental problems, see Steinbock 1995, 134–37; cf. Steinbock 2001, xxxii–xxxiv; Heinämaa 2010a and 2010b. For an account of *sexual difference* as a transcendental problem, see Heinämaa 2003, 21–23, and Heinämaa 2004.

structive approach to *The Coming of Age* aims at making a new contribution to the philosophy of aging but at the same time it is intended to demonstrate that we—as today's theorists of the human condition—have much to learn from Beauvoir's fearless approach and her clear insight.

In my understanding, *The Coming of Age* is a methodological twin sister of *The Second Sex*. In a very similar fashion as in her first extensive study of the human condition,[4] Beauvoir offers a double illumination of her subject matter. She tackles the problem of the old age—as she tackled the problem of sexual difference—in two different ways, first empirically and then philosophically. The first part of *The Coming of Age* discusses experiential findings, from the fields of natural and human-social sciences, biosciences, sociology, anthropology, ethnology, and history. The second part takes another approach and proposes a different task for reflection. Beauvoir starts from lived experiences and treats them as particular examples of experiencing. She does not proceed by inductive inferences or by empirical generalizations. Instead, she sees as her task to capture the necessary structural features of the experience of aging, "the constants" of "human reality," as she herself calls them.

This approach to lived and intentional experiences can best be characterized by classical phenomenological concepts: the philosopher begins from singular experiences and aims at capturing the first person givenness of experiencing; his[5] task is not to dwell on particulars or to generalize over them but to proceed to study the necessary structural features of all experience. The two reductions—the transcendental-phenomenological reduction and the eidetic reduction—are needed to liberate the investigation from all natural and habitual presuppositions concerning the experienced object and the experiencing subject. By purifying his consciousnesses from theoretical and practical positings and from traditional preconceptions, and by imaginatively varying the experience thus purified, the philosopher is able to bring into focus the constants of conscious life. He is not just interested in the structures of his own personal life, or of the lives of his contemporaries, but aims at finding the constants of all human

---

4 Beauvoir uses the term "la réalité humaine" ("human reality," in English). This is usually understood as a translation of Heidegger's "Dasein" but it covers what Husserl calls the *meaning* or the *sense* of human existence (e. g., Husserl 1993).
5 I use the male pronouns "he" and "his" in the neutral sense which refers to a human being. I have chosen to do this, because my quotes are from the English translations of Beauvoir's works which follow this problematic convention (the corresponding problem strains, of course, the original French text). In my own language (Finnish), personal pronouns lack gender marking so that this problem does not occur.

life—intimate and familiar life but also historically distant and culturally alien. In this enterprise, his best alliances are the historian, the novelist and the poet.[6]

We find this aim clearly explicated by Beauvoir at the beginning of the second part of *The Coming of Age*.[7] Beauvoir does not rest satisfied with reporting the plurality and richness of human experiences but proceeds to describe and analyze the universal features that transcend cultural and historical peculiarities. She writes:

> [w]e can try to isolate the constants and to find the reasons for the differences. ... To be sure, the state of the aged has not been the same in all places and at all times; but rising through this diversity there are constants that make it possible for me to compare various pieces of evidence independently of date. (279, italics in the original)[8]

To be sure, the investigation of the constants of human life is not Beauvoir's primary interest. Rather, her main goal is to put forward an ethical and political argument concerning the dignity and respectful treatment of human beings. However, her ethical and political claims rest on her existential-phenomenological insight into the universal structures of human life, and the critical development of this insight is goal of my essay.

Beauvoir's existential-phenomenological claim about aging is that it concerns three fundamental ontological structures of human life: its temporality, its objectification in interpersonal relations and its necessarily bodily dimension.[9] On the basis of her remarks, I will develop three arguments about the phenomenon of aging: first, the claim that aging presents itself to us originally as a personal metamorphosis; second, the idea that this metamorphosis involves a radical change in the habitual self-objectification of the person; and third, the thesis that aging affects not just our futural horizon but equally all temporal registers and ultimately the whole structure of lived time.

---

6 Cf. Beauvoir 2004a; Husserl 1983, § 70, 145–48; Merleau-Ponty 1964.
7 The methodological clarification is located in a similar way in *The Coming of Age* as in *The Second Sex*.
8 Cf. Beauvoir 1996, 361; 1989, xxxvi.
9 In the beginning of the second part of *The Coming of Age*, Beauvoir lists the following components of the experience of aging: body, image, time, history, praxis, others and the world, and argues that these are co-implicatory and cannot be studied in isolation (1996, 279).

The Event of Aging

The first crucial insight that we find in Beauvoir's treatment of old age concerns the ontic sense of aging: The phenomenon of getting old does not consists of any progressive deterioration or slow alteration but of a *sudden event* or series of such events. More precisely, aging is experientially not a gradual process but is an unexpected happening that takes us by surprise.

Beauvoir uses several different terms to emphasize the event-character of aging; she talks about "a surprise" (292), "a revelation" (290), "a metamorphosis" (283), "a transformation" (290) and "a crisis" (379), and writes: "The fact that the passage of universal time should have brought about a private, personal metamorphosis is something that takes us completely aback" (283). And in another section:

> We must assume a reality that is certainly ourselves although it reaches us from the outside and although we cannot grasp it. There is an insoluble contradiction between the obvious clarity of the inward feeling that guarantees our unchanging quality and the objective certainty of our transformation. All we can do is to waver from the one to the other, never managing to hold them both firmly together. (290)

Thus, Beauvoir offers a very different account of aging than the one we know from the empirical sciences of life and nature. The aging human body is not equated with deteriorating animal organisms or compared to vegetable life. The phenomenon of human age has its own meaning structures and it determines its own parameters of investigation that undermine all kinds of naturalistic and biologistic reductions.[10]

Beauvoir's philosophical approach differs also from that of the social sciences in which the person is studied primarily as an individual in a collective of individuals. Beauvoir accounts for aging in the first person perspective: she asks primarily how the change presents itself, or is given, to the person who undergoes it (279). Others are not excluded from this type of investigation, but they take part in the constitution of sense only as *co-constituters* and thus depend on the constitutive activity of the experiencing person. As co-constituters others cannot determine us from outside but need our active participation and communicative co-operation.

---

10 This methodological argument is best known by the powerful formulation that Heidegger gave to it in *Being and Time* (1992), but the argument has deep roots in the phenomenological and existential traditions. For these roots, see Heinämaa (2010a and 2010c).

Before proceeding to study the two other insights into old age that we find in Beauvoir's discourse, it is necessary to spend some time critically investigating the concepts with which she operates while describing aging as a metamorphosis. It is important to notice that the concepts that Beauvoir uses to emphasize the suddenness of aging are of two different kinds. On the one hand, she uses the ontological concepts of *metamorphosis* and *transformation* but, on the other hand, she also operates with epistemological concepts, such as *discovery, revelation,* and *realization.* These two types of concepts have different implications.

The concepts of *metamorphosis* and *transformation* propose that aging is, or involves, a change in one's fundamental way of being, i. e., an ontological change.[11] The epistemological concepts, on the other hand, give the impression that it is merely the cognitive experience of coming to know one's new state that is sudden and that the transformation itself is or may be gradual and relatively slow. So we must ask what Beauvoir's position really is on this matter: Does she argue that aging itself is sudden or does she just propose that our realization of the phenomenon comes unexpectedly? Was my judgment hasty, when I claimed that the first result of her reflection concerns the abruptness of aging?

In my understanding Beauvoir's philosophical discourse does not choose between the traditional alternatives of knowing and being or the epistemological and the ontological. The fundamental tension or ambiguity that she thematizes is not that between inner knowledge and external reality, or between inner sense and outer substantiation. Rather, the tension is between *two different forms of self-relating,* one proceeding by immediate experience and the other constituted via relations with other subjects (Beauvoir 1976, 55). Both ways of relating to oneself involve epistemological as well as ontological parameters. At the beginning of *The Ethics of Ambiguity,* Beauvoir thematizes the duality of the human condition as follows:

> "The continuous work of our life," says Montaigne, "is to build death." … Man knows and thinks this tragic ambivalence which the animal and the plant merely undergo. A new paradox is thereby introduced into his destiny. "Rational animal," "thinking reed," he escapes from his natural condition without, however, freeing himself from it. He is still a part of this world of which he is a consciousness. He asserts himself *as a pure internality* against which no external power can take hold, and he also experiences himself *as a thing* crushed by the dark weight of other things. (7, emphases added)

---

11 On the historical-philosophical problems involved in the concepts of metamorphosis, see Songe-Møller 2008.

The crisis of aging accentuates this necessary ambiguity of our existence, the transcendental fact that we are constantly given to ourselves both *directly* as a unique viewpoint to the whole world and *via others* as a worldly thing among other worldly things. At the same time the phenomenon exacerbates the cognitive tension between inner certainty and objective knowledge. Both tensions—the ontological and the epistemological—constantly characterize our condition, but the metamorphoses of maturation and aging bring them to the fore (Beauvoir 1996, 292–96). Thus understood, aging is a transition from one existential situation to another both of which involve an ontological as well as an epistemological duality: we are given to ourselves and we know ourselves directly; but due to our relations to others we are and we understand ourselves also through intersubjective mediation. This complex structure is brought to change in the event of aging. Thus we have to ask: What part of us, or who, exactly is changed in this metamorphosis? Beauvoir's *The Coming of Age* gives us an important clue also about the subject of the transformation.

Embodiment and its Two Aspects: Alienness and Normativity

The second important insight that we find in Beauvoir's discourse concerns the particular aspect of our selfhood that undergoes the metamorphosis of aging. Beauvoir argues that it is not the whole of me that changes in the event of aging but only one part of me, i.e. one moment or sense of selfhood. In her own words, it is "the other *in* me" who suddenly turns old (1996, 288/306 and 294/312, translation modified, emphasis added). She elaborates this insight further by stating: "Within me it is the other—that is to say the one that I am for others—who is old: and that other *is* myself [*moi*]" (284/302, translation modified, emphasis added). It is worth studying this paradoxical formulation in some detail while keeping in mind the existential question: Who is it exactly that turns old in this metamorphosis?

The first part of Beauvoir's formulation gives a simple answer to the question above: the aspect that turns old in me is the one that is given to others and exists primarily for them. This answer invites the notion that the aged person is like a mask or a role that we have to accept or assume because of our social dependences. Some sections of Beauvoir's reflection support this line of interpretation. Her quotes from Marcel Proust and André Gide, for example, introduce the metaphors of masks, costumes, disguises, roles and play-acting (cf. 1996, 289 and 296), and the Sartrean concepts of *image* and *the unrealizable* that she uses also suggest the idea of an imposed change (291–93).[12] The quote from Proust's *Time Regained* (*Le temps retrouvé*), in particular, is efficient in transmitting the alienating aspect of aging while picturing the aged person as if in a constant masquerade, wandering among acquaintances and friends whom she cannot recognize and who cannot recognize him:

> "At first I could not understand why I found some difficulty in recognizing the master of the house and the guests, and why everyone there was 'made up'—a make-up that usually included powder and that altered them entirely. The prince ... had provided himself with a white beard and as it were with leaden soles which dragged at his feet, so that he seemed to be playing the part of one of the Ages of Life." (Quoted in Beauvoir 1996, 289/307)

However, the second part of Beauvoir's formulation challenges the metaphors of masks, roles and play-acting by identifying the aging other with the subject itself. "Within me it is the other ... who is old," Beauvoir writes, but adds: "and that other is myself."

I want to argue that this paradox must be understood in the frame of Beauvoir's existential-phenomenological account of embodiment. The crucial idea here is that our own bodies are always given to us in a double way: originally and immediately as systems of sensibility and motility, and secondarily and mediately—via our relations with others—as perceptual and movable objects. These are not two separate realities but are two sides or dimensions of one complex phenomenon. This means that, when we speak about the "mask" of old age (296), we must keep in mind that this "mask" is not separate from our own flesh. Rather, it is the "outer side" of our own sensibility and motility, intertwined with the sensations, movements and affections that give us our own bodily processes as well as the external events. This "mask" can never be thrown off, never separated from our sensuous-motor and affective experiences. When we finally drop it, we must also let go of life.

The theatrical metaphors of mask, role, and play-acting are illuminative in thematizing an *internal fission* within the aged subject, between his cogito ("I suffer," "I cry") and his external appearance ("he suffers," "he cries").[13] But

---

12 Compare this argument to Beauvoir's and Sartre's interchange in *Adieux* where she ends up claiming that the experience of temporality that Sartre claims to have is "completely abnormal" (Beauvoir 1984, 418).

13 In *The Coming of Age*, Beauvoir distinguishes between two senses and two constitutive moments of selfhood, the self as the agent of *cogito* and the self (*moi*) as a transcendent object ("psychological pseudo-realities") (Beauvoir 1996, 291 and 398; cf. 1984, 420–21). I have argued elsewhere that, despite her loyalty to Sartre, she never accepted his early argument in his *The*

these metaphorical tools become misleading if we conclude or imply that being aged is a performance, a social or cultural convention or an artificial production. Being old does not mean that we have agreed to play the role of the aged person or have taken this role on us in order to adjust to the reactions, requirements and expectations of others. We do not *act* old. Why would we? We submit to old age and *become* old (cf. Beauvoir 1996, 375 and 540).

Beauvoir accounts for this paradoxical condition in Sartrean terms: she explains that we do not experience our age "in the for-itself mode" but encounter it in our being-for-others.[14] According to her, the disparity comes from the fundamental fact that we learn to differentiate between youth and old age in the faces and bodies of others, and only later come to realize that this distinction also applies to our objectified selves. We do not immediately connect the quality of age to ourselves but by mediation, via our perceptions of others and the other's perceptions of us. Moreover, Beauvoir suggests that we can never relate this quality to our absolute being-for-ourselves (291). She states: "Old age is particularly difficult to assume because we have always regarded it as something alien, a foreign species: 'Can I have become a different being while I still remain myself?'" (283)

The disparity that Beauvoir thematizes can be described more precisely in phenomenological terms in the following manner. The condition of "being old" concerns myself in so far as I am objectified as a perceivable and socially significant body, i. e., given to myself as part of the perceivable and instrumental world that is equally accessible to all agents. This objectified self is not the only aspect of my corporeality. In addition to it, and prior to it, I am given to myself as a touching-touched and moving-moved power. My primary corporeal self is neither a perceivable thing, given equally to all perceivers, nor an invaluable object of the communal world; rather my primary corporeal self is my lived body as it is constituted to me in tactile and kinesthetic sensations, in self-touching and in spontaneous movement.[15] The disparity is thus between my body as an intersub-

---

Transcendence of the Ego that the ego is nothing but a transcendent object (Heinämaa 2003, 57–61); cf. Björk 2008.

14 Also other types of conditions accentuate the tensions between being-for-oneself and being-for-others, e. g., mental and physical sickness and injury, exceptional ugliness and beauty and different types of deformation. Cf. Jenny Slatman's phenomenological interpretation of body-implants (Slatman 2009; Slatman and Widdershoven 2010), and Gail Weiss' discourse on Siamese twins (2008).

15 Cf. Sartre 1998, 404–45; Merleau-Ponty 1995, 90–97; Husserl 1993, 86 and 152–58; Husserl 1970, 213–15.

jectively given entity in the world and my body as the center of all my worldly attachments.

My situation in the perceivable world and in my personal environment changes constantly, throughout my whole life: I am now here in Helsinki working in my office and yesterday I was in Lisbon swimming in the Atlantic. I was sick and now I am well. I have been tired and exhausted but now I am happy and energetic. All these qualities are given in different ways both to myself and to others, and due to my relations with others I also gain an external perspective on my states and qualities.

Occasionally, my immediate self-givenness and my appearance in the intersubjective world may conflict. I may look tired but feel energetic; I may appear sad while just being attentive. Such partial conflicts do not usually mark any global, all-encompassing divergence between self-givenness and intersubjective appearance. Some events, however, inflict a comprehensive change or a crisis of existence. The fundamental equilibrium, established in childhood and youth between self-givenness and objective appearance, is then shaken (283–86). The bodily self that we grasp immediately and "internally" by sensations, movements and affects does not anymore correspond to the bodily self that we know "externally," by the mediation of others. In this sense my existential situation has changed.

Beauvoir argues that the disparity that marks the event of becoming old is *usually* inflicted by the reactions of others. She claims that the revelation of aging comes often from outside and is always connected to my existence for others. "The aged person comes to feel that he is old by means of others, and without having experienced important changes; his inner being does not accept the label that has been stuck to him—he no longer knows who he is." (292)

So according to Beauvoir, age concerns myself primarily insofar as I am for others. However, this objectified sense of self is not foreign to me or imposed on me, but is part of myself insofar as I live in relations with others and insofar as they take part in the constitution of the perceivable world with me (cf. Beauvoir 1984, 420–21).[16] In other words, my external appearance does not remain outer or alien to me—it cannot—as it always already is included in my being in the world.

Beauvoir emphasizes that no *actual* others, no scornful looks or pitiful talks, are needed to trigger the metamorphosis of aging. Our body—as it is given to us in our personal dealings with the world—always implies the look of the other. At the age of sixty, she writes, "Lou Andreas Salomé lost her hair after an illness: up

---

16 Cf. Beauvoir 1976, 55, 61, 71 and 91.

until then she had felt 'ageless'" (1996, 287). To enter the metamorphosis of aging, it is enough that we experience a disparity between the two aspects of our bodies: our bodies as our familiar practical and expressive means of accessing the world, on the one hand, and our bodies as publicly observable objects of the world, on the other hand.

The very same duality manifests itself abruptly already in the transformations of childhood and adolescence, but in old age it receives a specific function, that of announcing our death. The material objects that now fall off from our bodies, or appear on or in them, do not signal a rebirth, as they did in childhood and youth, but function as emblems of an ending: falling hair, cracking teeth, shaking spotted hands, dropped eyelids, thick yellow nails—shadows of our skull.

It is worth studying more closely the givenness of these peculiar "things" which oddly belongs to our bodies but at the same time are alien to us,[17] for they disclose something crucial about the metamorphosis of aging. My point is not that aging is restricted to such phenomena. In addition to them, it also involves drastic changes in our bodily powers and motor capacities. However, I believe that an important general feature about aging is more easily explicated by studying such ambivalent "body parts" than by focusing on the weakening of skills and capacities. This feature is the uncanny character of old age, its abnormal normality or "normal abnormality," as Beauvoir puts it. Distancing from Beauvoir's account, however, I want to argue that old age is not just given to us by the reactions of others and does not just concern our bodies-for-others but also involves changes in the habitual norms of lived bodiliness. So let us study how our most material body parts disclose themselves to us in the process of aging.

When teeth, hairs and nails are separated from our sensing, living bodies, they function as full-fledged material objects accessible to all perceivers equally. They fall to the floor in the very same manner as any worldly objects, and their destruction does not cause any sensations of physical pain or distress in our bodies. Moreover, these objects can be observed, manipulated and studied from different viewpoints—both by ourselves and by others. Usually, they are handled as

---

17 Julia Kristeva's term "abject" captures nicely the ambivalent character of such "body parts": "A massive and sudden emergence of uncanniness, which, familiar as it might have been in an opaque and forgotten life, now harries me as radically separate, loathsome. Not me. Not that. But not nothing, either. A 'something' that I do not recognize as a thing. A weight of meaninglessness, about which there is nothing insignificant, and which crushes me. On the edge of non-existence and hallucination, of a reality that, if I acknowledge it, annihilates me" (1984, 2).

waste, but sometimes they are preserved as memories; and in the developmental processes of childhood they have great symbolic value.[18]

On the other hand, as long as our teeth, hair and nails remain functioning parts of our sensing living bodies, they do not appear to us as full-fledged objects but serve as locations and means of sensation and as practical tools. Our teeth, for example, are less sensitive to touch and warmth than our skin but they still have proprioception as well as sensations of pain; and even if we do not have any feeling *in* our hair, it is constantly given on the scalp by its weight, warmth, position, and movement. In respect to sensibility, the function of these bodily elements is more integral to personhood than the function of incorporated devices, such as clothes and tools. When we lose them, we have to adapt to a change in the system of sensibility.

To be sure, such changes are alien and external to our freely willing self. My hair, for example, may block my vision, and my aching teeth may prevent me from focusing on reading and thinking. Thus our bodies and our body parts may appear as obstacles or hindrances to our freely chosen projects. Such experiences form an integral part of the phenomena of sickness and aging. In a similar way as an infected eye may prevent me from seeing things at a distance or at the margins of my normal visual environment, a dropped eyelid may also limit my familiar visual field. Weakness in legs may prevent me from running and dancing, and trembling hands cannot cut or hit as steady hands can.

In all these cases, my body appears as alien or contrary to my willing self, but it is crucial to notice that this willing self is not completely independent or separated from all sensibility. Two factors in particular must be emphasized here: First, my present lived body and its parts may appear as hindrances but this is possible merely because my willing self is habituated to a different body, a sensing and moving self with larger powers and broader environments. My eyelids are given to me now as dropped because they used to be light; my legs appear as stiff and weak because they were able to perform far-reaching movements. So my present embodiment appears as faulty against the background of my previous mode of embodiment and not against a general form characteristic of humans or against a disembodied, purely spiritual will. Second,

---

18 In all these cases, our body parts function as cultural objects with cultural values and meanings, and thus they can be compared to utensils and ritualistic objects. It is important to notice, however, that our body parts can also serve as nutrition for animals. This means that there are perceiving subjects in our environment that treat or can treat our bodies and organs as material for their own natural organic functions. Moreover, the experience of breast feeding demonstrates that this type of objectification is not restricted to our relations with animals: human beings also consume the bodily fluids of other human beings.

our weakening sense-organs and limbs are for us the necessary, although disappointing, means of accessing the practical and affective surrounding and monitoring the perceivable field. These sparse teeth are now our only means of masticating food; these eyes with falling eyelids are the ones that we have for seeing; these stiff crooked fingers and these trembling hands are our means of pointing, grasping and caressing, and the heavy legs are the ones that move us around in space.

The bodily means now available divert from the norms of our habitual perception and movement and from their optima.[19] Together they produce an "abnormal condition" (285), not in relation to any external standard—that of perceivable things, physical bodies or other similar selves—but in relation to the standards that we have established for ourselves in our perceptual-motor life.[20] At the same time, however, they institute another norm and another optimum. Thus old age can rightly be called a "normal abnormality" (286).

This analysis suggests that our mirror image is only secondarily infected by age. We cannot realize that we are old simply by staring at the mirror or at the faces of others; we must already feel, or suspect, that we have changed before we can detect and identify with our new appearance in the reflection. Here my analysis diverts from the main line of Beauvoir's discussion.[21] This means that aging is a complex phenomenon, and not simply captured by the distinction between being-for-itself and being-for-others. We appear as old in several different but related and dependent, ways: by certain objectivities that belong to the shared world, by departures from intersubjective optima, by deviations from our own habitual norms and by the establishment of new norms.

In *The Coming of Age*, Beauvoir's argues that the crisis of aging can be handled in several different ways, some more successful than others.[22] She points

---

19 On the phenomenology of norms and normality, see Heinämaa 2012b.

20 In *The Normal and the Pathological*, Georges Canguilhem emphasizes that the constitution of new profound norms is typical to childhood. This means that the condition of the child can be compared to the condition of the sick, or the old, but should not be identified with either one of them. Such an identification is "an absurdity because it ignores that eagerness which pushes the child to raise itself constantly to new norms, which is profoundly at variance with the care to conserve which directs the sick person in his obsessive and often exhausting maintenance of the only norms of life within which he feels almost normal" (Canguilhem 1991, 189).

21 Interestingly, Beauvoir includes also this idea in her account but does not work out its implications. She writes: "we must already have some cause for uneasiness before we stand and study the reflection offered us by the looking-glass" (1996, 287).

22 The argument is very similar to the one that we find in *The Second Sex* where Beauvoir shows that the feminine condition can be lived in several different ways, some more "happy" than others: the narcissist, the woman in love, the mystic and the independent woman (1989, 629–

out that we may live in different forms of self-deception clinging to our former habits and coining essences (362). Alternatively we can affirm the transformation and do the best possible with the means and capacities now available. We can also remain vacillating between our two modes of givenness—being for ourselves and being for others (291), or else we can try to find a new equilibrium between these two appearances and establish new norms for our self-relation and for our relations with others (cf. 540–43). In any case, a comprehensive change requires that we renew our engagement to our goals and values and to those of others. Beauvoir expresses this insight in *The Coming of Age* with the same resoluteness as in *The Ethics of Ambiguity:*

> There is only one solution if old age is not to be a derisory parody of our former existence, and that is to go on pursuing ends that give our life a meaning—devotion to individuals, to collectives, to causes, social, political, intellectual or creative work. ... One's life has value so long as one attributes value to the life of others, by means of love, friendship, indignation, compassion. (540–41/567; translation modified; cf. Beauvoir 1976, 67; Heinämaa 2012a)

We have seen that the transformation of aging includes several phenomena: operative organs loose their liveliness and get overloaded by their materiality; our actions and performances come constantly short by common standards but also by our own standards of normality; others react to us in unexpected ways, and we ourselves find it hard to recognize our reflection in mirror. We certainly get old in the eyes of others, as Beauvoir argues, but at the same time, we also get old by a fundamental transformation of our own lived bodies.

In addition to these bodily changes, external and internal, aging also involves a change in our temporal horizons of experiencing. Contrary to the common sense conception according to which aging means that our past grows and our future shrinks, I will develop in the following the Beauvoirian insight that aging affects both horizons equally and that it means, at worst, a collapse of the horizontal structure of lived time in whole.

715; cf. Heinämaa 2012a). These "justificatory types" should be compared with those that Beauvoir distinguishes in *The Ethics of Ambiguity:* the infantile, the serious, the nihilist, the adventurer, the passionate altruist and the artistic critic (ch. "Personal Freedom and Others," 1976, 35–73). I have clarified the Kierkegaardian background of this methodology of types in my *Toward a Phenomenology of Sexual Difference* (2003); cf. Björk 2008.

Temporality, Death, and Future

Beauvoir's third insight concerns the temporality of old age. She argues that the metamorphosis of aging brings with a radical change in the temporal form of experiencing, that is, a change in the tripartite structure of past, present, and future. She claims that both the lived future and the lived past undergo a fundamental change in this transformation: the future which has gaped open is suddenly closed, and the past which has felt light and vivid weights now heavy. The aged find themselves trapped between two monoliths: "A limited future and a frozen past" (378).[23]

Following Sartre, Beauvoir claims that the critical change in the metamorphosis of aging is the closure of the futural horizon. For the infant, the future is without limits (375–76). For the young person, the future is an *infinite* field for possible activities and happenings. The mature and the middle aged see the years in an *indefinite* series, coming one after another. The aged person, in contrast, is the one who is able to imagine an endpoint, and more: he is the one who sees an ending and must live in its proximity. The future has lost its stretch; life is *finite*; and each year, each day and each moment is framed by the idea of a final halt—impossible but inevitable[24]:

> [t]he very quality of the future changes between middle age and the end of one's life. At sixty-five one is not merely twenty years older than one was at forty-five. One has exchanged an indefinite future—that one tends to regard as infinite—for a finite future. In earlier days we could see no boundary-mark upon the horizon: now we do see one. (378/400, translation modified)

The closure of the future is immediately reflected in the lessened dynamism of the past. As our futural projects shrink and shorten, as their time-span diminishes, they cannot support our contact with the past anymore. In order to posses our past, Beauvoir argues, we must bind it to existence by futural projects (361). When death comes to limit our time span, the narrative structure of our life breaks down and our memories flout free without temporal anchors. Finally, instead of being remembered, the past is relived and repeated in empty gestures. Beauvoir compares the final past to a wreck and describes its foundering as follows:

---

23 Cf. Beauvoir 1996, 416; Beauvoir 1984, 420.
24 For the idea of death as an impossible possibility, see Martin Heidegger's *Being and Time* (1992); cf. Heinämaa 2010a.

As I was moving forward, so it was crumbling. Most of the wreckage that can still be seen is colourless, distorted, frozen: its meaning escapes me. Here and there, I see occasional pieces whose melancholy beauty enchants me. They do not suffice to populate this emptiness ... "the desert of the past." (365)

Usually we describe old persons by saying that they have many years behind, a long existence or even a whole history (361). Beauvoir rejects this commonplace notion and argues that instead of accumulating, the past collapses in the last phases of our life. Objective accounts can attach a long history to each present, but this is possible only in the third-person perspective.[25] For the aged themselves, the past is given in a completely different way. Rather than extending by length, it grows heavy, loses its flexibility and succumbs to an obscurity. The metaphors of weight and heaviness describe the experience more accurately than those of length: without the support of an open future, the living present cannot sustain the weight of the enormous past. Thus the whole structure of lived time trembles when the futural horizon is closing.

This Beauvoirian analysis of aging renders the aged person as an anomaly. It must be emphasized, however, that the old age is not a paradox as such, but presents itself in this way in the conceptual framework that defines human subjectivity by freedom and transcendence.[26] The aged person has come to the vicinity of a limit, which cannot be overcome (Beauvoir 1984, 420).[27] Moreover, he must live in the nearness of this limit, and find or create meaning despite her inability to transcend death. Thus, his existence questions the idea of life as pure transcendence.

Despite the negative tone of her descriptions, Beauvoir claims that meaningful life is possible at the frontier of death. She argues, however, that this possibility remains empty or merely conceptual unless we transform our individual and communal lives completely:

Once we have understood what the state of the aged really is, we cannot satisfy ourselves with calling for a more generous "old-age policy", higher pensions, decent housing and organized leisure. It is the whole system that is at issue and our claim cannot be otherwise than radical—change life itself. (1996, 543)

Beauvoir contends that in the nearness of death, our future horizon can open onto new dimensions. Our activities and projects can refer, trans-generationally,

---

25 Cf. Heinämaa 2010c, 81–85.
26 Cf. Beauvoir 1976, 70 and 90–91.
27 Cf. Beauvoir 1996, 371–72.

to the lives of future others, successors and descendants, in several generations (379).[28] However, according to Beauvoir, this possibility is merely conceptual for most of us. We may imagine such openings, and we can find them described in historical, anthropological and ethnographic sources, but when we look around in the present, we notice that such prospects are given merely to few exceptional or privileged individuals. The trans-generational futurity is not an essential possibility of all humans as Sartre suggests nor a structural feature of human life as Levinas argues in *Time and the Other* (1987) and *Totality and Infinity* (1994). Beauvoir's analysis suggests that it is merely a *historical possibility*, an option for some but not all: "Generally speaking," Beauvoir argues, implicitly challenging Levinas' view, "the father does not see himself in his son. Nothingness swallows him entirely" (1996, 380, translation modified).[29]

The trans-generational opening of the future is a cultural and historical variable for Beauvoir, and not a constant of human life. She points out that it has been, and still is, possible for some people in some cultures, but she asserts that in modern industrial and technological societies this type of futurity is an inessential exception. Only certain specific and rare practices allow the development of personal achievements and accomplishments which can operate as starting points for new projects, not just for ourselves but also for others who follow us in time.

Beauvoir argues that in modernity all production is subjected to consumption and tends to become mechanical (1996, 380 – 82), and that only individuals engaged in highly intellectual or spiritual activities are able to project a future which transcends the prospects of immediate utility. She discusses five examples of such professions: the scientist, the philosopher, the writer, the artist and the politician (388 – 434). Only in these few professions, can personal time, already barred by death and weighted down by the past, reopen and retain its reference to the future of descendents and successors. The majority of old people live barren, deserted lives in isolation, repetition and boredom. Beauvoir's disillusioned view is almost devastating:

> Past events, acquired knowledge retain their place, but in a life whose fire has faded: they have been. When memory cracks, the events sink and vanish in a ridiculous darkness; life unravels stitch by stitch like a frayed piece of knitting, leaving nothing but formless strands of wool in the old person's hands. (539 – 40/566, translation modified)

---

28 Cf. Beauvoir 1976, 60. For Beauvoir's philosophy of futurity, see Heinämaa 2010b.
29 Cf. Levinas 1987, 91; 1994, 267; cf. Sartre 1985, 535 – 39. For Levinas' discourse of transgenerational relations, see Heinämaa 2010b.

The insight that only privileged people can gain a future from younger generations is operative already in *The Coming of Age*. It is not fully explicated or defended by arguments but it is clearly stated and well articulated in a few forceful paragraphs. I have provided a systematic explication here and have developed Beauvoir's view further. I have done this, not only for exegetic reasons but more importantly for systematic ones: I believe that Beauvoir offers us a fresh insight which is more accurate than the analyses of Sartre and Levinas. Both Sartre and Levinas argue trans-generational future is a structural feature of human life, but Beauvoir challenges this notion and claims that this form of lived temporality is not a constant but is a variable dependent on historical and social parameters.

In order to see this controversy more clearly, I will turn to a later text by Beauvoir, in which the topic of aging and time comes forth with a new acuteness. This is *Adieux: A Farewell to Sartre* (*La céremonie des adieux*, 1981) that Beauvoir wrote after Sartre's death on the basis of her notebooks from the 1970s. In *The Coming of Age*, the idea of trans-generational future is discussed in abstract terms, but in *Adieux* the topic has a concrete setting and a personal emphasis: Beauvoir argues against Sartre, who functions in the dialogue as the main topic but also as a lifelong philosophical companion and interlocutor already marked by death.

> At the end of June Sartre began to suffer cruelly from his tongue. He could neither eat nor speak without pain. I said to him, "Really, this is a horrible year; you have troubles all the time." "Oh, it doesn't matter," he replied. "When you're old it no longer has any importance." "How do you mean?" "You know it won't last long." "You mean because one's going to die?" "Yes. It's natural to come to pieces, little by little. When you're young, it's different." The tone in which he said this overwhelmed me; he already seemed to be on the far side of life. (Beauvoir 1984, 19)[30]

I will end my discussion of the metamorphosis of aging by studying how the idea of trans-generational future that Beauvoir introduced in *The Coming of Age* is developed by her in the farewell-dialogue with Sartre. By this extension, we can further our understanding of the evolution of Beauvoir's thought but more importantly we gain a better understanding of the constants and the variables of the phenomenon itself.

---

30 Cf. Beauvoir 1984, 131 and 445.

The Adieux

Adieux can rightly be called Beauvoir's last philosophical dialogue with Sartre. The book is composed of two parts. The first part is a notebook and a biography of the last ten years of Sartre's life, starting with the aggravating symptoms of Sartre's illness in 1970 and ending in Sartre's death in 1980. The second part consists of Beauvoir's philosophical and personal conversations with Sartre, made in August and September 1974. Sartre is already very sick and almost blind. Beauvoir invites him to discuss a variety of different topics, philosophical, literary, political and personal. Old age is one of them.

The "conversations" function as a recording of Sartre's final thoughts but they also witness a dialogue between two thinkers. Beauvoir proposes a topic, one after the other; she asks questions, presents her position, and thus invites Sartre to present his own views. Sometimes the answer is short and definite, and the two proceed together to the next topic. At other occasions, Beauvoir presses Sartre and argues against him or refuses to abandon a problem that she finds important. The themes of the conversations range from concrete to abstract and they move between the personal to the universal: work, writing and thinking; novelists and philosophers[31]; food, eating and sexuality; life, birth and death; politics, freedom and equality; memory and recollection; childhood and old age.

The two last conversations focus on the topic of human life. Beauvoir starts by asking Sartre how he sees his "life as a whole" (1984, 425). Sartre answers by outlining a basic structure of human life that opens in birth and closes in death, but interestingly he also describes a final phase of old age in which life broadens toward the intersubjective and the universal:

> Generally, I see not only my life but all lives roughly in this way—a threadlike beginning that slowly broadens with the acquisition of knowledge and the earliest experiences, adventures, and a whole range of feelings. Then from a certain age that varies according to the person, partly because of himself, partly because of his body, and partly because of circumstances, life moves toward its close, death being the final closing as birth was the opening. But as I see it this time of closure is accompanied by a continual broadening toward the universal. A man of fifty or sixty who is traveling toward death, is at the same time learning and also experiencing a certain number of relations with others and with society, relations that grow wider and wider. (1984, 425–26)

---

31 Sartre and Beauvoir discuss the works of Husserl, Heidegger, Merleau-Ponty and Camus, but also Proust, Gide, Genet and Flaubert.

Here Sartre proposes that, in the nearness of death, a new intersubjectivity and through it a new futurity is constituted for the aging person. The perspective of the young and the mature adult are broadened and opened, and as a result the time of the experiencing subject can refer in a new way to the lived times of other diachronic subjects. Sartre's reflection suggests that this is a structural feature, a constant, of all human life: facing the impossible possibility of its own cessation, the singular human life opens onto the universal and futural humanity. He continues:

> A certain form moves forward its completion, and at the same time the individual acquires knowledge or patterns of thought ... that go in the direction of universality. He acts either in favor of a certain society or for its preservation, or in favor of the creation of another society. And this society will perhaps only appear after his death. In any event its development will take place after his death. In the same way most of the undertakings [projects] that concern him in the last part of his life will be successful if they are carried on after his death ... but will come to nothing if they end before it. (426)

In another section, Sartre describes a naïve notion that he had of his existence in his early adult years. He believed that he could gain eternity by his literary and philosophical creations. He describes this notion as a secularized version of the Christian idea of immortality and explains that he rejected it already by his concept of *committed writing* (152–53).[32]

Motivated by the social and political turn in his thinking, Sartre now entertains the idea that we can choose to participate in long-term communal projects in which our successors continue and prolong our work for common goods or universal ends. In *Adieux*, he makes clear that such sharing is possible only in political and social activities, that is, in activities that are co-operative by definition. Whereas artistic creations remain tied to individual and personal interests, political and social activities point beyond the limits of one's personal life. Sartre summarizes his mature view by claiming that "there is a future that lies beyond death and that almost turns death into an accident in the individual's life, a life that goes on without him" (426). He seems to think that this is a general possibility, an option open in principle to all humans, even if realized only by few.

Beauvoir intervenes here and points out that Sartre's "general" description applies merely to certain "privileged people" (426). She claims that in modernity,

---

32 Cf. Beauvoir 1984, 413. In *The Ethics of Ambiguity*, Beauvoir attributes this attitude to the personal type that she calls "the adventurer". She writes: "When he dies, the adventurer will be surrendering his whole life into the hands of men; the only meaning it will have will be the one they confer upon it. He knows this since he talks about himself, often in books" (Beauvoir 1976, 63).

trans-generational future is possible but merely for intellectuals and artists such as Sartre and herself. For most people, all productive and creative activities with long futural perspectives and intersubjective bearing end with retirement, and the world as a whole is replaced by a shrinking personal environment. Old age, she states, rarely has the enlarging or broadening form that Sartre describes (426).

In the light of these paragraphs, it seems to me that Beauvoir's understanding of the futurity of human life differs from the accounts offered by her contemporaries. Whereas Sartre and Levinas describe the trans-generational opening as a structural feature of human existence, Beauvoir argues that this type of temporality is not given with humanity but achieved in certain specific modes of co-existence. It is not a constant of the human condition but a variable.

Beauvoir's view is informed by her historical comparisons but also by her sensitivity to personal, social and cultural differences. In *Adieux* it is accentuated by the contrast to Sartre's conception. The methodological lesson that we can learn from this interchange is that historical, cultural and interpersonal comparisons assist critical philosophical reflections by challenging our preconceptions of human nature. The work on free variation that aims at identifying the structural features of experience is not any armchair activity but is a demanding exercise that requires that we question our conceptions repeatedly. Exchange with empirical science and with history and the arts is indispensable since it strengthens our imagination and cures us of the overestimation of our own capacities of fantasizing.

Conclusions

I have argued, on the basis of Beauvoir's remarks, that experientially aging involves three characteristic factors that concern our whole existence and affect our conscious life in a comprehensive way. This implies that aging has a philosophical significance and that it cannot, as a phenomenon, be adequately handled by empirical life-sciences or social sciences. The three existential facts about aging explicated in this essay are the following: First, aging as a phenomenon is not a slow gradual alteration but is a sudden and thorough transformation. Second, aging affects our bodily self in its two central dimensions: we change both in our bodily being-for-others and in our being-for-ourselves. And finally aging does not just diminish our future expectations but also problematizes our relation to our own past. Thus understood, aging is a fundamental and all-inclusive personal metamorphosis and is not a contingent change in our outer appearance or social role. Further, the analysis implies that human life is not a continuous process of generation, blooming and decay, comparable to the life of a plant, but includes a series of radical transformations in which the self is lost and regained.[33]

References

Bachelard, Suzanne. 1968. *A study of Husserl's formal and transcendental logic*. Trans. Lester Embree. Evanston, IL: Northwestern University Press [*Logique formelle et logique transcendentale: Essai d'une critique de la raison logique*. Paris: Presses Universitaires de France 1957].

Beauvoir, Simone de. 1965. *The prime of life*. Trans. Peter Green. Harmondsworth, Middlesex: Penguin [*La force de l'âge*. Paris: Gallimard 1960].

Beauvoir, Simone de. 1976. *The ethics of ambiguity*. Trans. Bernard Frechtman. New York: Citadel Press / Kensington Publishing Corp. [*Pour une morale de l'ambiguïté*. Paris: Gallimard 1947].

Beauvoir, Simone de. 1984. *Adieux: A farewell to Sartre*. Trans. Patrick O'Brian. New York: Pantheon Books [*La céremonie des adieux, suivi de entretiens avec Jean-Paul Sartre août-septembre 1974*. Paris: Gallimard 1981].

Beauvoir, Simone de. 1989. *The second sex*. Trans. and ed. H. M. Parshley. New York: Vintage Books [*Le deuxième sexe I: les faits et les mythes*. Paris: Gallimard 1949; *Le deuxième sexe II: l'expérience vécue*. Paris: Gallimard 1949].

Beauvoir, Simone de. 1996. *The coming of age*. Trans. Patrick O'Brian. New York, London: W. W. Norton & Company [*La vieillesse*. Paris: Gallimard 1970].

Beauvoir, Simone de. 2004a. Literature and metaphysics. Trans. Veronique Zaytzeff and Frederick M. Morrison. In Simone de Beauvoir: *Philosophical writings*, ed. Margaret A. Simons with Marybeth Timmermann and Mary Beth Mader. Urbana and Chicago: University of Illinois Press [Littérature et métaphysique. *Les temps modernes* 1 (7) (1946): 1153–63].

Beauvoir, Simone de. 2004b. A review of *The phenomenology of perception* by Maurice Merleau-Ponty. Trans. Marybeth Timmermann. In *Simone de Beauvoir. Philosophical writings*, ed. Margaret A. Simons with Marybeth Timmermann and Mary Beth Mader. Urbana and Chicago: University of Illinois Press, 159–64 [La phénoménologie de la perception de Maurice Merleau-Ponty. *Les temps modernes* 1 (2) (1945): 363–67].

Björk, Ulrika. 2008. *Poetics of subjectivity: Existence and expressivity in Simone de Beauvoir's philosophy*, Philosophical studies from the University of Helsinki 21, Department of Philosophy, University of Helsinki.

---

33 Bonnie Mann's critical comments on an earlier version of this essay helped me to clarify my ontological and epistemological interests in Beauvoir's discourse on old age. I am thankful to Professor Mann as well as to Professors Debra Bergoffen, Christina Schües and Beata Stawarska for clarifying discussions on the different levels and goals of Beauvoir's argumentation. I own special thanks to Professor Anthony Steinbock for his encouragement which helped me to highlight my own insight into the phenomenon of aging.

Canguilhem, Georges. 1991. *The normal and the pathological.* Trans. Carolyn R. Fawcett, in
    collaboration with Robert S. Cohen. New York: Zone Books [*Le normal et le
    pathologique.* Paris: Presses Universitaires de France 1966].

Heidegger, Martin. 1992. *Being and time.* Trans. John Macquarrie and Edward Robinson.
    Oxford: Blackwell [*Sein und Zeit.* Tübingen: Max Niemeyer (1927) 1993].

Heinämaa, Sara. 2003. *Toward a phenomenology of sexual difference.* Lanham: Rowman &
    Littlefield.

Heinämaa, Sara. 2004. The soul-body union and sexual difference: From Descartes to
    Merleau-Ponty and Beauvoir. In *Feminist reflections on the history of philosophy,* ed. Lilli
    Alanen and Charlotte Witt. Dordrecht: Kluwer, 137–52.

Heinämaa, Sara. 2010a. Being towards death. In *Birth, death, and femininity,* ed. Robin May
    Schott. Bloomington: Indiana University Press, 98–118.

Heinämaa, Sara. 2010b. Future and others. *Birth, death, and femininity,* ed. Robin May
    Schott. Bloomington: Indiana University Press, 119–52.

Heinämaa, Sara. 2010c. The sexed self and the mortal body. In *Birth, death, and femininity,*
    ed. Robin May Schott. Bloomington: Indiana University Press, 73–97.

Heinämaa, Sara. 2012a. Ambiguity and difference: Two feminist ethics of the present. In
    Phenomenology and materiality: Beauvoir and Irigaray, ed. Emily Parker and Anne van
    Leeuwen (submitted to Oxford University Press).

Heinämaa, Sara. 2012b. Two senses of normality: Concordance and optimality. An
    unpublished manuscript.

Husserl, Edmund. 1960. *Cartesian meditations.* Trans. Dorion Cairns. Dordrecht, Boston:
    Martinus Nijhoff [*Cartesianische Meditationen und Pariser Vorträge,* Husserliana I, ed.
    Stephan Strasser. The Hague: Martinus Nijhoff 1950].

Husserl, Edmund. 1968. *Phänomenologische Psychologie, Vorlesungen Sommersemester
    1925,* Husserliana IX, ed. Walter Biemel. The Hague: Martinus Nijhoff.

Husserl, Edmund. 1970. *The crisis of European sciences and transcendental phenomenology:
    An introduction to phenomenological philosophy.* Trans. David Carr. Evanston:
    Northwestern University Press [*Die Krisis der europäischen Wissenschaften und die
    transzendentale Phänomenologie: Eine Einleitung in die phänomenologische
    Philosophie,* Husserliana VI, ed. Walter Biemel. The Hague: Martinus Nijhoff 1994].

Husserl, Edmund. 1978. *Formal and transcendental logic.* Trans. Dorion Cairns. 2nd printing.
    The Hague: Martinus Nijhoff [*Formale und transzendentale Logik. Versuch einer Kritik der
    logischen Vernunft,* Husserliana XVII, ed. Paul Janssen. The Hague: Martinus Nijhoff
    (1929) 1974].

Husserl, Edmund. 1983. *Ideas pertaining to a pure phenomenology and to a
    phenomenological philosophy, First Book: General introduction to pure phenomenology.*
    Trans. F. Kersten. The Hague: Martinus Nijhoff Publishers [*Ideen zu einer reinen
    Phänomenologie und phänomenologischen Philosophie, Erstes Buch: Allgemeine
    Einführung in die reine Phänomenologie (1913),* Husserliana III/1, ed. Karl Schuhmann.
    The Hague: Martinus Nijhoff 1976].

Husserl, Edmund. 1989. *Aufsätze und Vorträge (1922–1937),* Husserliana XXVII, ed. Thomas
    Nenon and Hans Rainer Sepp. Dordrecht, Boston, London: Kluwer Academic Publishers.

Husserl, Edmund. 1992. *Die Krisis der europäischen Wissenschaften und die transzendentale
    Phänomenologie, Ergänzungsband, Texte aus dem Nachlass 1934–1937,* Husserliana
    XXIX, ed. Reinhold N. Smid. The Hague: Kluwer Academic Publishers.

Husserl, Edmund. 1993. *Ideas pertaining to a pure phenomenology and to a phenomenological philosophy, Second Book: Studies in the phenomenology of constitution*. Trans. Richard Rojcewicz and André Schuwer. Dordrecht, Boston, London: Kluwer Academic Publishers [*Ideen zu einer reinen Phänomenologie und phänomenologischen Philosophie, Zweites Buch: Phänomenologische Untersuchungen zur Konstitution*, Husserliana IV, ed. Marly Biemel. The Hague: Martinus Nijhoff 1952].

Kristeva, Julia. 1982. *Powers of horror: An essay on abjection*. Trans. Leon S. Roudiez. New York: Columbia University Press [*Pouvoirs de l'horreur*. Paris: Editions du Seuil 1980].

Levinas, Emmanuel. 1987. *Time and the Other*. Trans. Richard A. Cohen. Pittsburgh: Duquesne University Press [*Le temps et l'autre*. Paris: Quadrige / Presses Universitaires de France 1947].

Levinas, Emmanuel. 1994. *Totality and infinity*. Trans. Alphonso Lingis. Pittsburgh: Duquesne University Press [*Totalité et infini: Essai sur l'extériorité*. Dordrecht: Kluwer Academic 1961].

Merleau-Ponty, Maurice. 1964. Metaphysics and the novel. In *Sense and non-sense*, trans. Hubert L. Dreyfus and Patricia Allen Dreyfus, 26 – 40. Evanston, Illinois: Northwestern University Press [Le roman et la métaphysique. In *Sens et non-sens*. Paris: Gallimard (1948) 1966, 45 – 71].

Merleau-Ponty, Maurice. 1995. *Phenomenology of perception*. Trans. Collin Smith. New York: Routledge & Kegan Paul [*Phénoménologie de la perception*. Paris: Gallimard (1945) 1966].

Sartre, Jean-Paul. 1960. *The Transcendence of the ego: An existentialist theory of consciousness*. Trans. Forrest Williams and Robert Kirkpatrick. New York: Hill and Wang [La transcendance de l'ego: Esquisse d'une description phénoménologique. *Recherches Philosophiques*, VI, 1936 – 37].

Sartre, Jean-Paul. 1985. *Critique de la raison dialectique II: l'intelligibilité de l'histoire*. Paris: Gallimard.

Sartre, Jean-Paul. 1998. *Being and nothingness*. Trans. Hazel Barnes. New York: Washington Square Press [*L'être et le néant: Essai d'ontologie phénoménologique*. Paris: Gallimard 1943].

Slatman, Jenny, and Guy Widdershoven. 2009. Being whole after amputation. *The American Journal of Bioethics–Neuroscience* 9 (1): 48 – 49.

Slatman, Jenny, and Guy Widdershoven. 2010. Hand transplants and bodily integrity. *Body & Society* 16 (3): 69 – 92.

Sokolowski, Robert. 1964. *The formation of Husserl's concept of constitution*. The Hague: Martinus Nijhoff.

Songe-Møller, Vigdis. 2008. Metamorphosis and the concept of change: From Ancient Greek philosophy to the Apostle Paul's notions of the resurrection of the body. In *Complexity: Interdisciplinary communications 2006/2007*, ed. Willy Østreng, Center for Advanced Study, Oslo, 84 – 86.

Steinbock, Anthony J. 1995. *Home and beyond: Generative phenomenology after Husserl*. Evanston, Illinois: Northwestern University Press.

Steinbock, Anthony J. 2001. Translator's introduction. In Edmund Husserl: *Analyses concerning passive and active synthesis: Lectures on transcendental logic*, trans. Anthony J. Steinbock. Dordrecht, Boston, London: Kluwer Academic Publishers, xv–lxvii.

Weiss, Gail. 2008. "Intertwined identities: Challenges to bodily autonomy," a paper presented at *Intercorporeality and Intersubjectivity*, 6 – 7 June, University College Dublin.

Bonnie Mann
Revisioning Classical Phenomenology
Comment on Sara Heinämaa

The following comments focus on the beginning and the end of Sara Heinämaa's essay and leave the middle, which I consider to be unassailably insightful, untouched. There is a tension between the beginning and the end of the paper that raises decisive questions about how we should understand Beauvoir's project and how we should characterize Beauvoir's relation to the tradition of classical phenomenology.

Heimämaa argues at the beginning of her essay that the second part of *The Coming of Age* "takes another approach and proposes a different task" (168) than the first part, which is focused on the empirical, social and political realities of aging. I take this claim to be part of an important feminist reaction to critics who have tended to read Beauvoir's work as reductively sociological or empirical, but not philosophical. Heinämaa's book on Husserl, Merleau-Ponty and Beauvoir, *Toward a Phenomenology of Sexual Difference*, begins with the important claim that Beauvoir's project is "not a socio-historical explanation ... but a philosophical inquiry" (Heinämaa 2003, xi). Yet the effort to recuperate the philosophical depth of Beauvoir's work seems here to require a careful surgical operation which separates the conjoined projects, thus freeing the philosophical project from its symbiotic socio-historical partner.

The post-operative move is to situate Beauvoir among the philosophers of the phenomenological tradition: Heinämaa argues that Beauvoir's approach to lived intentional experience "can best be characterized by Husserlian concepts: the philosopher begins from personal experience and aims at capturing" the necessary structural features of that experience, i.e., "the constants" of human reality (168). Beauvoir is engaged, on Heinämaa's reading, in a "reduction" in the tradition of classical phenomenology. Beauvoir's goal, like that of the classical phenomenologists, is a purification of consciousness of its natural and habitual beliefs, so the investigator can encounter the phenomena as they are given. There is a strong suggestion here; we might even call it an assumption, that Beauvoir's project is philosophical precisely because such bracketing takes one *beneath* the cultural and historical particularities of experience to its general structures.

But Heinämaa's own conclusion seems to destabilize this beginning claim. She argues that along with the closing of the future that the aged person experiences as death draws nearer, there is also the possibility of an opening onto the future rooted in sociality. "[T]he time of the experiencing subject can refer in a new way to the lived times of the other diachronic subjects" (185)—a new temporality opens the future in the lives of others for the one approaching death.

There are two significant developments noted by Heinämaa. First, Beauvoir insists that this kind of futurity is not a general feature of human experience. Second, Beauvoir's project is consequently *not* consistent with approaches in other phenomenological work. In other words, Beauvoir seems to move backwards through the reduction, back into the realm of the contingent. Here the surgical separation of the two projects seems to have failed, as we find ourselves contending with that which we previously excised.

I would like to suggest that Beauvoir, while working in the tradition of classical phenomenology, actually transforms the approach of that tradition and that this allows her to do what classical phenomenology has so often failed to do, i. e., to give an account of the human experience of oppression. In my own view, the task of feminist thinking is to articulate the "emancipatory aspirations of women" (Benhabib 1995, 29). While there are many ways of talking about women that may be important, an investigation does not become *feminist* unless it is linked to and has repercussions for those emancipatory aspirations. Phenomenology is only suited to feminism insofar as it becomes capable of such an account. Beauvoir makes phenomenology feminist by making it capable of addressing the phenomenon of oppression.

There are two things that seem to me to decisively distinguish Beauvoir's phenomenology from that of her predecessors and contemporaries. First, Beauvoir's reduction has a different character than that of the classical phenomenologists. Second, her reduction allows her to encounter the general features of human experience in a radically different way than through the classical reduction.

In the history of the practice of phenomenology, no aspect of the practice is more difficult to grasp, or more contentious, than the so-called "reduction," which is sometimes understood to be a *set* of practices rather than one practice. These practices are understood to be acts of "setting aside," whether of the taken-for-grantedness of a phenomenon, ready-to-hand interpretations of it, previous knowledge (including scientific knowledge) about it, theories or beliefs about it, incidental meanings that attach contingently to it, and accepted investigative approaches to the study of it. The point of this setting aside is to restore a sense of wonder in one's encounter with the phenomenon, to uncover the essential features of the experience of it, and to investigate its meaning free of presuppositions. How does one "bracket" one's presuppositions? In classical phenomenology the answer to this question is notoriously unsatisfactory. The philosopher engages in imaginative variation to discover what is essential about the phenomenon in question, or settles into a kind of meditative reflection on it. Feminists will understandably be skeptical of claims to have "set aside" prejudices through an imaginative or meditative process, given that these prejudices are not only deeply entrenched, but are tied to real material interests and entangled with profoundly personal and prereflective processes of identity formation. For Beauvoir, an imaginary purification of consciousness would be an abstract fantasy, outside the context of more serious work. This might function well enough when the object of investigation is a ball of wax, but fails utterly when the object of investigation is a complex, historically rooted human experience like becoming woman or becoming old. Here, setting aside our preconceptions is tedious, enraging, exhaustive hard work. Those hundreds of pages addressing the data of biological sciences, history, literature, specific case studies, and the myths of old age are that work. For Beauvoir, this work ties her social and philosophical projects together.

The point of such labor is a call to arms against "a whole mutilating system of life that provides the immense majority of those who make part of it with no reason for living" (Beauvoir 1996, 224), a system of life governed by "the machine, the crusher of men" (543). We cannot separate the social from the philosophical aspects of the work, because we discover through our investigation that the general features have been deployed by the "crusher of men," animated by the interests of the powerful in the project of justifying and stabilizing relations of exploitation. Our investigation reveals that injustice is not a superficial empirical contingency floating above the general features of experience. Right at the heart of experience, crisscrossing and ensnared with its *most* general features are the sedimented historical and social meanings generated by a social order that feeds on the criminal appropriation of some humans by others.

Beauvoir's reduction leads into, not away from, messy political realities. Any phenomenology that follows Beauvoir's approach will not find pure experience even in pure experience. At the heart of lived experience, in the very way those general features are lived, we find the footprints of injustice.

The tension between the first and last parts of Heinämaa's paper shows that Beauvoir's reduction is not Husserl's, and that her phenomenology is not "classical." Beauvoir's phenomenology is *feminist* precisely insofar as it revisions classical phenomenology.

References

Beauvoir, Simone de. 1996. *The coming of age*. Trans. Patrick O'Brian. New York and London: W. W. Norton & Company.

Benhabib, Seyla. 1995. Feminism and postmodernism: An uneasy alliance. In *Feminist contentions: A philosophical exchange*. Co-authored with Judith Butler, Drucilla Cornell and Nancy Fraser. New York: Routledge, 17–34.

Heinämaa, Sara. 2003. *Toward a phenomenology of sexual difference: Husserl, Merleau-Ponty, Beauvoir*. Oxford: Rowman & Littlefield.

Silvia Stoller
We in the Other, and the Child in Us
The Intersection of Time in Beauvoir and Merleau-Ponty

At the very beginning of Simone de Beauvoir's *The Coming of Age* (1996) we are confronted with a remarkable idea that reminds us of another remarkable idea that can be found in Maurice Merleau-Ponty's *Phenomenology of Perception* (1962). Both ideas correspond to temporality and aging. They are intriguing and call for closer inspection. I believe that behind these thoughts lies valuable insight into the philosophy of age and aging. Beauvoir asks us to recognize the Self in the Other, strictly speaking, to recognize oneself in one's older other. Merleau-Ponty stresses the meaning of the Other within the Self, that is, the meaning of one's own past in the present. Both deal with a theory of Self-Other relation, and they address the topic of the young-aged relation, and in so doing they introduce a theory of temporality in regard to the issue of age and aging. In my opinion, these ideas apply very productively to *gerontological ethics*. What exactly are Beauvoir and Merleau-Ponty trying to get at, how are their ideas related to one another and where do they part ways? At a first glance, they seem to be dealing with the same subject matter, but closer examination reveals that different aspects are being emphasized: Beauvoir and Merleau-Ponty do not only differ from each other in that the former turns towards the outside, and the latter towards the inside, Beauvoir apparently seems to support a pessimistic account of the past, while Merleau-Ponty avoids judging negatively on the past. However, regardless of this discrepancy, I argue that they complement each other in their humane approach to growing old. My objective is to start by introducing Beauvoir's, then to be followed by Merleau-Ponty's idea, to then draw parallels and come to a conclusion.

Beauvoir: We in the Other

> Let us recognize ourselves in this old man or in that old woman. It must be done if we are to
> take upon ourselves the entirety of our human state.
> —Simone de Beauvoir

In her work *The Coming of Age*, Simone de Beauvoir begins with the premise that our society suppresses and represses old age. People "evade those aspects of it that distress them. And above all they evade old age" (Beauvoir 1996, 1). As can be read in the introduction, it is this denial that explains why Beauvoir herself had decided to delve into an analysis of aging. It is an attempt to speak out against the silence surrounding this subject: "And that indeed is the very reason why I am writing this book. I mean to break the conspiracy of silence" (2).

From the onset, the essay seems to be built upon a solid ethical foundation. The attitudes towards the elderly in our society are "scandalous" (216). Beauvoir paints a bleak picture of our culture's attitude towards aging people. In a society of workers (today it would be better to speak of neo-capitalism or global economics) a human being is viewed not as a person but as a worker who is only valuable for society as long as she or he contributes to a productive economy and the increase of capital in a work-orientated system. But the result is the same: when she or he is no longer providing "material value" to the society, she or he stops being a productive member of society, is no longer valued and —as a result—treated as useless. To go one step further, "he [she] is no longer anything but a burden" (89). Alienation and expulsion from society are the consequence: "Some exploited, alienated individuals inevitably become 'throw-outs,' 'rejects,' once their strength has failed them" (542). They become outsiders within society, and from now on live the life of the "other." "When [the worker] loses his powers he takes on the appearance of *another*" (89).[1] Undoubtedly, since Western democratic societies are still capitalist working societies, Beauvoir's critical statement against the capitalist exploitation of workers and the disrespectful treatment of aged people is as valid, or even more valid, now as when she first wrote it.

Beauvoir takes an uncompromising position, accusing society and making it aware of the consequences of such an attitude towards aging. She speaks of a "crime" against the elderly, and of a "fault" that society commits by treating the elderly in such a way (542). Beauvoir is not stingy with her accusations, and she asks: "What should a society be, so that in his last years a man might still be a man? ... The answer is simple: he would always have to been treated as a man" (542). With these words Beauvoir sets her standards fairly high. Treating a person as a person, without regard to her or his social and economic function—and that throughout a life-time—means treating her or him, especially at old age, in a humane way. As such Beauvoir has expressed a tremendously important ethical demand with respect to the future treatment of the aged in Western societies.

---

1 The "old man" taking on the appearance of "another" through loss of value is reminiscent of Beauvoir's statement about a woman as "another" in *The Second Sex* (Beauvoir 1989). However, in *The Coming of Age* Beauvoir contends that the old man's transformation into "another" is much greater than the woman's, since the old man (see Beauvoir 1996, 89) no longer has a function in society.

The ethical-humanistic claim of Beauvoir is tied into an ethical approach to aging which should be taken up by each person in society and which will be described in the following. It is highly interesting to note that Beauvoir's example of this comes not from the West but from Eastern cultures, namely from Buddhism. This is a surprising fact, and it pops up so quickly in the introduction that it is easily overlooked. Beauvoir's essay in regard to philosophy, though doubtlessly influenced by Jean-Paul Sartre, as well as by Hegel's dialectics and Merleau-Ponty's phenomenology, differs in this decisive point in that she refers to a non-European, Buddhist tradition. I consider this extraordinary and a not to be underestimated aspect of Beauvoir's ethics of aging.

At the very beginning of her essay Beauvoir writes about Buddha and one of his childhood experiences. She goes on to refer to this episode repeatedly in her writing and puts her own ethical spin on this Buddhist wisdom, tying it into observations on aging. Beauvoir recounts the first time Buddha, that is, Siddhartha, who leaves his father's palace to go on a ride in the royal carriage. During the trip he and the coach driver meet a fragile old man. The coach driver tells young Siddhartha what an aged man is. Siddhartha cries and responds: "It is the world's pity ... that weak and ignorant beings, drunk with the vanity of youth, do not behold old age! Let us hurry back to the palace. What is the use of pleasures and delights, since I myself am the future dwelling-place of old age?" (1).

The sobriety of this hits home to Siddhartha. In the old man, Siddhartha recognizes himself at old age. The old man Siddhartha has seen is a reminder of old age to come. He serves as a mirror of his own future. Siddhartha realizes that he will not remain the child he presently is. He realizes that from now on all the joys of childhood, the pleasure of a sheltered life within his family, will not remain the same: that there is another world brought on by aging. But he would not be Siddhartha if he just stopped at this somber tragedy of aging. Siddhartha's first sobering encounter with old age is linked to the following wisdom: The "vanity of youth" prevents young people from grasping the entire truth about life, i. e. aging. It is unfortunate that people "drunk with the vanity of youth" cannot see aging.

Beauvoir continues her analysis of the reckless manner in which we deal with aging in our society by contending that it concerns us all, not just the elderly: "We carry this ostracism so far that we even reach the point of turning it against ourselves: for in the old person that we must become, we refuse to recognize ourselves" (4). In this passage she argues that if we face aging in an inhumane way, this will also have negative consequences for us. We are already refusing to recognize the old person we will be some day. Here is where Buddhist teachings greatly influence Beauvoir's ethics of aging: if we refuse to recognize ourselves in the old man (or woman), then we not only disapprove of aging but, ultimately, of ourselves.

A few lines later she goes on to emphasize this point, referring to Buddha again: "unlike Buddha, when we are young or in our prime we do not think of ourselves as already being in the dwelling-place of our own future old age" (4). To a certain degree, it is only natural that young people are not preoccupied with aging and do not take on the whole responsibility of the future. "Until the moment it is upon us old age is something that only affects other people. So it is understandable that society should manage to prevent us from seeing our own kind, our fellow-men, when we look at the old" (5). Nonetheless, Beauvoir sees the lie behind this fact, hidden in a denial of the future. Exposing myths and revealing cultural constructions behind the myths is the power that lies behind all of Beauvoir's work: it is her driving force, her main motivation. This applies to *The Second Sex* as well as to *The Coming of Age*. Hence Beauvoir vehemently warns that:

> We must stop cheating: the whole meaning of our life is in question in the future that is waiting for us. If we do not know what we are going to be, we cannot know what we are: *let us recognize ourselves in this old man or in that old woman*. It must be done if we are to take upon ourselves the entirety of our human state. And when it is done we will no longer acquiesce in the misery of the last age; we will no longer be indifferent, because we shall feel concerned, as indeed we are. (5, emphasis added)

As can be seen in this quote, Beauvoir's tale of Siddhartha's meeting with the old man is not accidentally included in her work. It serves to support her thesis of the repression of old age in our society. This leads her to the conclusion that suppressing and denying aging actually conflicts with the truth about our entire existence. Using Buddhist wisdom as a reference, people are unmistakably called upon to recognize themselves in the other: "Let us recognize ourselves in this old man or in that old woman!"

The idea behind it is that we must recognize ourselves in older people when we ourselves are young or younger, if we want to measure up to our human existence. In this way we attain not only self-knowledge ("If we do not know what we are going to be, we cannot know what we are") but also an understanding of humans in general ("It must be done if we are to take upon ourselves the entirety of our human state"). Beauvoir argues that only this way the shameful situation of old people in our society can be changed ("And when it is done we will no longer acquiesce in the misery of the last age; we will no longer be indifferent"). Thus, for her, to recognize oneself in old people is a basic condition upon which an ethics of aging should be built.

Merleau-Ponty: The Child in Us

What we have experienced is, and remains, permanently ours; and in old age a man is still in contact with his youth.
—Maurice Merleau-Ponty

While Beauvoir counts as the "grande dame" of French feminism, Maurice Merleau-Ponty counts among the main representatives of French phenomenology.[2] In his main work *Phenomenology of Perception* (1962), Merleau-Ponty deals with three major sections: "The Body," "The World as Perceived" and finally "Being-for-itself and Being-in-the-world." In the third part he develops a phenomenological theory of temporality based on his phenomenology of corporality. Time is analyzed from the perspective of lived experience.[3] More precisely, for Merleau-Ponty it concerns time *in statu nascendi* (415), that is, interpreting time "as it comes into being" (415). In Merleau-Ponty's opinion and from the perspective of lived experience time is not a line, meaning time as a series of single events, but a "network of intentionalities" (417), wherein the past and the future are woven together in the present. This means that the past is never wholly past but contained in the present, and at the same time it also means that future is never wholly future but already outlined in the present. The past and the future form, from a phenomenological viewpoint, temporal "horizons" of the present.[4]

Even though Merleau-Ponty does not attach higher significance to either of the two horizons of time, I would like to narrow in on the following question: how are we to understand the past in Merleau-Ponty's phenomenology of tempo-

---

2 Merleau-Ponty attended the École Normale Superieure in Paris, together with Simone de Beauvoir, and they worked together for many years on the editing committee of the magazine *Les Temps Modernes*, which was founded by Merleau-Ponty and Sartre. As is well known, Simone de Beauvoir and Maurice Merleau-Ponty cultivated a mutual intellectual exchange over a period of many years. Merleau-Ponty's writing repeatedly cross-references to the work of Beauvoir can be found, and in turn she has been inspired, notably so, by Merleau-Ponty's phenomenological approach. For more on the interrelation between Beauvoir's feminism and Merleau-Ponty's phenomenology, see Stoller 2010, especially part I on "existence." How much she was particularly inspired by his phenomenological analysis of *time* and *temporality*, however, is less clear.

3 The perspective of lived experience is a main characteristic of Merleau-Ponty's phenomenology. In appreciation of the *Phenomenology of Perception,* Simone de Beauvoir also treats femininity in her work on *The Other Sex* from the perspective of experience and even gives the second part of her work the title "L'expérience vécue" (for more on experience in Merleau-Ponty's work, see, e. g., Kruks 2001).

4 For more on time and temporality in Husserl's phenomenology, see Lohmar and Yamaguchi 2010.

rality? It should be pointed out up front that Merleau-Ponty places great emphasis on the past. He claims that everything we have ever perceived, thought or
done remains an implicit dimension in our present life. As past experiences
they can be called "traces." However, these traces, as Merleau-Ponty argues,
do not simply refer to the past, "they are present" (413).[5] Even if we cannot remember our past perceptions, our previous thoughts, or actions we once under-
took at some point in time, there is still no doubt about the fact that these perceptions, thoughts and actions belonged individually to *us*. Put differently, the
simple fact that something is not remembered does not mean that this experience did not happen, that it no longer exists, or that it no longer influences
our present life. The no longer recalled experience exists at least as something
"no-longer-remembered." For something in the past exerting influence on us
does not require that it is necessarily remembered. Furthermore it means that
we are and remain those who at one point had this perception or thought or carried out this action. To put it differently: we are everything that we have once perceived, thought or done, and we, in a certain way, remain the person we once
were: "[I]f I am mistaken at this moment, it is for ever true that I am mistaken"
(393), Merleau-Ponty argues. Having once seen a painting by Van Gogh, I have
forever incorporated this painting into myself, being somebody who once has
seen it somewhere, under certain circumstances and in a certain way: "[e]ven
though I retain no clear recollection of the pictures which I have seen, my
whole subsequent aesthetic experience will be that of someone who has become
acquainted with the painting of Van Gogh" (393). Nothing in life can undo what
happened in life.

To turn to the topic of aging, it can be concluded, following Merleau-Ponty:
If once I was a child, then even in old age I will be someone who has been a
child. Even as an old person I am still none other than the one I once was, despite all the transformations my life has brought with it. Merleau-Ponty summarizes this insight by the following sentences: "What we have experienced is, and
remains, permanently ours; and in old age a man is still in contact with his
youth" (393).

---

5 Sigmund Freud speaks of unconscious "mnemic traces" (German: "Erinnerungsspuren")
which are, literally, "traces of memory." The English translation provided by Strachey speaks of
"memory-traces": "A trace is left in our psychical apparatus of the perceptions which impinge
upon it. This we may describe as a 'memory-trace'; and to the function relating to it we give the
name of 'memory'" (Freud 1993, 537). Such "mnemic traces" or "memory-traces" are representations of an absent object *in* the present. As long as they belong to the unconscious
system, however, they are incapable of emerging into consciousness (Laplanche and Pontalis
2006, 247–49).

Let us concentrate on this wording: "and in old age a man is still in contact with his youth." In the French original it is: "le vieillard touche à son enfance" (Merleau-Ponty 1945, 450). What does Merleau-Ponty intend to express through this? First of all it expresses the irrefutability of the past. We can never leave the past behind in the same way as we overtake a car. We cannot discard it like a piece of old clothing. Indeed, we wear the past everyday and every year of our lives, in every moment of our present age. Or to give another example: although we grow out of our baby shoes, our feet are still the same—we are still one and the same person. The "wonder" of aging is not that once you were someone else who is now no longer there but that you are the person who you once were: the old man is still in contact with his childhood, the childhood is a "permanent acquisition," as Merleau-Ponty points out (1962, 392).

On the other hand, this statement also comments on the special quality of the irrefutable past. *How* is this past always there for me? The wording "in old age a man is still *in contact with* his youth" (emphasis added) provides a clue to answer this question. That the old man is in "contact" with his past and does not take possession of it is a major point. This sort of "contact" or better "touch" (*attouchement* in French) is only a *soft* kind of contact, often just a first closeness, and associated with a feeling of carefulness and respect. For this reason it also differs from other forms of contact such as grasping. From this we can conclude that the past is only present for us in a very subtle, sensitive way.[6]

However, it is never wholly there for us, even though it always represents an acquisition to us. Certainly, the past withdraws mostly from our conscious perception. We can never remember all our past experiences. And try as hard as we might, even when we actively recall our memories, a large part of our past will still remain in the dark. Vice versa, we can say that the past is not "reducible to the express memories" (393), "whereas in fact we feel it [the past] behind us as an incontestable acquisition" (419), as Merleau-Ponty states.

The past Merleau-Ponty examines can be described as a *latent knowledge*. It is intrinsic to the knowledge we posses about ourselves, without explicitly having knowledge of it. The Latin verb *latere* means "to lie hidden": something is there, but it is hidden. This past can also be termed an *anonymous* knowledge. It is anonymous in that it is not called into being through reflection or an act

---

6 It is important to note that the English translation of Merleau-Ponty's "le vieillard touche à son enfance" into "and in old age a man is still in contact with his youth" is misleading. To "touch somebody or something" is not the same as "to be in contact with somebody or something." While "being in contact" does not say much about the quality of the contact, the verb "to touch" denotes a special form of contact.

of recognition: it is simply there without us ever having given this knowledge a concrete description or name. The Greek *an ónyma* means "having no name," "unnamed," which does not mean the same as "unknown." It *is* known but not in a conscious manner.[7]

As outlined above by way of Merleau-Ponty's philosophy, phenomenology is based on the premise that the past is a temporal horizon *of* the present. According to phenomenology, a horizon is a domain which withdraws from our direct knowledge or experience, but which is inherent to every knowledge or experience. Thus, a perceived object appears, for example, only in perspectival adumbrations (*Abschattungen*). I can see the front of an object, but other sides of the object are not visible to me. With every change in perspective new sides become invisible, that is, they become anonymous horizons.[8] There remains always something invisible left. An object can never be viewed simultaneously from all its perspectives and with all its adumbrations. Despite this, we never perceive only the "front side" but the object as a whole. The invisible sides of the object contribute to the identification of the object itself. These phenomenological ideas are consistent with psychoanalysis, which is based on the idea that the past that has not been remembered—in the language of psychoanalysis: the unconscious —but still leaves its traces in the present life of a person.[9] This unconscious, as is generally known, is not directly accessible to us but can only be made available indirectly, through our dreams, for example.

The Intersection of Time in Beauvoir and Merleau-Ponty

In this essay, I have juxtaposed Beauvoir and Merleau-Ponty by introducing two different ways of discussing time and temporality. In this respect, I concentrated on two claims which both of these French philosophers asserted in regard to aging. Now I would like to pursue the question as to how these two claims differ

---

7 I have elsewhere applied this phenomenological concept of latency and anonymity to gender and sexuality, arguing that gender identity and sexuality should not only be described in terms of explicit knowledge but also in terms of "latent" and "anonymous" knowledge (Stoller 2008a, 2013).

8 It was Husserl himself who, in various sections of his work, characterized the horizon as being anonymous. The anonymous horizon is depicted as "determinable indeterminacy" (Husserl 2001, 42). For more on anonymity with regard to gender and temporality, see Stoller 2011, and on anonymity in phenomenology in a more general sense, see Stoller 2008b.

9 For Merleau-Ponty's interpretation of psychoanalysis throughout his work, see Stoller 1999.

and how they could both apply to a kind of gerontological ethics. In the following I will argue that Beauvoir and Merleau-Ponty address two different aspects of aging, but that they are both conducive to developing an ethics of age and aging.

When Beauvoir calls upon us to recognize ourselves in old people, then she is speaking on a *social* level, addressing the relationship between "self" and "other." From the very beginning of her work *The Coming of Age*, the social dimension of aging plays a central role. One of her main ideas is that one's own age is conveyed, in the first instance, through the social world (*Mitwelt*). That means it is others who make us aware of our own age and aging process. Beauvoir mentions, on numerous occasions, one of her key experiences connected to aging: At the age of 50 she heard someone call out in surprise: "So Simone de Beauvoir is an old woman, then?" (Beauvoir 1996, 288)[10] At that moment Beauvoir became confronted with her own age. She contends that the experience of being old is, generally, determined through social relationships, that is, when old meets young.

In addition to the meaning the social world (*Mitwelt*) has for the realization of one's own age, Beauvoir also emphasizes the role of objects of the external world (*Außenwelt*). One example, familiar to most of us, would be looking at old photographs. Usually we are not aware of our age—but when we look at old pictures we inevitably become aware of an age difference: This was me before; now I am older. Both cases—that of social interaction as well as the case of the perception of objects (*Gegenstandswahrnehmung*)—comprise elements of the external world (*Außenwelt*). In sum, it is somebody or something outside myself that or who is capable of reminding me of my own current age. It is either an object or a person. In terms of philosophy, the experience of aging, according to Beauvoir, is primarily built upon the experience of the world and of the other.

But it is also important to stress another aspect not yet mentioned. When Beauvoir proposes that we shall recognize ourselves in the other, notably the older person, then she is doing so out of an *ethical claim*. As mentioned in the first part of this essay, Beauvoir contends that recognizing ourselves in older people is crucial to a humane approach to them. It is the first step in that we no longer treat old people in our society with indifference, ignorance or disrespect. As soon as we focus more on the social perception of older people, the situation itself will move us. Just to refresh our memory, here is the quote again.

> [l]et us recognize ourselves in this old man or in that old woman. It must be done if we are to take upon ourselves the entirety of our human state. And when it is done we will no lon-

---

10 See also Beauvoir 1996, 288.

ger acquiesce in the misery of the last age; we will no longer be indifferent, because we shall feel concerned, as indeed we are. (1996, 5)

The assertion Beauvoir ultimately makes in this particular work is to call for a special *attitude* towards older people. This does not happen on its own but demands a conscious inner attitude towards the older generation—a change of the attitude, which should lead to a break with the habitus. It presupposes the moral will to engage ourselves with older people and the aged. Certainly, it also needs a certain practice, that is, practice in perceiving older people. This means that recognizing one's elders or older generations is not a matter of course: it very often requires a certain awareness of the existence of older people and their specific life-worlds, which goes hand in hand with an inner attitude towards them. This inner attitude and this practice of perception mean a responsible social attitude and are both of an ethical nature. Regarding Simone de Beauvoir, we can conclude that by taking account of Beauvoir's call upon us to recognize ourselves in the other, her approach is explicitly ethical.

This leads back again to Merleau-Ponty. He emphasizes the aspect of one's own childhood in later years. According to Merleau-Ponty, childhood, that is, each person's past in itself, is an integral part of a person's present age. The fact that the old man or old woman is still in touch with his or her own childhood indicates that one's own past is never really over because it still plays a role in the present. Merleau-Ponty's perspective represents the perspective of the old man or the old woman who looks back upon his or her own childhood. His view is not directed—like Beauvoir's—at the external in the objective and social world, the world of things and people, at least not if one considers his quote about the old man.[11] His sight is set *inward*, and as such it does not express an inter-subjective but an *intra-subjective* relationship.

The philosophical differentiation between the "relation to the world" (*Weltbezug*), the "relation to the other" (*Fremdbezug*), and the "relation to oneself" (*Selbstbezug*) is quite helpful in order to understand what kind of relation Beau-

---

11 I am aware that Merleau-Ponty's phenomenology cannot be reduced to this aspect. As I mentioned at the beginning, Merleau-Ponty in his *Phenomenology of Perception* takes into account, in the corresponding parts, both dimensions—that of the past as well as that of the future. It would also be wrong to assume that he places greater emphasis on the relation to itself or the relation to the other. This, of course, is not the case. On the other hand, here I am not striving for completeness. The subject of this essay is not to compare Merleau-Ponty and Beauvoir as a comprehensive system. I would like to stress again that I have only examined two aspects which are found in the works of Merleau-Ponty and Beauvoir and try to discuss their content so as to formulate some useful ideas for a gerontological ethics.

voir and Merleau-Ponty actually refer to in their accounts of the experience of being old. What follows from this differentiation is that Merleau-Ponty places eminent significance on the relation to itself, while Beauvoir in the sections cited in this essay pays attention to the other person and outer objects. One moves towards the external, the other turns inward: Simone de Beauvoir focuses on other people and things, Merleau-Ponty focuses on the other within oneself.

The way in which Merleau-Ponty conceives the past also demonstrates a further difference between him and Beauvoir. As I have illustrated, Merleau-Ponty sees the past as a temporal horizon which is an essential element determining our present experience, even if we cannot remember the past and its events specifically. As a rule, for us the past is only there as an anonymous, inexpressible knowledge, for only seldom do we fully remember our past. However, Merleau-Ponty avoids making a value judgment when it comes to the anonymous or latent past, and his phenomenological description of the temporal structure of human existence remains entirely free from any explicit ethical consideration.

Certainly, Beauvoir in her work *The Coming of Age* too emphasizes the past, however she does so in a different way than Merleau-Ponty does. In fact, the past, according to her, plays an important role in the lives of older people. "This delight in former days is characteristic of most old people, and indeed it is often this that makes their age most evident" (1996, 362). The "intimate solidarity with the past," according to Beauvoir, "applies to most old people" (1996, 362). She even speaks of a kind of return of "childhood" in the life of an "aged man": "It is his childhood above all that returns to haunt the aged man" (370). Interestingly, she also says that in old age "he recognizes himself in the baby" (372). These remarkable aspects remind us of Merleau-Ponty. However, Beauvoir also claims that old people are intensively "fixed" to the past if not to say caught in it: "They set up a fixed, unchanging essence against the deteriorations of age, and tirelessly they tell stories of this being that they were, this being that lives on inside them" (362). She seems to say that the past is a kind of prison in which the aged are captured: "At his point the whole of a long life is set and fixed behind us, and it holds us *captive*" (373, emphasis added). Moreover, she describes the life of the elderly as being mainly characterized by boredom. The retired people are victims of what she called a "terrible curse" of boredom (541).

In my opinion, this might well be an appropriate description of the experiences of old people. But the point here is that Beauvoir makes a value judgment: she seems to see the orientation of the elderly towards the past as something *negative*. This means that she does not simply perceive the old people's orientation towards the past in a neutral way; in my opinion, she instead refers to a certain kind of elderly people only, and hand in hand evokes a negative image of them in general. Apparently, she also shares a certain popular view of psychology: the more attached a person is to his or her past, the less capable is he or she to cope with everyday life.

Beauvoir's widely negative account of the past in the life of the ages goes well with the concept of "project" in existential philosophies, such as Sartre's existentialism, according to which a "project" is always directed at the future. According to Sartre, each of us must determine his/her own project in order to transcend our current life and continue with our existence. Individual choice and transcendence are highly recommended existentialist values; they guarantee a future life in satisfaction while avoiding stagnation and frustration. In my opinion, only in light of Beauvoir's existentialist attitude are we able to understand Beauvoir's formula for a "solution" at the end of her study *The Coming of Age:* "There is only one solution ..., and that is to go on pursuing ends that give our existence a meaning" (540). It seems as if Beauvoir, at this point, follows Sartre's account of the project and supports a *future-directed* perspective. In the chapter "Old Age and Everyday Life" she quotes Sartre's notion of "nausea" which is to be understood as a result of a life without future projects: "If life does not transcend itself, moving towards given ends, and if it falls back, dull and motionless, upon itself, then it brings about that 'nausea' which Sartre has described" (459). For this reason she claims that people whose old age is most favored "are those whose interests are many-sided" (453). The greatest luck for the old person, according to Beauvoir, "is to have his world still inhabited by projects," and she adds that this luck is even greater than health (cf. 492).

Again, also at the point of the search for a solution Beauvoir is directed towards the outside, meaning towards something else but to oneself, in particular to the social world: She recommends "to go on pursuing ends that give our existence a meaning—devotion to individuals, to groups or to causes, social, political, intellectual or creative work" (540). Here she trusts in "passions" which allow the aged to stay active and engaged with other people and avoid them to pay too much attention to themselves: "in old age we should wish still to have passions strong enough to prevent us turning in upon ourselves" (540). Thus, Beauvoir is not only saying that it is good to care for one's passions, she is also saying that turning in upon ourselves is less recommendable if one has reached a certain age. This is why she seems to indirectly recommend avoiding it. She claims that existence is worth to be lived only if it is connected to the social world: "One's life has value so long as one attributes value to the life of others, by means of love, friendship, indignation, compassion" (541). As I have mentioned above, Beauvoir does have a certain sense of the past, and the idea, e.g., that the childhood returns to the aged person, certainly should not go unnoticed. However, it seems to me that, at the end, her philosophical commitment to Sartre's existentialism and the need for transcendence does not fully allow her to make a more *positive* use of it.

At this point I would like to depart from Beauvoir's standpoint and follow another path of thinking. To be clear: I do not intend to say that being directed to the future and staying engaged with the social world is not helpful in order to live a good life as an aged woman or man. There is nothing wrong with this so far. Beauvoir's solution of a certain way of "active aging" certainly avoids depression and stagnation. However, when it turns out that future-directed life implies a distance from the past, it must be asked if this must necessarily be the case. In my opinion, moving to the future must not go at the expense of moving to the past. Rather, living a good life at an advanced age does require a *double movement:* being directed to the future as well as being directed to the past. As indicated above, there is a tendency in Beauvoir's account to deliver a negative account of the past. Several passages in her book evoke the impression that Beauvoir cannot pull anything good out of the past and sees it, first and foremost, as a hindrance. If we take into consideration Beauvoir's view of old people's neurotic fixation to the past and her belief in the existential concept of aiming only at the future—then it follows that she supports a more negative understanding of the past. Beauvoir seems to say that, contrary to the miserable fixation to the past, if old people want to live in dignity they have to project themselves into the future and leave behind all the hindering past. Thus, according to Beauvoir, you can have a future only if you give up the past.

In contrast, Merleau-Ponty does not seem to have such a negative attitude towards the past. If the past keeps on playing a role in the present, then it is not as a "burden" that we must bear into the present. He avoids placing a value judgment on the past. Contrary to Beauvoir, he refrains from making a judgment.[12] A human being is all that he or she once was, regardless of whether their lives up to that point have been good or bad, whether the past is painful or pleasant to recall. When he says that the old man is still in touch with his childhood, then he wants to say that we can never make an end to our past because it is always present within the present.

Contrary to Beauvoir, however, Merleau-Ponty did not develop an explicit ethics of age and aging. Beauvoir has put forward the claim that we must recognize ourselves in other old people. This calls for an especially sensitive attitude towards older people, a kind of *openness* towards them, which could, as a con-

---

12 Perhaps this is typical of the manner of the "phenomenological epoché." The "phenomenological epoché" is a term derived from Edmund Husserl and is part of the so-called "phenomenological reduction." It refers to the methodological act of suspending judgments about the perceived world.

sequence, lead to a humane understanding. We could say that Beauvoir's ethics of aging starts with just such an openness towards the other. In my opinion, this is one of the most valuable demands in Beauvoir's essay. However, although Merleau-Ponty does not place any such ethical demands, we could still argue that his ideas on the phenomenology of temporality at least contain an *implicit ethics*. We could interpret his statement "in old age a man is still in contact with his youth" as an implicit call to be open towards the past. What would such an implicit ethics look like?

In the spirit of Beauvoir's statement that one must develop a special inner attitude towards the other we can also claim that one must take on a special inner attitude towards one's own past. However, it is impossible to simply dictate sensitivity towards old people. In the same way one cannot force sensitivity towards one's own past. The past, usually, is not presented to us in its full transparency. As I mentioned in the second part of this essay, we must speak of the past as an *anonymous knowledge*. Behind this anonymous knowledge there lie the dormant past experiences as well as the repressed parts of our past.

However, psychoanalytical experience, especially, demonstrates that we can access these hidden pieces of the past—though only if we open our inner selves up to them, after we have stopped resisting and, if we allow ourselves to do so, by approaching them indirectly, and by reaching them through free association or dreams. This also means an openness towards the unknown, towards that which might come, even if it is threatening, as we know it can be. In my opinion, this kind of openness towards the past ("the child in the old man") can be termed an ethical attitude. It is an ethical attitude because it allows for an open encounter with the other within myself and makes change possible—a transformation that ultimately also shapes and redefines our relationship to the world and to people.

Perhaps it is at this point that Beauvoir and Merleau-Ponty intersect again in their different attitudes. Beauvoir demands openness towards the other, Merleau-Ponty demands openness towards one's own past. And although Beauvoir's ethics of the other, on the one hand, is more explicit since it obviously results in a changed lived relation to the aged, Merleau-Ponty's recognition of the other within oneself, on the other hand, supports an implicit ethics of the self. Yet both philosophers argue for a challenging openness towards an otherness, if not to say strangeness, an otherness and a strangeness that allows for an ethical attitude in and towards the world.

In the preface of her work *The Coming of Age* Beauvoir makes her point clearly, namely that age and aging can only be captured "as a whole," that they should be treated not only as a biological fact but also as a cultural fact (1996, 13). I share this view. Perceiving age in its entirety, however, can also mean examining it according to the three already mentioned aspects: in relation to the world (*Weltbezug*), in relation to the other (*Fremdbezug*) *and* in relation to itself (*Selbstbezug*). If one of these relations is underexposed, it would seem to me to lead to the whole perspective being undetermined, since every relation to the world or relation to the other effects the relation to itself. Naturally, the opposite is also true: The type of relation to itself deeply shapes the relation to the world and the relation to the other. To put it differently, if we do not have a negative attitude towards our past but accept it as a part of our life, with all its ups and downs, then we are on our way towards finding satisfaction in life. At this point I would like to refer especially to what we have learned from psychoanalysis: Only by channeling through the past can the future be (re)lived.[13]

To me, an ethics of age and aging seems to be incomplete if it is limited solely to social relationships and social values, that is, in relation to the world and in relation to the other. For an ethics of age and aging to be comprehensive, it must be complemented with the dimension of a relation to oneself. This way our view is not only directed towards the outside, towards the external world, but also towards the inside, the inner world; not only towards the future but also towards the past. Somewhere in the middle the future meets the past, and this encounter determines the quality of our age and aging and, I believe, our attitudes towards the elderly.[14]

Translated by Ida Černe

---

13 From this the conclusion can be drawn that Merleau-Ponty had much closer ties to psychoanalysis than did Beauvoir. It is documented in *The Other Sex,* that Beauvoir was a great skeptic of psychoanalysis. She made it very clear that she preferred existential perspectives to psychoanalytic approaches, as did most other French existentialists at the time. Directed at the future, existentialism is incompatible with psychoanalysis which emphasizes the past. Merleau-Ponty's attitude is completely different. From the very beginning of his career in philosophy, in the 1930s, he became interested and involved with psychoanalysis and even integrated it into his phenomenological theory. His occupation with psychoanalysis does not only contain Sigmund Freud's psychoanalytical theory, but goes beyond it to the works of post-Freudians such as Melanie Klein or Jacques Lacan. Here it seems appropriate to mention a statement Beauvoir made in 1986, three weeks before her death. In an interview she was asked what projects still interested her. She answered: "But there's something else I would very much like to do if I were thirty or forty now, and that is a work on psychoanalysis. I would not take Freud as my starting point, but go right back to basics and from a feminist perspective, from a feminine rather than a masculine viewpoint. But I shan't do it. I don't have enough time ahead of me. Other women will have to do it" (Schwarzer 1984, 88–89). Did Beauvoir perhaps, in her old age, become aware that psychoanalysis could do more for her than she had previously believed?
14 For extensive comments I would like to express my sincere thanks to Ida Černe, Helen Fielding, Dorothea Olkowski, and Christina Schües.

References

Beauvoir, Simone de. 1989. *The second sex*. Trans. H. M. Parshley. New York: Vintage Books.
Beauvoir, Simone de. 1996. *The coming of age*. Trans. Patrick O'Brian. New York and London:
    W. W. Norton & Company.
Freud, Sigmund. 1953. *The interpretation of dreams (second part) and on dreams*. In *The
    standard edition of the complete psychological works of Sigmund Freud*, vol. V
    (1900–1901). Trans. James Strachey. London: The Hogarth Press and the Institute of
    Psycho-analysis.
Husserl, Edmund. 2001. *Analysis concerning passive and active synthesis: Lectures on
    transcendental logic*. Trans. Anthony J. Steinbock. Dordrecht: Kluwer Academic
    Publishers.
Kruks, Sonia. 2001. *Retrieving experience: Subjectivity and recognition in feminist politics*.
    Ithaca, London: Cornell University Press.
Laplanche, Jean, and Jean-Bertrand Pontalis. 2006. *The language of psychoanalysis*. Trans.
    Donald Nicholson-Smith. London: Karnac Books.
Lohmar, Dieter, and Ichiro Yamaguchi, eds. 2010. *On time: New contributions to the
    Husserlian phenomenology of time*. New York: Springer.
Merleau-Ponty, Maurice. 1962. *Phenomenology of perception*. Trans. Colin Smith. London and
    New York: Routledge (originally published as *Phénoménologie de la perception*. Paris:
    Gallimard 1945).
Schwarzer, Alice. 1984. *After The Second Sex: Conversations with Simone de Beauvoir*. Trans.
    Marianne Howarth. New York: Pantheon Books.
Stoller, Silvia. 1999. Merleau-Pontys Psychoanalyse-Rezeption. *Phänomenologische
    Forschungen*, Neue Folge 4, 1. Halbband (1999): 43–76.
Stoller, Silvia. 2008a. Latentes Geschlechterwissen. In *Geschlechterwissen und soziale
    Praxis: Theoretische Zugänge—empirische Erträge*, ed. Angelika Wetterer.
    Königstein/Taurus: Ulrike Helmer, 64–81.
Stoller, Silvia. 2008b. Anonymität als Bestimmung von Welt. In *"Welten": Zur Welt als
    Phänomen*. Ed. Günther Pöltner and Martin Wiesbauer. Frankfurt/Main: Peter Lang,
    51–68.
Stoller, Silvia. 2010. *Existenz—Differenz—Konstruktion: Phänomenologie der Geschlechtlichkeit
    bei Beauvoir, Irigaray und Butler*. München: Wilhelm Fink.
Stoller, Silvia. 2011. Gender and anonymous temporality. In *Time in feminist phenomenology*,
    ed. Christina Schües, Dorothea E. Olkowski, and Helen A. Fielding. Bloomington and
    Indianapolis: Indiana University Press, 79–90.
Stoller, Silvia. 2013. The indeterminable gender: Ethics in feminist phenomenology and
    poststructuralist feminism. *Janus Head*, vol. 13 (1) (Winter/Spring), special issue on
    Feminist Phenomenology, ed. Eva M. Simms and Beata Stawarska, 17–34.

Marieke Borren
Towards a Gerontological Ethics of Existence?

Comment on Silvia Stoller

The aim of Stoller's article is to sketch the outlines of a "gerontological ethics" that conceives of aging and old age "as a whole," which means that it takes into account three dimensions: one's relation to the world (*Weltbezug*); to others (*Fremdbezug*), and to oneself (*Selbstbezug*). She does so by staging a dialogue between Simone de Beauvoir and Maurice Merleau-Ponty, regarding them as offering potentially complementary perspectives. Somewhat more in the background is a third intellectual source, psychoanalysis, though it is no less important to the overall argument.

Interestingly, implicit in Stoller's account are two different though not incompatible ethical approaches, each of them related to a different "spatial" and temporal perspective on our experience of the process of aging in general and of our own age in particular. The one perspective is turned *inward*, towards the *self*; it concerns one's relationship to oneself. More particularly, it takes the perspective of elderly people to their *former* selves, the children they once were and whom they could—and should—learn to see as a self that they still embody. Hence temporally, this perspective is directed towards the *past*, invoking the mostly pre-reflexive or, "anonymous," as Stoller calls it, operation of memory and remembrance. The past becomes a *topos* of openness here, provided we open ourselves to it. This resonates with the narrative strand of thought within the phenomenological tradition that holds that our past experiences are never fixed or determined but always remain open to interpretation and reinterpretation, although it is bound to basic factual givens.

The other perspective reverses this approach of aging both spatially and temporally. It is turned *outward*, to *others* and the *world*, both of which inevitably mediate our evaluations and experiences of old age. Typically the young (that is: not-yet-old) could—and should—learn to recognize in others the old people they will become themselves. In its primary orientation towards the *future*, anticipation replaces the retrospective mood of the first perspective. The future here becomes a *topos* of closure, of redundancy and decline.

The former perspective Stoller associates with Merleau-Ponty and psychoanalysis, the latter with Beauvoir. Beauvoir's account of old age contains the explicit and quasi-Kantian moral demand to put ourselves in the place of the elderly—since they reflect our own future. Stoller argues that appealing to the cultivation of an attitude of openness towards the past, Merleau-Ponty's ethical agenda is merely implicit.[1] This distinction runs parallel to the one between a Kantian deontological moral code on the one hand and what later Foucault alternately called "ethics of existence," "art of living" or "care for the self" on the other (Foucault 1986, 1988a, 1988b). Whereas a moral code formulates absolute, universalistic principles and rules of conduct that apply to our relationship to others, an ethics of existence encompasses a non-rule-guided *ethos* concerned with one's relation to oneself, one's own particular existence.[2] Beauvoir already demonstrated that these two ethical approaches may be compatible. Karen Vintges has convincingly reconstructed the development of a concept of ethics as art of living throughout Beauvoir's work, alongside a more conventional moral code. This Beauvoirian art of living she defines as follows: "In the name of our freedom, we must create ourselves as an individual identity, styling and developing our daily behavior in all its aspects, with the aim of contributing concretely to the quality of the life of others" (Vintges 1996, 94). More and more in the course of her work, Beauvoir came to add a positive ethos of existence to the absolute moral stance that she took on a number of social and political issues. In addition, she increasingly formulated this moral code in exclusively *negative* terms: one may not impede others' freedom to develop as free ethical subjects.[3] This double ethical perspective is also reflected in the very outline of *The Coming of Age:* whereas the first part of the book, "Old age seen from without," is indeed devoted to the depreciatory view of old people which society imposes on us, the perspective is reversed in the second half of the book, "The being in the world," in which Beauvoir turns her attention inward, to the lived experience of aging of the elderly themselves.

However, Beauvoir knew very well that we do not shape ourselves in a void: our existence is *situated*, which means that we are always already *weltbezogen* (related to the world). In *The Coming of Age* she analyzes how the social circumstances of elderly people block their abilities to shape their own existence, in a way very similar to her analysis of the fate of women in patriarchal society in *The Second Sex* more than twenty years before. Hence, it is no surprise that Beauvoir's normative assessment of old age is more negative than Merleau-Ponty's. She argues that socio-economic rather than biological factors determine the sad fate of old people. By exposing the scandal of the de-humanizing way

---

1 Cf. the insistence within psychoanalysis on "working through" one's personal past.
2 Interesting parallels exist between a "gerontological ethics of existence" and "narrative gerontology," an approach recently developed by Gary Kenyon, Phillip Clark and Brian de Vries (2001) and William Randall and E. Elizabeth McKim (2008).
3 See, Vintges 1996, especially chapter 6.

late-capitalist society treats old people, she attempts to raise critical awareness by breaking the "conspiracy of silence" (Beauvoir 1996, 2) on old age and to change society. As Beauvoir writes in the introduction of *The Coming of Age*, "[T]he fact that for the last fifteen or twenty years of his life a man should be no more than a reject, a piece of scrap, reveals the failure of our civilization" (6). She goes on, saying: "Insisting that men should remain men during the last years of their life would imply a total upheaval of our society" (7). An integrated gerontological ethics, of which Stoller has beautifully sketched the *existential* outlines, requires, I think, a critical *social* theory of old age alongside an ethics of existence, since social views on old age are hardly any less unfavorable than at the time of the publication of *The Coming of Age*.

References

Beauvoir, Simone de. 1996. *The coming of age*. Trans. Patrick O'Brian. New York, London: W. W. Norton & Company.

Foucault, Michel. 1986. *The care of the self: The history of sexuality*, vol. III. London, Harmondsworth: Penguin.

Foucault, Michel. 1988a. The ethic of care for the self as a practice of freedom. In *The final Foucault*, ed. James Bernauer and David Rasmussen. Cambridge, Massachusetts: MIT Press 1988, 1–20.

Foucault, Michel. 1988b. Technologies of the self. In *Technologies of the self: A seminar with Michel Foucault*, ed. Luther H. Martin, Huck Gutman and Patrick H. Hutton. Amherst: University of Massachusetts Press, 16–49.

Kenyon, Gary, Phillip Clark, and Brian de Vries, eds. 2001. *Narrative gerontology: Theory, research, and practice*. New York: Springer.

Randall, William L., and A. Elizabeth McKim. 2008. *Reading our lives: The poetics of growing old*. Oxford: Oxford University Press.

Vintges, Karen. 1996. *Philosophy as passion: The thinking of Simone de Beauvoir*. Bloomington: Indiana University Press.

Christina Schües

Age and Future

Phenomenological Paths of Optimism

If aging means to be old, then age and having a future are contradictions—this is a common assumption. If age belongs to the young, then the future is wide open. Those who are older have a shortened future, and those who are old do not have any future. Having a future, that is, making plans, being optimistic, and looking forward, is not a sentiment old people have. In her book *The Coming of Age*, Simone de Beauvoir confirms and explains this sentiment: old people are confronted with finitude. "Confronted" means "having a front," a limit before, literally in front of, the eyes. However, the concept of *future* seems to suggest infinitude and openness. When we see older people, then we see the past. But when we look more closely, we see our own future. And we wonder if our future will be miserable once it is transformed into the present.

The future (*avenir*), from which something comes, seems to have vanished for old people. Hence, this phase of life seems rather lost and empty, without prospects or optimism. Aging, we know, is a biological fact, a cultural phenomenon; it has a social dimension, and, most importantly for this discussion, an existential dimension. Generally, the social organization of elderly people could be, as Beauvoir admits, considered more optimistically if a society were to distribute sufficient resources for the elderly. However, the experiences elderly persons *must* existentially make with themselves and with their own temporality are typically difficult and frustrating. Consequently, it seems that bad habits and appalling traits, depression and misery almost become inevitable. With this consideration, Beauvoir positions her thinking within the negative-pessimistic reflective tradition which starts from the Greek melancholic lyric (such as Mimnermus) and extends to her existential-philosophical study.[1] This discourse of pessimism regards life as a history of decay. The alternative, optimistic view is rooted in the stoic-epicurean tradition, which begins with Solon. Its protagonists, such as, for example, Epicurus, Seneca, and Cicero, favor a lifelong learning process of maturity. In this essay I would like to consider Beauvoir's concept of the inner experience of the relation between aging and having a future with regard to questions of pessimism or optimism, decay or learning, loss or activity; then I like to present a third way between optimism or pessimism. Beauvoir claims that she describes the concrete experiences of aging from inner experi-

---

1 See also Améry (1994) and Bobbio (2001).

ence. Rather than providing a definition, she wants to tell stories, stories told from the subjective perspective of inner experiences, and these stories show a certain plurality of individuals. However, especially when considering the relation between aging and having a future she proposes very *specific* theses, which she supports with different stories.

In the following, my essay is divided into three parts. In the first part, I take up the question: When are you old? In the second part, I address a question that follows immediately from the response to the first question, namely: Is the future *really* lost? This question will reconsider the question of when someone is old. With respect to this question about the future I will consider two theses. First, I will discuss the thesis that, for aging, the future is in the process of *becoming* lost. Second, I will discuss the thesis that there is *no* more future. Finally, in the third part, I will reorient the phenomenology of time and activity by introducing a particular concept of temporal order.

When Are You Old?

Simone de Beauvoir makes rather precise observations about the inner experience of old people, derived from her reading and from what she has been told. She claims to discuss the human situation not merely from the outside but rather from an inside perspective. Emphasizing the subjective perspective, she formulates how the individual takes the existential human situation to be. This existential dimension can be considered with regard to the world, to history, and to time. I will reflect upon all three components, but mostly I will emphasize the question of time, and here especially the future.

World: Conflict and Contradiction

The external surrounding world is that which I am not. Namely, my self is confronted with the external body, the other with its gaze and the surrounding world. When I am old, when I am becoming old, I come into *conflict* with the external, which I am not. We all come into conflict with reality that inevitably presents the objective situation, according to Beauvoir. But this reality is there for the other, but not for myself. There is a contradiction between the inner evidence which stands for our duration, and the objective evidence of our transformation: "Whether we like it or not, in the end we submit to the outsider's point of view" (Beauvoir 1996, 290). This is when our old age begins:

> We must assume a reality that is certainly ourselves although it reaches us from the outside and although we cannot grasp it. There is an insoluble contradiction between the obvious clarity of the inward feeling that guarantees our unchanging quality and the objective certainty of our transformation (Beauvoir 1996, 290).

However, even though we might *try* to grasp the view from the outside reality, we will never be able to do so, because, as Beauvoir argues with Sartre, old age belongs to the category of the *unrealizable*. The un-realizable stands for that which I am not for myself; it stands for the outside aspect, for the reversal of my situation as I *live* it. The unrealizable stands for the objective form as it is realized by the body in the form of its slow but sure *decay*. My body is apprehended by the look of the other who regards my feeble body with its pains and weaknesses, its wrinkles and stiffness; it is forced upon me by society which makes up my surrounding world. Hence, the unrealizable, i.e., aging, exists for the other but not for myself. It is not an object of my inner experience.

The basis for Beauvoir's description of the unrealizable is a strict dualist thinking of objective condition and subjective feeling, external and inward evidence, of for-itself and in-itself, of the world that escapes me. The *other* in me is old, and this other I cannot realize. This contradiction, Beauvoir calls it also asymmetry, is supposed to be typical for elderly people. The result is that the force from the external—the body, the other, and the surrounding world—forces the old person into this contradictory situation to which he or she can either be blind or defensive.

Sometimes, for those who take up a defensive attitude, the unrealizable can provoke the assertion that "I am different" to other "old people"; but mostly old men and old women are frustrated. Certainly, men and women are frustrated in different ways; each individual lives his/her own frustration. Yet, each frustration is based on the unrealizable that is invoked by such a conflict.

This frustration has to do with the fact that societies change; our modern society tosses the aged person into his or her outdated past, and it does so while he or she is still alive (380). Overemphasizing the biological fate, modern society often decides, before she or he is even aware of any age phenomenon, that somebody is to be excluded from *present* daily life. With the difficulty of finding employment from the age of fifty-five on and retirement expected by the age of sixty-five, depending on vocation, older people are more or less "condemned to idleness because of this prejudice" (385). With respect to these issues, political questions could be posed: How do we structure and organize (*gestalten*) the world? Do old or elderly people have a place in the world other than exclusionary institutions like homes for the old-aged?

History: Weight and Imperatives

An old person's relation to history changes. He/she no longer has any control over the story of his/her own life. History slips out of memory; it becomes frozen and stiff, full of clichés and is not alive anymore (Beauvoir 1996, 365). The past *has* the old person; he/she wants to plunge back into his/her earlier years (372). Beauvoir describes how the old person internalizes his/her past in the form of pictures, fantasies, and emotions.[2] Thus, in a way, Beauvoir explains that history becomes ambiguous, frozen and stiff, and yet more alive than the present. The past is the base from which I project myself and which I must go beyond—this holds for every phase of life. The whole of what I have done, what I am, my knowledge, the mechanisms and the cultural tools I have learned, as well as the way in which I have been shaped by things, activities, and my relation with the world, is called the "practico-inert" by Beauvoir (following Sartre) (372). What is specific for the elderly person? He/she, according to Beauvoir, is much more burdened by the practico-inert than younger people; but the realization of a shortened future does not allow him/her to overcome the "imperatives of the past" and change them for the future. A close look at the following citation will reveal how Beauvoir distinguishes the heavy past from any possibilities of maturity or further projections of the self, which may include changes:

> Projects are frozen. This description suits old age, though old age is still more weighed down than maturity. At this point the whole of a long life is set and fixed behind us, and it holds us captive. Imperatives have increased in number; and the reverse of these imperatives are impossibilities (Beauvoir 1996, 373).

Thus, we are captured by the past, yet, as Beauvoir pessimistically suggests, the future which has evolved from the past has often enough disappointed our expectations.[3] My practico-inward and the imperatives of the past certainly do not guarantee that what is present or future directly grows out of the past; the longer I live, the more often my projects have been thwarted: the sudden death of family members or friends, perhaps even younger people, wipes out relationships, even whole sections or networks of relations of someone's life. Thus,

---

2 The French original reads in the following way: "l'homme âgé intériorise son passé" (Beauvoir 1970, 394). For the translation I prefer the English term "internalize" instead of "inward experience," because it includes a movement (Beauvoir 1996, 372). The German translator writes *verinnert* (Beauvoir 2004, 484).

3 "Not only has this past's future ceased to be a future, but in becoming the present it has often disappointed our hopes" (Beauvoir 1996, 366).

on the one hand, everyone is guided by her or his practico-inertia and the imperatives of the past, and, on the other hand, everyone is distressed and frustrated or disappointed by the adversities of a long life. And the older someone is, the heavier the past and the stronger the frustration can be, and the more the "contrast between the present and the past may become intolerable" (369). Beauvoir's argument is that, if the past is frozen and its imperatives strong, and if the future of this past is not realized, then the old person stands "bound hand and foot" in front of his/her future which is thereby lost and too short anyway (373).[4] Most significantly, the *concept of future* is Beauvoir's pivot for her stories about old people.

The Inner Experience of Time: Loss

Generally speaking, for Beauvoir time is basic to our existence. She begins her chapter on "Time, activity, history" with the following sentence: "For human reality, existing means *temporally existing:* in the present we look towards the future by means of plans that go beyond our past, in which our activities fall lifeless, frozen and loaded with passive demands" (Beauvoir 1996, 361, emphasis added, translation modified).[5] Aging changes our relation to time and specifically to the future. For young people the future is wide open and infinite, so Beauvoir suggests, but for the old person the future is finite and short, and this has profound consequences for the inner experience of life. Aging means aging in time, and age is a temporal form of life. If age is a temporal form of life, then questions arise concerning what form of time and what sort of experience of time Beauvoir proposes. For, certainly aging means a change of the temporal form of life.

Being old means to be confronted with one's own finitude with regard to the temporal dimension; the spatial dimension is always finite but the temporal dimension is, for the young, without limit. But—and here Beauvoir must assume a reflective act in inner experience—when we realize that we are old, then we also *realize* that our future is finite and that we are restricted to one epoch. Thus in this context it seems, even though age itself might not be an object of inner experience, that nevertheless the old person *must realize* that his/her concept of the future has changed fundamentally. Thus, she writes: "Once a certain thresh-

---

4 Cf. French original: "se trouve ligoté" (Beauvoir 1970, 395).
5 The English translation states that we exist in time. Time is not just prior or some sort of basket. "Temporal existing" is closer to the French: "Exister, pour la réalité humaine, c'est se temporaliser" (Beauvoir 1970, 383).

old has been passed—a threshold that varies according to the individual—the elderly man becomes aware of his biological fate: the number of years of life that remain to him is limited" (373). Having a limited or finite future means, for Beauvoir, that the future is short and closed: "It is the more closed the shorter it [the future] is, and seems all the shorter for being the more closed" (373). In other words, when the elderly person becomes conscious of the biological process of his/her age and of society's perception, *then* he/she is confronted with a twofold finitude: one is contingent and results from facticity. The limit is a biological fact, imposed from an objective perspective. The other sense of finitude is an ontological structure of the for-itself (377). Until old age these two senses remain separate, but when the elderly person acknowledges old age, both become apparent at the same time. The old person realizes, and I think this means acknowledges, his/her "own age," that his/her years are numbered, and that he/she will never escape (378). That is, if the future is closed and the past is frozen and full of imperatives, then the openness of the future is actually lost, and this means: life has lost its threefold structure of past-present-future.

A young person directs his/her hopes into the future that is open for him: "For an old man the stakes are down;" he cannot do anything fundamentally about what is lacking at his work because, so I assume reading Beauvoir, he realizes he does not have a sufficient future. The future is closed. Hence, so the argument goes, the future is lost. Very explicitly, Beauvoir commented in an interview with Alice Schwarzer, "But old age means taking a step out of the infinite into the finite. One has no future—that is the worst thing" (Schwarzer 1984, 88).[6]

The experience of time has discovered finitude; finitude guarantees my singularity, but at the same time, according to Beauvoir, the old person has only his/her past and realizes that the stakes are down, that the future is lost. When the future is lost, you are old.

Is the Future Really Lost When You Are Old?

Are "the stakes down"? Let me turn to a structural alternative in order to show a conception which accounts for aging from an inner perspective without relying upon the physical body, the world, and the other, that is, the generally objective perspective. However, just to clarify from the start, my own proposition about the temporal structure of life or age will differ from this one.

---

6 In this interview Beauvoir emphatically says in reference to Cocteau: "The bad thing about growing old is staying young" (Schwarzer 1984, 87).

Losing the Future: Structural Alternative

Max Scheler focuses on the inner process of one's "own" structure of consciousness.[7] He describes temporality as a threefold structure which finds itself in each immanent moment of experience, thus we find an immediate presence according to an act of consciousness, such as perception, and a past and future accord for the acts of remembering and expectation. In each of our moments of experience, these three modes exist in the form of a total content (*Gesamtinhalt*). Differently regarded from this total content is the temporal scope (*Zeitumfang*) which refers to the whole life process. Since the presence of every event is connected with past and future, and since the process of life is directed towards the future, the individual temporal scope is constantly redistributed. That is, the scope of the past grows constantly, and the content of the future constantly declines. Hence, with every experienced progress of time, the future horizon becomes narrower in its experienced content (*erlebbaren Fülle*). Scheler defines this phenomenon of the increase of the past and decline of the future as nothing other than the essence of "aging" (Scheler 1957, 16 and 21).[8] Being aware of the difference between these two total scopes in favor of the range of the past is the "experience of the death direction" (20). Even if someone were not to know his or her date of birth, she or he still would be conscious of his or her age. Age is not experienced because of external circumstances such as date of birth, wrinkles and a feeble body; rather it is *intuitively felt*, i.e. inwardly experienced, on the ground of the constant drain of future life by way of the lived life and its increasing past.[9] Since intuitively sensed, aging accords with the experience of the direction of death. I, therefore, even have knowledge of my own death which I approach by getting older. This knowledge is evident and does not need any proof by external observation or associations on the basis of, for example, a bad illness. Dying would simply mean the "more or less *contingent realization*" of "death" being the essence which had already been anchored in the structure of life

---

7 Max Scheler was widely read at the time and well known by the French phenomenologist Maurice Merleau-Ponty; Beauvoir does not mention Scheler.
8 For the following discussion I refer especially to Scheler's chapter on "Tod und Fortleben" (Scheler 1957, 9–64). The translations of the citations are mine.
9 For Scheler, the evidence of death is a self-experience which is bound to the death direction that is essential for the life structure. It is questionable, however, whether the consciousness of aging is founded on a difference of the increasing of the scope of the past and decreasing of the scope of the future. In my consideration, the experience of temporal scope must be distinguished from its content. If many events have passed and we followed them enthusiastically, then we experience the temporal flow as running very fast. Looking back, however, it seems as if a lot of time has passed *because* of its full content (see Bergson 1988, 133–77).

(18). For Scheler, the evidence of having to die manifests itself in each moment of life.

Scheler's conception is interesting for us but also problematic. It is interesting insofar as he tries to elicit intuitive evidence of the limit of life—death—as being evident in each moment of life. Thus, for him internal life always carries its own limit, i. e. its own finitude. Finitude is always there and cannot confront me from an external point of view which is grounded on some biological base. The problematic side here is the following: "Having to die" would find its evidence by actual death. However, the realization of dying does not have the same essence of death as would be experienced by the evidence of death. The realization of death changes structures which were given in life. Thus, a phenomenological account could never get a grip on the essence of the limit of life. Yet, for Scheler, the evidence of death includes also the having-to-die. But if the "must" is an essential element of the evidence of death, then the "must" is only realized by dying. Dying is the affirmation of a claim of evidence. However, dying as the ending of a direction of consciousness and "having-to-end" are incompatible with each other. If the "must," the necessity, the "having-to" of death is an essential element of death, then death would be a *factum tremendum*, a horrible fact, but not an experience of necessity that the human can approach with an affirmative evidence of death and that she or he can actually realize.[10] Thus, death in its realization remains to be a *factum brutum*, a wild fact, because it can never be fulfilled in any structure of experiences; hence, its act of consciousness (which it does not have) can never be adequately experienced. Death as a *factum brutum* is absent from consciousness; therefore death, or the limit of life, is surely an important topic for philosophical investigations, but it makes a fool of a philosophical thinking which tries to ground its account on it. Death remains by itself in its wildness and strangeness, even though, for Scheler, life has a definite direction which is intuitively sensed, its limit cannot be realized even though it is there in the future.

The Future is Lost

The differences between Scheler and Beauvoir are interesting: Both focus on inner experience; for both time seems to be subjective. However, for Scheler the time of life has the order or the *Gestalt* of an hourglass. In the beginning we have much time, a bucket full, and we *intuitively* feel that time runs through

10 See also the insightful essay by Elisabeth Ströker (1968).

us and that we lose it. Yet, as we have discussed, he finds it difficult to give reason to the necessity of dying and death. For Beauvoir, the loss of time is based on a more or less sudden internalization (*Verinnerlichung*) by way of becoming aware of the external gaze of society and the other, the biological phenomena, the body and the calculation of clocks and calendars. But in Beauvoir's view, *intuitively* we feel always young. We would never *realize* the time of age, if physical concepts, for example, the calculation of time (which is best done by digital clocks) did not remind us of the fact that it is *time* to be old. Thus, we come into conflict between the inner experience of having been released from the "nothing" (from where we come) somewhere (spatial term) behind us and the continuation into the infinite and objective time by physics. Thus, realizing finitude as a shock and frustration means that the I, the soul of the elderly person, subjugates itself (or is subjugated) under an objective physical time concept. If the elderly person is shocked by the "attack" of the external world and by finitude and closedness, then this means that his/her ego is confronted with objective time. She or he feels trapped by the conflict between the ego and the physical, between an inner time concept (mentalism) and the concept of objective time (physicalism).

Augustine was the first to propose an inner time concept in order to explain movement (Augustine 1998, 221–45). For him, time is not in the world or a property of the world but rather the *extension of the soul*. The soul measures the time of movements in the form of continuous presence: "The present considering the past is the memory, the present considering the present is immediate awareness, the present considering the future is expectation" (235). They are psychic or mental functions which do not have their corresponding temporal order in the world. The soul measures impressions which are found in the soul, in consciousness, and hence only the soul has time, and therefore time has a subjective structure.[11]

Phenomenologists such as Edmund Husserl and Henri Bergson have more or less followed this initiative by Augustine; all of them made the temporality of consciousness or experience in terms of a threefold structure of past, present, and future a topic of discussion. Empirical time, i.e. the time which is constitutive of our experience, is built *in* time, which itself is not the form of this experience. Thus, on the one hand, time is *in* the soul, or respectively it is the temporality of consciousness[12], but it is not in the world, and on the other hand time is

---

11 Thus, for Augustine, the one who has a spiritual life and who is close to God lives most in the present.

12 Martin Heidegger, of course, intends to break out of the philosophy of consciousness. But it would be a different discussion to ask more carefully whether he actually succeeds. Certainly he distinguishes physical, objective time from the temporality of "Dasein."

to be taken as objective, physical time which is measured by clocks and which is one-dimensional and continuous.[13] Humans generally have to deal with the (epistemological) conflict between objective and subjective time, and they are often trapped in this very conflict which becomes their confrontation and frustration. Keeping in mind this long tradition of two opposing time concepts in Western history, Beauvoir's descriptions are not surprising: It is in the nature of this confrontation between opposing time concepts that any subjugation of inner experience under the calculation of the one-dimensional, oriented, physical time structure can only be felt—because of its finitude (based on the biological facts), externality and abstraction—as an attack on self-consciousness and as an "empty experience." Hence, if this is called "aging," then it must remain "unrealizable."[14] Thus, the limit of life (*death!*) can neither be realized from inner experience nor from an objective perspective. But does this mean "the stakes are down"?

Paths of Optimism

Beauvoir suggests two paths of optimism, both of which are attached to the belief that the future is the key to optimism, to a "good life." The first path does not take time as being problematic because aging passes silently for someone. This idea is grounded in the observation that sometimes one is not really bothered by the external world (the body, the other, society) and one continues to fit smoothly into the "objective world" and the biological facts. This is certainly a reassuring thought, but philosophically not very interesting. The second possibility is based on a different social time order: If a society has a circular time structure, then the idea of post mortal benefits for the next generation can allow the future to remain extended and open for an old person. Thus if, for instance, a farmer can count on his children to keep his farm going after his death, then his work seems to have a concrete meaning that even exceeds his death. This is also a reassuring idea based on a different socio-historical structure of society.

In the following, I would like to consider a different perspective on temporality and revalorize the present. A comment by Seneca gives insight into a different time concept: "The greatest hindrance to living is expectancy, which depends upon the morrow and wastes to-day" (1932, sec. IX). Or perhaps more

---

13 Certainly, there are different concepts of physical time, but these differences, which mostly relate to questions about the essences of laws of nature, shall not be of concern in this essay.
14 But actually I am sure we find more experiences or phases of life in which this phenomenon of a time-clash is the base for an "empty experience."

generously stated: It is important to live in the present which supposedly only the future promises. The value of life, the meaning of life, lies in the present. Beyond Beauvoir's reflections I will focus on a phenomenological concept of time which is structured according to the order of activity. I call it the "order of time."

Time of Human Activity: Order of Time

The "power of time" is very central to human beings; we cannot experience anything without time, yet time is not a property of things.[15] Nevertheless, we are temporal beings and we exist temporally. Therefore, time has power over us. But, as people so often complain in their everyday lives, time can be stolen. The condition for the experience that someone, a technical devise or a system, can steal one's time is the measurement of time by clocks and the transformation of temporality in quantifying time sequences. Then economic pressure, tight time schedules or individual demands by other people or fixed time constraints can consume and rule personal time. For a person who accordingly feels temporally under pressure, this pressure results in experiences of having to run after time, of having no time of one's own or of having to work faster and faster. Michael Ende, the author of the fantasy novel *Momo*, explains this phenomenon in a dialog between Meister Hora and little Momo about the gentlemen in gray: "They live on people's time, as you know, but time dies—literally dies—once it has been wrested away from its rightful owners. All human beings have their own share of time, but it survives only for as long as it really belongs to them" (Ende 1988, 129). Momo understands. The gray men are actually dead. They do not have their own time, and without the stolen time, "they'd disappear into thin air, which is where they come from" (Ende 1988, 129).[16] We learn from this story that someone who does not have time anymore is nobody. Human beings have their own time, time is not a property, but time—and this is a very important phenomenological observation—has its order. The order of time becomes something like a second nature (cf. Schües 2011, 68). Each being, but also each activity, has its different and specific order of time. A human is not simply in the world; rather, he/she is constituted through human activities which are always temporally structured. Without time human existence would be nothing; the loss of time means non-existence, existence means to be in time and to have time. If it is true that everybody has his or her *own* time, then this means, firstly, that the

---

15 For a further analysis, see Schües 2011.
16 The men in gray have the Gestalt or the order of time of human beings.

order of time changes according to situations, actions and life phases. So far, Beauvoir would agree. But secondly, it would mean that neither a physical time concept nor a strictly subjective or inner time concept is suitable to explain a different order of time that is found in between human activity and experience.

What does "order" mean in regard to the issue of time? The term "order" stands for a *particular* temporal organization of activity, i.e. physical or mental activity which is elevated from its context by means of its specific order and which presents a certain *finite unity* in experiences. The order of time has a *quality* and not just a quantity. The quality of an order can be transposed by simultaneously holding onto the same rhythm. For example, a melody can be transposed in a different tone, or the way of telling a funny story has a specific internal time order. When speaking of our experiences, we often distinguish between light, boring or hard times.

Hence, phenomenologically seen, every activity has its own temporal order which is distinct from the quantity of time or clock time. Certainly, activities take place *in* time. But this external observation refers only to a quantity measured by calculation, for instance, the duration of the action. More essential to an activity is its own time, its temporal quality: For instance, when you read a book, it is not important how long you read and at what time you read which sentence. More fundamentally, you have to forget your watch and focus on the meaning of the text in order to understand and enjoy it. Or, when you repair your bicycle you must proceed in a certain way; the aspects "before" and "after" are understood in terms of the ground of the task and the structure of a bicycle repair. Or finally, the dialog between two lovers is certainly carried away from any time considerations; it does not have particular goals and rules that have been calculated beforehand.

Consequently, calculated time is not a constitutive element of any of these examples.[17] Between the organization of time (*Zeitgestaltung*) and the particular activity concerning a concrete being there is an *interrelation*. The order is neither *simply* my time nor *simply* the time of the other but always *more or less* suitable and constitutive for the activity in its concrete context and always *more or less* suitable for the way *I am doing it*.

Sometimes we act according to an order of time which is not at all our own time and not at all suitable for an activity because someone else has the *power of time* over us. Then we do not feel as though we are ourselves; we feel alienated and oppressed by the power of the time of the other. *Sharing time* means trying

---

17 Certainly there are exceptions, some games, for example, chess against the clock, use clocks as constitutive elements.

to live and to act according to a similar order of time. It means combining one's own time and the time of the other; it means being in accord with the order of time of the other.[18] Living in society, living with other people means being subjected to different orders of time (*Zeitgestaltungen*): the time of one's own and the other, but also the time of activities and things, for instance, reading a difficult book, simply needs a certain order of time; when somebody speaks too slowly, it makes us nervous.

Growing up means becoming accustomed to the order of time in society. It is not simply my time or the social time that are constitutive for the sense of an action but the time order of that activity. Each activity has its own proper time (Mittelstraß 1992, 394). And each person has also her personal way of carrying out an activity. Thus, thinking is different from repairing bicycles; sorrow is different from melancholy; sleeping is different from boredom, and so on.

Even more drastically considered, if activities, but also life processes and natural processes, did not have their own time order (*Gestalt*), then we would not understand what time means and we would not sometimes have the sentiment that other people, or certain institutional structures, could steal our time from us or the time which is appropriate for a particular activity.

Hence, my argument is that a time conception which is restricted to physicalistic calculation or to the inward ego cannot possibly account for different phases of life or different activities respectively. If I were to argue that each activity, each life process, even each natural process, had its own temporal order, then I would also have to assume that age has its own temporal order. The fact that things need their time according to their "nature" can also be understood when we refer, for instance, to our lived body: For speaking we need our vocal cords, for listening we use the ears (in the broad sense), for human interaction we use this "natural" ground, yet we do not focus on the natural grounds—we take them for granted and act accordingly, e. g. we speak in a certain rhythm (unless we have a cough or ear problems). Or, for instance, take happiness, love, and depression: they are not properties of an individual life but each sentiment has a particular *Gestalt* under which life appears. That is, it is not time that flows but the activities, the things of human life that move, as already the Greeks knew. The experiences of human beings are expressions of active time, or *Gestalt* time; they are not adequately captured by quantifying physical time or the temporality of an inner ego (or the soul).

---

18 This can be thought in reference to Wittgenstein's phrase: "And they agree in language they use" (Wittgenstein 1969, § 241). Compare also the essay by Gail Weiss (2011).

Consequently, aging and its activities also have their own *Gestalt* time. In order to sharpen the difference between my view and Beauvoir's, I will briefly advance my thesis: Beauvoir believed, as stated above, that because of the confrontation of interiority and exteriority age *cannot be realized* and that someone feels old when she or he *realizes* that the future is lost. Her perspective assumes that the external worldview gains the upper hand over the inner experience and that in fact we are firmly convinced by the prospect of a finite future, an understanding of which we get by means of calculation. The clock and the calendar are our paradigm of transformation from a concrete time to an abstract time. This transformation takes her out of the concrete activity of life and confronts her with the existential limit of death, which is indeed not part of life.

My suggestion is the following: If we were to *learn* to consider activities according to their appropriate time order (*Zeitgestalt*), and if we were to acknowledge that each activity is temporally organized (*zeitlich gestaltet*) in the present and not just in the future, then we could learn to take each phase of life according to its particular time and realize it in its own rights and values. Of course the decay, stiffness and weaknesses of the body cannot be made beautiful by means of discussion, and certainly illness can make life difficult and miserable at any point. However, if age is regarded as its own phase of life with its own temporal Gestalt, if the "men in gray" (mainly economists, or also insurance agents) who try to steal the order of time are resisted, and if the inner voice that feels young and yet believes in external calculation can be convinced to look at the *order of time* (*Gestaltungszeit*) of activities *now*, i.e. in the present, then we could learn to construe and order the proper *Gestalt* time of all activities in the light of being young or old, slow or fast. Thus, we would focus on the present of the activities and on their own temporal order.

The temporality of the I does not properly account for the temporal order of activities, and also it might not be strong enough to withstand the objective time concept of the gray men because the I in this internalist conception has nothing to hold onto in the world. The knowledge of our own death is not an object of experience; it cannot be deduced from an objective time structure, nor is it knowledge thought by the I of an internal time-consciousness. Yet we know that we have to die.

Finally, the thesis is that it is not the future which is supposed to be the source of optimism, and it is not the "loss" of future which is the source of misery and frustration, because future "loss" is actually not sufficiently grounded. Rather, the sources of optimism are experiences *with* activities and experiences *in* activities in *their* temporal order (*Gestaltzeit*). Thus optimism—whether it be that of someone young or someone old—is grounded neither on a physicalist nor an internalist (mentalist) conception of time nor in a net of bureaucratic time. These conceptions are merely abstractions.

What is important to *realize,* is the character of the activity and the *Gestalt* of time in my experiences in life. If humans live their lives according to their time of order, then they understand what time means. And if an old person is allowed to live his/her life in its and in his/her time order, then he/she feels that he/she is not just part of a biological dimension but is actually and essentially a member of a human world with its temporal dimensions of activities. In light of this thought, aging and its activities also have the character of the *Gestalt time* which needs its worldly room and care. Humans age as differently as they live. The "stakes are down" when the present is lost to them, but that can happen at any time.

In short, my proposal is for a temporal world of activity in which the "men in gray" cannot steal our time, whether it be the phase of age or any other time of our parents, grand-parents, children, or ourselves.[19]

References

Améry, Jean. 1994. *On aging: Revolt and resignation*. Bloomington and Indianapolis: Indiana University Press.

Augustine. 1998. *Confessions*. Trans. Henry Chadwick. Oxford: Oxford University Press.

Beauvoir, Simone de. 1996. *The coming of age*. Trans. Patrick O'Brian. New York: W. W. Norton & Company [*La vieillesse*. Paris: Gallimard 1970].

Bergson, Henri. 1988. *Matter and memory*. Trans. Nancy Margaret Paul and W. Scott Palmer. New York: Zone Books.

Bobbio, Norberto. 2001. *Old age and other essays*. Trans. and ed. Allan Cameron. Cambridge: Polity Press.

Cicero, Marcus Tullius. 2009. *Cicero's Cato the elder on old age*. Charleston, South Carolina: BiblioBazaar.

Ende, Michael. 1988. *Momo*. Trans. Maxwell Brownjohn. Garden City, New York: Doubleday.

Heidegger, Martin. 1996. *Being and time*. Trans. Joan Stambaugh. Albany: State University of New York Press.

Husserl, Edmund. 1966. *The phenomenology of internal time-consciousness*. 2nd ed. Trans. James Churchill. Bloomington and London: Indiana University Press.

Mittelstraß, Jürgen. 1992. Zeitformen des Lebens: Philosophische Unterscheidungen. In *Zukunft des Alterns und gesellschaftliche Entwicklung. Forschungsbericht* 5, ed. Paul B. Baltes and Jürgen Mittelstraß. Berlin and New York: Walter de Gruyter, 386–407.

Mimnermus. 1996. Fragment 1. *The fragments of Mimnermus*. Text and commentary by Archibald Allen. Stuttgart: Franz Steiner Verlag, 31–41.

---

19 I thank Helen Fielding, Dorothea Olkowski, and Silvia Stoller for their comments on the text.

Sartre, Jean-Paul. 1993. *Being and nothingness*. Trans. Hazel E. Barnes. Washington: Washington Square Press.

Scheler, Max. 1957. *Zur Ethik und Erkenntnislehre. Gesammelte Werke*, vol. 1, ed. Maria Scheler. Bern: Francke.

Schwarzer, Alice. 1984. *After* The Second Sex: *Conversations with Simone de Beauvoir*. Trans. Marianne Howarth. New York: Pantheon Books.

Schües, Christina. 2011. The power of time. In *Time in feminist phenomenology*, ed. Christina Schües, Dorothea E. Olkowski and Helen Fielding. Bloomington: Indiana University Press, 60–78.

Schües, Christina, Dorothea E. Olkowski, and Helen A. Fielding, eds. 2011. *Time in feminist phenomenology*. Bloomington, Indianapolis: Indiana University Press.

Seneca. 1932. *On the shortness of life*. Trans. John W. Basore. London: William Heinemann. http://www.forumromanum.org/literature/seneca_younger/brev_e.html (accessed September 8, 2011).

Ströker, Elisabeth. 1968. Der Tod im Denken Max Schelers. *Man and World: An International Philosophical Review*, vol. I, ed. John M. Anderson, Joseph J. Kockelmann and Calvin Schrag. Dordrecht: Kluwer, 191–207.

Weiss, Gail. 2011. Sharing time across unshared horizons. In *Time in feminist phenomenology*, ed. Christina Schües, Dorothea E. Olkowski and Helen A. Fielding. Bloomington: Indiana University Press, 171–88.

Wittgenstein, Ludwig. 1969. *Philosophical investigations*. Trans. Gertrud Elisabeth Margaret Anscombe and Rush Rhees. Oxford: Blackwell.

Beata Stawarska
Ambiguous Future

Comment on Christina Schües

Few phenomenologists addressed the developmental dimension of temporal existence in the context of aging, and took up the questions of childhood and old age as weighty existential themes. Beauvoir's philosophy is exceptional in this regard, and provides us with a concrete, situated phenomenological analysis of age and aging, broadly construed.

Following Beauvoir, old age is an existential temporal drama that aggravates our finitude by producing a kind of a contraction of the future. As she puts it, "One has exchanged an indefinite future—and one has a tendency to look upon it as infinite—for a finite future" (1996, 378). The ontological finitude of human existence seems therefore to reach its paroxysm in the old age, which unlike illness or fatigue, is stamped with irreversibility. This sense of aggravated finitude and contracted future applies especially to a Western society where the future is unpredictable and loosely tied to the present. Writing in the France of 1960s, Beauvoir emphasizes an insurmountable ignorance regarding what kind of social order will ensue, and whether the future society will end in socialism, technology, or barbarism (410). Only a repetitive society, as she terms it (410), has the comfort of reading the future from the present, with the father justified in his hope that the progeny, and the progeny of the progeny, will carry on traditional, familial tasks. In that sense, a repetitive society dictates a futural orientation for their members, in that it opens the possibility of trans-generational renewal in which an individual life fits into a larger inter-personal chain of interconnected projects, and aspirations. Within a non-repetitive and individualist society of Western Europe, the possibilities of such renewal appear minimal and insignificant. As Beauvoir notes, "ignorance alone is certain," and all hypothesis about the future is "idle and trifling" (411). The writer cannot predict the verdict of posterity, and her posthumous fate is in principle foreclosed from her knowledge. It would be naïve, it seems, to project oneself into this posthumous future, which could spell fame equally well as misunderstanding or oblivion.

In her reading of Beauvoir's analysis of old age, and its contracted future, Christina Schües proposes to re-think the present as a site of meaning and value for the old and the young alike. For example, she notes that:

> If we were to *learn* to consider activities according to their appropriate time order (*Zeitgestalt*), and if we were to acknowledge that each activity is temporally organized (*zeitlich ge-*

staltet) in the present and not just in the future, then we could learn to take each phase of life according to its particular time and realize it in its own rights and values. (228)

Schües agrees that the inherent temporal patterning or "Gestaltung" of activities such as a conversation between lovers, or working on a bike, may not succeed in de-contracting the future. And yet it opens up the possibility of actively tempo-ralizing the present by means of a participatory engagement in its flowing, intri-cately rhythmed, virtually self-organizing, temporality. Considering the daily haste of our tragically overburdened professional existence, where we seem per-petually too late for life, old age appears to contain the promise of the present fully lived, savored, in its proper time. This is a vision of old age that I am, thanks to Christina Schües' original reading, looking forward to. It is a future of aging which opens up a possibility of a more authentic engagement with time.

And yet I wonder whether a focus on the present does not confine us to a uni-generational perspective on old age, and to a synchronous conception of time. This may be a methodological limitation of a phenomenological inquiry conducted in the first person, which limits the experiential field to an individual life-span. Beauvoir's suspension of judgment regarding the future, embedded as it is in an unstable societal context, would be a logical result of her rigorous em-ployment of the phenomenological method. A positive vision of the present of-fered by Schües would be similarly motivated. And yet, I wonder whether such limitation does not overshadow the complex ways in which the future and the past are entangled when viewed from a trans-generational perspective, and its diachronous time—that is a time that is oriented towards an other whose life transcends the span of my life. Beauvoir may be right that the future is un-decipherable, and nothing constrains future generations to carry on the projects of their progenitors. And yet, are we not responsible for future generations, and if so, are we not ethically oriented towards the future in ways that exceed the epistemological limitation of not knowing what this future will bring? This dia-chronous time of the other which a phenomenological subject will not be there to witness may still regulate and impact the projects undertaken in the present. These projects carry an ethical futural dimension within them. In this sense, we are responsible for the future which we cannot know.

Put differently, there may be an ethics of aging to be modeled on Beauvoir's ethics of ambiguity, or there may be an ambiguity in aging when regarded in eth-ical terms. This ethical ambiguity is situated by Beauvoir at the crossroads of freedom and facticity, insofar as the individual freedom is weighed down by the very world it transcends in the concrete choices and decisions made. To act ethically is therefore to accept the consequences of one's fundamental free-dom within the entangled destinies shared by the self and others. This ambiguous admixture of freedom and facticity translates into an ambiguous admixture of the present and the future, since to act freely means to orient oneself towards the facticity of the futural implications of one's present choices, even though the future, like facticity, is inherently beyond individual control. Needless to say, such futural orientation should not be read in the ethically dangerous terms of some mythical historical end in the name of which individual lives could be endangered in the present. The appeal is not made to what Beauvoir terms a stationary future (cf. Beauvoir 2000, 118), with its false promises of perfection and universal harmony, which have historically been used as justification for violence and sacrifice of truth and justice. Beauvoir was rightly concerned about such a congealed conception of the future used for ideological purposes. And yet the ethical ambiguity of a situated freedom contains, I believe, an inescapable futural orientation, and an ethically pregnant analysis of temporality intertwines the present and the future. This trans-generational future may bring some comfort in the old age, for it expands temporality beyond the gradually contracting span of one's own life.

Furthermore, as children, we are the future of the past. Reading Beauvoir on the old age, I was often flooded with memories of my grandmothers. Their cooking, their stories, seemed to create or perpetuate a repetitive society of sorts, with its traditional meals served over the holidays, and narratives of war and liberation I soon knew by heart. I received these stories and nourishments without being able to reciprocate them in my grandmothers' time, another example of an inescapably diachronous temporality at work across the generations. I carry the gifts of my grandmothers' love with me in the present, but they belong to an ancestral past which was orientated towards a pro-generational future. These complex trans-temporal entanglements with a larger-than-individual life seem inescapably caught up in the present and suggest that the present is inherently ambiguous both in its futural orientation of responsibility for what is to come and its retroactive recognition of dept and gratitude for one's own life.

References

Beauvoir, Simone de. 1996. *The coming of age.* Trans. Patrick O'Brian. New York and London: W. W. Norton & Company.
Beauvoir, Simone de. 2000. *The ethics of ambiguity.* Trans. Bernard Frechtman. New York: Kensington Publishing.

Contributors

Debra Bergoffen is Emerita Professor of Philosophy at George Mason University and Bishop Hamilton Lecturer in Philosophy at American University (USA). She is the author of *The Philosophy of Simone de Beauvoir: Gendered Phenomenologies, Erotic Generosities* (Albany: State University of New York Press, 1997) and *Contesting the Politics of Genocidal Rape: Affirming the Dignity of the Vulnerable Body* (New York: Routledge, 2012). Her co-edited volumes include a special issue of *Hypatia* (vol. 26, no. 3, Summer 2011) titled "Ethics of Embodiment" with Gail Weiss; *Confronting Global Gender Justice: Women's Lives Human Rights* (New York: Routledge, 2011) with Paula Ruth Gilbert, Tamara Harvey and Connie L. McNeely, and a special issue of *New Nietzsche Studies* (vol. 7, no. 3–4, Fall 2007/Winter 2008) titled "Nietzsche and the Jews," with David Allison and Babette Babich. Her most recent articles include: "Simone de Beauvoir and the Marquis de Sade: Contesting the Logic of Sovereignty and the Politics of Terror and Rape," in *Beauvoir and Western Thought from Plato to Butler*, ed. Shannon Mussett and William Wilkerson (Albany: State University of New York Press, 2012, pp. 75–90), "Simone de Beauvoir in her Times and ours," in *Situating Existentialism*, ed. Jonathan Judaken, Robert Bernasconi (New York: Columbia University Press, 2012, pp. 360–85).

Marieke Borren teaches philosophy and gender studies at the Universities of Nijmegen, Groningen and Amsterdam (Netherlands). Her main areas of research include the work of Hannah Arendt, feminist philosophy, political philosophy and phenomenology. In 2010 she obtained her PhD at the University of Amsterdam for her doctoral thesis on Hannah Arendt's hermeneutic phenomenology of the political, titled *Amor Mundi: Hannah Arendt's Political Phenomenology of World*. Her most recent publications include "'A Sense of the World': Hannah Arendt's Hermeneutic Phenomenology of Common Sense," *International Journal of Philosophical Studies*, vol. 21 (2013), no. 2, pp. 225–55, and "Feminism as Revolutionary Practice: From Justice and the Politics of Recognition to Freedom," *Hypatia: A Journal of Feminist Philosophy*, vol. 28 (2013), no. 1, pp. 97–214.

Penelope Deutscher is Professor of Philosophy at Northwestern University (USA). She is the author of *Yielding Gender: Feminism, Deconstruction and the History of Philosophy* (London: Routledge, 1997), *A Politics of Impossible Difference: The Later Work of Luce Irigaray* (Ithaca: Cornell University Press, 2002), *How to Read Derrida* (London: Granta Publications, 2005) and *The Philosophy of Simone de Beauvoir: Ambiguity, Conversion, Resistance* (Cambridge: Cambridge University Press, 2008). She also co-edited (with Kelly Oliver) *Enigmas: Essays on Sarah Kofman* (Ithaca: Cornell University Press, 1999), and (with Françoise Collin) *Repenser le politique* (Paris: Campagne Première, 2005).

Helen A. Fielding is Associate Professor in the Departments of Philosophy and Women's Studies and Feminist Research at The University of Western Ontario (Canada). Her main areas include continental philosophy, feminist philosophy, phenomenology, embodiment, Merleau-Ponty, Irigaray and Heidegger. She has co-edited (with Gabrielle Hiltmann, Dorothea Olkowski and Anne Reichold) *The Other: Feminist Reflections in Ethics* (Basingstoke: Palgrave Publishers, 2007), (with Christina Schües and Dorothea E. Olkowski) *Time in Feminist Phenomenology* (Bloomington: Indiana University Press, 2011) and a special issue on "Vie et Individuation" in *Chiasmi International: Trilingual Studies Concerning Merleau-Ponty's Thought* (vol. 7, 2005). She has published articles in journals such as *Hypatia, Continental Philosophy Review* and the *Journal of the British Society for Phenomenology*, as well as articles in various collections such as *Feminist Interpretations of Maurice Merleau-Ponty*, ed. Dorothea Olkowski and Gail Weiss. She is currently working on a book manuscript titled *The Cultivation of Perception*.

Linda Fisher is Associate Professor in the Department of Gender Studies at Central European University, Budapest (Hungary). Her research areas include continental philosophy, phenomenology, hermeneutics, feminist philosophy and gender studies, philosophy and literature, and aesthetics. Her current work in feminist phenomenology explores the intersections of embodiment, difference, temporality, and intersubjectivity, with the aim of developing a phenomenology of gendered experience. She is co-author (with Leo A. Groarke and Christopher W. Tindale) of *Good Reasoning Matters!* (Toronto: Oxford University Press, 2nd ed., 1997), co-editor (with Lester Embree) of *Feminist Phenomenology* (Dordrecht: Kluwer Academic Publishers, 2000) and (with Silvia Stoller and Veronica Vasterling) *Feministische Phänomenologie und Hermeneutik* (Würzburg: Königshausen & Neumann, 2005) and has written on Husserl, Gadamer, Merleau-Ponty, and Beauvoir, embodiment, difference, identity and alterity, disability, multiculturalism, and opera. She is currently working on a monograph entitled *In Her Own Voice: A Feminist Philosophy of Voice and Vocality*, examining vocality as a locus of identity and intersubjectivity.

Annemie Halsema is Assistant Professor at the Department of Philosophy of VU University Amsterdam (Netherlands). Her research focuses on the notion of the self, embodiment and the self-other relationship in contemporary hermeneutics and feminist philosophy. She is the author of *Luce Irigaray and Horizontal Transcendence* (Amsterdam: SWP, 2010) and another monograph on Luce Irigaray in Dutch; she is co-editor (with D. Van Houten) of *Empowering Humanity: State of the Art of Humanistics* (Utrecht: De Tijdstroom, 2002) and of four co-edited volumes in Dutch. Other publications include "Phenomenology in the Feminine: Irigaray's Relationship to Merleau-Ponty," in *Intertwinings: Interdisciplinary Encounters with Maurice Merleau-Ponty*, ed. Gail Weiss (Albany: State University of New York Press, 2008, pp. 63–83), "Understanding the Body: The Relevance of Gadamer's and Ricœur's View of the Body for Feminist Theory" (co-author Louise D. Derksen), in *Gadamer and Ricœur: Critical Horizons for Contemporary Hermeneutics*, ed. Francis J. Mootz III and George H. Taylor (London: Continuum, 2011, pp. 203–25), "The Time of the Self: A Feminist Reflection on Ricœur's Notion of Narrative Identity," in *Time in Feminist Phenomenology*, ed. Christina Schües, Dorothea E. Olkowski, and Helen A. Fielding (Bloomington: Indiana University Press, 2011, pp. 111–34).

Sara Heinämaa is Senior Lecturer and Docent in Theoretical Philosophy and the leader of the research community "Subjectivity, Historicity, Communality" at the University of Helsinki (Finland). Presently she works as Professor of Philosophy at the University of Jyväskylä. She is the author of *Toward A Phenomenology of Sexual Difference: Husserl, Merleau-Ponty, Beauvoir* (Lanham: Rowman & Littlefield Publishers, 2003) and of "Part II: Phenomenologies of Mortality and Generativity," in *Birth, Death, and the Feminine* (Bloomington: Indiana University Press, 2010). She is co-editor (with Mirja Hartimo and Timo Miettinen) of *Phenomenology and the Transcendental* (Routledge, forthcoming), (with Vili Lähteenmäki and Pauliina Remes) of *Consciousness: From Perception to Reflection in the History of Philosophy* (Dordrecht: Springer, 2008) and (with Martina Reuter) of *Psychology and Philosophy: Inquires into the Soul from Late Scholasticism to Contemporary Thought* (Dordrecht: Springer, 2008). At the moment she is working on a book on personhood, generativity, and perfection.

Ulrike Kadi is Assistant Professor in the Department of Psychoanalysis and Psychotherapy at the Medical University of Vienna and University Lecturer in the Department of Philosophy at the University of Vienna (Austria). Her main areas are post-structuralism, psychopathology and psychoanalysis (Lacan). She has co-edited (with Gerhard Unterthurner) *Wahn: Philosophische, psychoanalytische und kulturwissenschaftliche Perspektiven* (Vienna: Turia + Kant, 2012). Recently published articles include "Begehren gebären: Überlegungen zur dunklen Vorgeschichte des Subjekts," in *Obskure Differenzen*, ed. Marlen Bidwell-Steiner and Anna Babka (Gießen: Psychosozial Verlag, 2013, pp. 39–58) and "Affekt und

Körper: Zu Jacques Lacans Spinoza-Lektüre," in *Spinoza: Affektenlehre und amor dei intellectualis*, ed. Violetta Waibel (Hamburg: Felix Meiner, 2012, pp. 146–66).

Sonia Kruks is the Robert S. Danforth Professor of Politics at Oberlin College (USA) where she teaches political theory and philosophy. She has served as the Director of the Women's Studies Program at Oberlin. Her research has, for many years, focused on French existential phenomenology and its intersections with feminist theory. Her books include *The Political Philosophy of Merleau-Ponty* (Hassocks, UK: Harvester Press / Atlantic Highlands: Humanities Press, 1981), *Situation and Human Existence: Freedom, Subjectivity and Society* (London: Unwin Hyman / Routledge, 1990), *Retrieving Experience: Subjectivity and Recognition in Feminist Politics* (Ithaca: Cornell University Press, 2001) and *Simone de Beauvoir and the Politics of the Ambiguity* (New York, Oxford: Oxford University Press, 2012). In addition, she has published many articles on French philosophy and feminist theory. She presently serves on the editorial boards of *Hypatia: A Journal of Feminist Philosophy* and *Sartre Studies International*.

Bonnie Mann is Associate Professor of Philosophy in the Department of Philosophy at the University of Oregon, Eugene (USA). Her work is in feminist philosophy and continental philosophy, with a focus on post-structuralism, phenomenology and feminist materialism. She is the author of *Women's Liberation and the Sublime: Feminism, Postmodernism, Environment* (Oxford: Oxford University Press, 2006), *Sovereign Masculinity: Gender Lessons from the War on Terror* (Oxford: Oxford University Press, forthcoming), and many articles.

Dorothea Olkowski is Professor and Chair of Philosophy at the University of Colorado, Colorado Springs and Director of the Cognitive Studies Minor (USA). She is a former Chair of the Department of Philosophy and former Director of Women's Studies. Specializing in feminist theory, phenomenology and contemporary French philosophy, she has been a Fellow at the University of Western Ontario, Rotman Institute of Philosophy and Science and the Australian National University in Canberra. She is the author of *Gilles Deleuze and the Ruin of Representation* (Berkeley: University of California Press, 1999), *The Universal: In the Realm of the Sensible* (Edinburgh: Edinburgh University Press, 2007) and *Postmodern Philosophy and the Scientific Turn* (Bloomington: Indiana University Press, 2012). She is editor of *Resistance, Flight, Creation: Feminist Enactments of French Philosophy* (Ithaca: Cornell University Press, 2000) and has co-edited (with Gail Weiss) *Feminist Interpretations of Maurice Merleau-Ponty* (University Park: Penn State University Press, 2006); (with Helen Fielding, Gabrielle Hiltmann, Dorothea Olkowski and Anne Reichold) *The Other: Feminist Reflections in Ethics* (Basingstoke: Palgrave Publishers, 2007) and (with Christina Schües and Helen Fielding) *Time in Feminist Phenomenology* (Bloomington: Indiana University Press, 2011).

Gertrude Postl is Professor of Philosophy and Women's Studies at Suffolk County Community College, Selden, NY (USA). Her main areas include feminist philosophy, in particular theories of language and the body. She is the author of *Weibliches Sprechen: Feministische Entwürfe zu Sprache und Geschlecht* (Vienna: Passagen, 1991) and editor of *Contemporary Feminist Philosophy in German*, a special issue of *Hypatia: A Journal of Feminist Philosophy* 20/2 (Spring 2005). She also co-edited (with Elisabeth Schäfer and Esther Hutfless) a collection of articles on Hélène Cixous' essay *The Laugh of the Meduse* (Vienna: Passagen, 2013).

Kristin Rodier is Doctorate candidate at the University of Alberta (Canada) under the supervision of Professor Cressida J. Heyes. Her main areas include feminist philosophy, critical theory, phenomenology, existentialism and psychoanalysis. Her master's thesis was published by the University of Saskatchewan's University Press. It is entitled *Simone de Beauvoir and Biologism: A Phenomenological Rereading of "The Givens of Biology"* (2007). Selected presentation: "De Beauvoir and the Possibility of a Materialist Feminism" at the Canadian Society for Continental Philosophy 2010.

Elisabeth Schäfer is University Lecturer at the Department of Philosophy at the University of Vienna (Austria). In 2012 she finished her dissertation thesis on Jean-Luc Nancy's thinking of a new ontology of touch. Her main teaching and research areas include deconstruction, feminist philosophy, ontology, and *écriture féminine*. She is the author of *Die offene Seite der Schrift: J. D. und H. C. Côte à Côte* (Vienna: Passagen, 2008) and she has co-edited (with Bernd Bösel and Eva Pudill) *Denken im Affekt* (Vienna: Passagen, 2010) and (with Sophia Panteliadou) *Gedanken im freien Fall: Vom Wandel der Metapher* (Vienna: Passagen, 2011). Recently, she co-edited (with Esther Hutfless and Gertrude Postl) a volume on Hélène Cixous' "Laugh of Medusa" entitled *Das Lachen der Medusa: Zusammen mit aktuellen Beiträgen* (Vienna: Passagen, 2013) which includes the first German translation of Cixous' famous essay and other related articles.

Christina Schües is Associate Professor at the Institute for the History of Medicine and Science Studies, University of Luebeck and Adjunct Professor at the Institute for Philosophy and Science of Art, Leuphana University, Lueneburg (Germany). Her research areas are devoted to the history of philosophy, phenomenology, political and feminist theory, anthropological philosophy, time, ethics, and medical ethics. She is the author of *Philosophie des Geboren-*

seins (Freiburg: Alber, 2008) and *Changes of Perception: Five Systematic Approaches in Husserlian Phenomenology* (Frankfurt: Peter Lang, 2003); she co-edited (with Birgit Hartmann, Steffi Hobuß, Nina Zimnik and Julia Patrut) *Die andere Hälfte der Globalisierung: Menschenrechte, Ökonomie und Medialität aus feministischer Sicht* (Frankfurt: Campus, 2001), (with Rudolf Rehn and Frank Weinreich) *Der Traum vom "besseren" Menschen: Zum Verhältnis von praktischer Philosophie und Biotechnologie* (Frankfurt: Peter Lang, 2003) and (with Dorothea Olkowski and Helen A. Fielding) *Time in Feminist Phenomenology* (Bloomington: Indiana University Press, 2011). Currently, she is working on a project about the well-being of children in the medical context, the human condition and enhancement practices, and peace theory.

Beata Stawarska is Associate Professor in the Department of Philosophy at the University of Oregon, Eugene (USA). Her main areas include contemporary European philosophy, phenomenology, philosophical psychology, and feminist phenomenology. She is the author of *Between You and I: Dialogical Phenomenology* (Athens: Ohio University Press, 2009) and a number of articles and book chapters dealing with the phenomenology of Merleau-Ponty and Sartre, including "From the Body Proper to Flesh: Merleau-Ponty on Intersubjectivity," in *Feminist Interpretations of Maurice Merleau-Ponty*, ed. Dorothea Olkowski and Gail Weiss (University Park: Penn State University Press, 2006, pp. 91–106), as well as articles dealing with the intersections between phenomenological and empirical approaches to sociality (published in *Phenomenology and the Cognitive Sciences, Philosophy Today, Continental Philosophy Review, CHIASMI International*, and elsewhere). Beata Stawarska's recent monograph *Ferdinand de Saussure's Philosophy of Language: Phenomenology, Structuralism* is currently under review.

Silvia Stoller is University Docent in the Department of Philosophy at the University of Vienna (Austria). Her research areas are phenomenology, feminist philosophy, gender studies, feminist phenomenology and philosophical anthropology (pain, love, age, laughter). She is the author of *Existenz – Differenz – Konstruktion: Phänomenologie der Geschlechtlichkeit bei Beauvoir, Irigaray und Butler* (Munich: Wilhelm Fink, 2010). She has co-edited (with Helmuth Vetter) *Phänomenologie und Geschlechterdifferenz* (Vienna: WUV-Universitätsverlag, 1997), (with Eva Waniek) *Verhandlungen des Geschlechts: Zur Konstruktivismusdebatte in der Gender-Theorie* (Vienna: Turia + Kant, 2001) and (with Veronica Vasterling and Linda Fisher) *Feministische Phänomenologie und Hermeneutik* (Würzburg: Königshausen & Neumann, 2005). Selected English publications include: "Asymmetrical Genders: Phenomenological Reflections on Sexual Difference," *Hypatia: A Journal of Feminist Philosophy* 20 (2), Spring 2005 (ed. Gertrude Postl), pp. 7–26;

"Phenomenology and the Poststructural Critique on Experience," *International Journal of Philosophical Studies* 17 (5), 2009, pp. 707–37; "Expressivity und Performativity: Merleau-Ponty and Butler," *Continental Philosophy Review* 43 (1), April 2010, pp. 97–110; "Gender and Anonymous Temporality," in *Time in Feminist Phenomenology*, ed. Christina Schües, Dorothea E. Olkowski and Helen A. Fielding (Bloomington: Indiana University Press, 2011, pp. 79–90); "The Indeterminable Gender: Ethics in Feminist Phenomenology and Poststructuralist Feminism," in *Janus Head* 13 (1), 2013, pp. 17–34.

Veronica Vasterling is Associate Professor in the Philosophy Department and at the Institute for Gender Studies at Radboud University Nijmegen (Netherlands). Her main areas are feminist philosophy, gender studies, phenomenology, hermeneutics, philosophical anthropology and political theory. She is co-editor of *Practising Interdisciplinarity in Gender Studies* (York: Raw Nerve Books, 2006), co-editor (with Silvia Stoller and Linda Fisher) of *Feministische Phänomenologie und Hermeneutik* (Vienna: WUV-Universitätsverlag, 1997), co-editor of a book on women philosophers (*Vrouwelijke filosofen: een historisch overzicht*) (Amsterdam: Atlas, 2012) and author of numerous articles, including "Contingency, Newness and Freedom: Arendt's Recovery of the Temporal Conditions of Politics," in *Time in Feminist Phenomenology*, ed. Christina Schües, Dorothea E. Olkowski and Helen Fielding (Bloomington: Indiana University Press, 2011, pp. 135–48), "The Psyche and the Social: Judith Butler's Politicizing of Psychoanalytical Theory," in *Sexuality and Psychoanalysis: Philosophical Criticisms*, ed. Jens de Vleminck at al. (Leuven: Leuven University Press, 2010, pp. 171–82) and "Political Hermeneutics: Hannah Arendt's Contribution to Hermeneutic Philosophy," in *Gadamer's Hermeneutics and the Art of Conversation*, ed. Andrzy Wierciński (Berlin: LIT Verlag, 2011, pp. 571–82).

Anja Weiberg is Assistant Professor in the Department of Philosophy at University of Vienna (Austria). Her main areas include research on Wittgenstein and applied ethics. She is the author of *"Und die Begründung hat ein Ende": Die Bedeutung von Religion und Ethik für den Philosophen Ludwig Wittgenstein und das Verständnis seiner Werke* (Vienna: WUV-Universitätsverlag, 1998/2002); (with Esther Ramharter) *"Die Härte des logischen Muß": Wittgensteins Bemerkungen über die Grundlagen der Mathematik* (Berlin: Parerga, 2006) and (with Monique Weissenberger-Leduc) *Gewalt und Demenz: Ursachen und Lösungsansätze für ein Tabuthema in der Pflege* (Vienna, New York: Springer, 2011).

Gail Weiss is Chair of the Department of Philosophy and Professor of Philosophy and Human Sciences at The George Washington University, Washington, D.C. (USA). Her main research areas are phenomenology, existentialism, feminist theory, and philosophy of literature. She is the author of *Refiguring the Ordinary* (Bloomington: Indiana University Press, 2008) and *Body Images: Embodiment as Intercorporeality* (London, New York: Routledge, 1999); she is editor of *Intertwinings: Interdisciplinary Encounters with Merleau-Ponty* (New York: State University of New York Press, 2008) and co-editor (with Debra Bergoffen) of the "Ethics of Embodiment" special issue of *Hypatia: A Journal for Feminist Philosophy* (Summer 2011, vol. 26, 3) and of the *Hypatia* cluster "Contesting the Norms of Embodiment" (Winter 2012, vol. 27, 2). She has also co-edited the following anthologies: (with Dorothea Olkowski) *Feminist Interpretations of Maurice Merleau-Ponty* (University Park: Pennsylvania State University Press, 2006), (with Jeffrey Jerome Cohen) *Thinking the Limits of the Body* (New York: State University of New York Press, 2003) and (with Honi Fern Haber) *Perspectives on Embodiment: The Intersections of Nature and Culture* (London: Routledge, 1999).

Index of Names

www.ingramcontent.com/pod-product-compliance
Lightning Source LLC
Chambersburg PA
CBHW070028100426
42740CB00013B/2627